MYTHS AND ANCIENT STORIES

MYTHS AND ANCIENT STORIES

NARRATIVE, MEANING AND INFLUENCE IN THE WEST

Kevin Mills

BLOOMSBURY ACADEMIC
LONDON • NEW YORK • OXFORD • NEW DELHI • SYDNEY

BLOOMSBURY ACADEMIC
Bloomsbury Publishing Plc
50 Bedford Square, London, WC1B 3DP, UK
1385 Broadway, New York, NY 10018, USA
29 Earlsfort Terrace, Dublin 2, Ireland

BLOOMSBURY, BLOOMSBURY ACADEMIC and the Diana logo are trademarks of Bloomsbury Publishing Plc

First published in Great Britain 2024

Cover design and illustration by Rebecca Heselton

A catalogue record for this book is available from the British Library.

ISBN: HB: 978-1-3503-4684-0
PB: 978-1-3503-4685-7
ePDF: 978-1-3503-4687-1
eBook: 978-1-3503-4686-4

Typeset by Deanta Global Publishing Services, Chennai, India
Printed and bound in Great Britain

To find out more about our authors and books visit www.bloomsbury.com and sign up for our newsletters.

To the students, past and present, in whose company I have travelled in the realms of gold.

CONTENTS

ACKNOWLEDGEMENTS

This book has taken shape over more than twenty years, during which I have worked with too many colleagues to mention, and taught more students than I can remember. Each has played their part in its production, and blame should be shared evenly among them.

In the latter stages of composition, I have been fortunate enough to find willing and percipient readers for some chapters, who have provided invaluable comment. Heartfelt thanks, then, to Alice Entwistle, Damian Walford Davies and Nic Dunlop. I am grateful, too, to all of my colleagues at the University of South Wales, among whom I have enjoyed a supportive and enabling working environment for the last fifteen years. To Vic Mills and our good companions in Contemporancient Theatre, I owe thanks for help in developing the material on *The Life of St Cadoc*. Diolch yn fawr iawn i chi gyd. Thanks too to Isla, Kirsty, Alf and Clem for putting up with long answers to polite questions.

Most of all, I want to thank the students who, over the last two decades, have sat through my classes on these texts, stimulated my thinking, asked tricky questions, and, just occasionally, left me doubting my ability to teach them anything at all.

INTRODUCTION

In the beginning

The first myths I ever came across were those of Creation, Fall and Redemption, as told in the biblical books of Genesis and the four gospels (Matthew, Mark, Luke and John). They were part of my childhood and shaped my life in ways too many to recount or even recall. I was taught that God made the world, made me and that I had, from the moment of my conception, inherited from Adam and Eve a fallen condition. I could be redeemed only by accepting Jesus Christ as my Saviour. My Christian parents were committed to the truth and efficacy of these ancient stories and, as a result, my experience, imagination and intellectual life have been profoundly affected by them.

My parents, of course, would not have referred to the stories of Adam, Eve and Jesus as myths. To do so would have seemed to them to deny their divine inspiration and to make them comparable with tales they considered untrue and deceptive. For them, the stories told by the gospels, like those they read in Genesis, were sacred history, worthy of unqualified acceptance; they were pristine utterances, uninfluenced by, and incomparable with, any non-biblical sources.

My experience is far from unique. Even today, in scientifically informed and technologically advanced societies, many people's lives are given meaning, purpose and structure by such stories, call them myths, histories, revelations or fictions. Perhaps that is part of what myth means. In the next chapter, we will look at the rich and teasing complications involved in trying to define it, but, for me, one highly significant aspect of its meaning is made plain by the extent to which stories from the Bible have fashioned my mind, my will, my imagination and my values. Even though I no longer believe the most ancient stories to be true in any literal sense, nor even that they bear a single, unequivocal meaning to which I might give assent, I remain a product of their moulding force. Myths, then, seem to me to be stories made not so much to entertain as to live by.

There are, of course, many reasons to suspect, question and reinterpret ancient stories. If nothing else does so, their power to harm and hurt as well as to nourish and nurture imposes a duty on the reader to look at them critically. They are neither neutral nor innocent in their representation of the world. They encode beliefs about the existence and characters of gods, about natural phenomena, morals, social order, power relations, sex, death and what might come after. If they are occasionally beautiful, rewarding and life-enhancing, they often confront us with the impossible, the improbable, the unlikely and the (frankly) undesirable. As well as earth mothers, creator spirits, overcomers of chaos, magical healers, helpful deities, mentors and city builders, they can portray ruthless killers, torturers, gangsters, rapists, both divine and human, as heroic, laudable and glorious figures. Modern fiction, especially, though not exclusively, that written by women, should teach us to think twice about what myths release into the cultures in which they circulate. I am thinking of those novels which have given voices to the silenced, marginalized, objectified and brutalized women of classical mythology: Margaret Atwood's Penelope, Pat Barker's Briseis, Madeline Miller's Circe, to name but a few. Once we begin to see in such critically astute, creative responses that our founding texts sometimes portray corrupt and damaging ideals, the task of re-examination becomes urgent. Myths are stories to live by, but they are also stories to expose, to challenge and to resist.

Literary representation

But I am writing of myth as if it were identical with ancient narrative, as if Genesis, the *Odyssey*, *The Epic of Gilgamesh* and all the rest were myths. They are, in fact, literary compositions in which myths play integral roles. Myth is woven into the fabric of these ancient works, but they are not, in themselves, myths. The distinction is an important one, because myth has a life outside of the stories in which we most commonly encounter it. As a literary critic, my interest is in those imaginative texts which have borne myth to us in tales of adventure, conflict, violence, redemption, mystery, terror, worship, wonder and magic, preserving aspects of prehistoric culture and society through the ages, and allowing modern readers to glimpse unfamiliar, sometimes incomprehensible, worlds. My reader should be aware that other approaches to myth are just as valid and no less interesting.

Among the most compelling accounts of myth as a matter of cultural belief and practice are books by Thorkild Jacobsen, Richard Buxton and Sarah Isles Johnston, each of which offers what might be called ethnographic insights. Jacobsen's *The Treasures of Darkness: A History of Mesopotamian Religion* (1976) has become a classic, and while its focus is on literary representations, it depicts Mesopotamian religious ideas and activity more broadly. Jacobsen describes the religious experience of the Mesopotamians as an encounter with the 'Wholly Other', the numinous, or that which is beyond everyday reality. Their belief system developed over 4,000 years, shifting from a perception of the gods as providers to seeing them as rulers, then as parents, and finally as tyrants. Underlying these metaphors was the observation and worship of natural phenomena and the need to cultivate good relationships with those forces which determined human survival.

Buxton's *Imaginary Greece: The Contexts of Mythology* (1994) draws on a wide range of evidence for how myth was used and understood in ancient Greek culture, outside of epic poetry. He shows myths being used in the education and socialization of children, in entertainment at banquets, in performances at public festivals, in the songs of travelling 'lyre singers' and in tragic drama. It featured, too, in visual representations: in designs for jewellery, vases, wine vessels and murals (especially in religious sanctuaries). Preserving for posterity the great figures and deeds of the past, passing on wisdom about the world and the human condition, furnishing persuasive examples which could be used in argument, offering consolation in the face of sorrow and suffering, myths could also be used to explain the present in terms of its origins.

Johnston's *The Story of Myth* (2018) sets out to explore the relationship between the stories told by Greek epics, tragedies and other compositions, and the religious beliefs of the society for which they served as instructive or devotional. She resists traditional approaches which emphasize the aesthetic achievement of the literature but reject the idea that it could have served religious causes, arguing that the engaging character of the stories made them powerful conduits for key beliefs. As told in various modes, Greek myths had the 'ability to engage their audiences emotionally and cognitively', giving them the potential 'to bring about changes in the outlook and behaviour' of listeners (Johnston 2018: 66–7).

As important as such approaches are to the understanding of myth, my concern in the following chapters is with ancient narratives and their cultural and literary influence. Questions of their truthfulness, historical accuracy, plausibility and their pertinence to religious systems are not under scrutiny here. What interests me in this context are the origins, development and functions of literature, and so I will seek to outline and interrogate the patterns, structures, themes and ideas expressed in the stories, leaving aside their value as sacred texts. These compositions, emerging as they do from the immemorial past, encode ways of seeing and understanding the world which are remote from our own, and while they open a gulf between ancient and modern which can never be fully closed, I hope to foster interest in, as well as a greater understanding of, what these extraordinary works offer contemporary readers.

Cultural significance of myth

Although this book is literary in focus, the cultural significance of myth is far broader than its impact on imaginative writing. It gave rise not only to literature but also to philosophy and history (and probably just about every other area of study). Myths have always been part of human cultures, used to explain natural phenomena and the mysteries of existence, proving fundamental to the development of religion, and, eventually, to science. Both continue to make use of myth in various ways, some of which I will explore in due course.

As well as being of great historical importance, myth is geographically universal. David Leeming's *Oxford Companion to World Mythology* (2005) gives an overview of the range and diversity of traditions and provides an invaluable resource for students of the subject. Obviously, a book such as this one can explore a very limited number of texts and cannot touch on the vast majority of mythological formations. I have selected texts based on my experience of teaching literature for many years. I asked myself: Which ancient works would it be most useful for my students to know about? Which traditions have had the most widespread and long-term influence on cultural productions in the West? Traditionally, Western culture has been fed by a range of mythologies, the most significant of which for English literature have been Classical (Greek and Roman), ancient Near Eastern (biblical) and Celtic (Irish and Welsh). I have concentrated on these three cultural sources. Others, such as Egyptian and Norse, have played a part, but arguably, a smaller one.

The picture has changed a good deal in recent decades. The twentieth century saw the broadening and enriching of English – both the language and its literature – by postcolonial writing from the Indian subcontinent, Africa, Australia and South America. Previously unfamiliar mythologies and folk traditions were thus introduced into the mix. Works by writers with non-white, non-European heritage have made an enormous contribution to the canon and approaches to its study. Nonetheless, understanding English literature in its historical dimensions, as well as film, games and TV, is immeasurably enhanced by a degree of familiarity with the texts discussed in this book.

Texts in translation

The following chapters work with English versions of the selected texts. Many significant issues are raised by translation, but, for the most part, I ignore them. I do so not because I believe them unimportant, but because I am not competent in the original languages and because my interest is, primarily, in the literary and cultural significance of the English versions. Where points of translation raise unavoidable issues which have had an impact on the reception and interpretation of the text, I discuss them by drawing on more than one translation and by attending to expert opinion. The book of Job presents a particularly thorny case: its language is difficult, sometimes obscure, and it confronts translators with a number of insuperable problems. These challenges are outlined in the chapter devoted to that book.

Multiple English versions are available of each of the texts discussed here, and consulting as many different translations as possible has been crucial to my way of writing about them. A list of translations used is appended to each chapter. In quoting from the primary works, I draw on each of these translations as seems appropriate, rather than following the more familiar practice of sticking to a single source. I do so in order to include what has seemed to me the clearest, most aesthetically pleasing, or most verbally or syntactically appropriate extract, and as a way of offering my reader a taste of the variety on offer. In most cases, the general sense-making process varies little between versions of the texts, and the translator's preferences are often aesthetic or technical. Such choices can, of course, be highly significant to the reading experience. To render Homer's epic poem, the *Odyssey,* in prose, for example, as many English versions do, offers the reader something very different from the poetic versions of Richmond Lattimore (1967), Robert Fagles (1996) and Emily Wilson (2018), but since my aim is to provide broad introductions to the works, I have focussed on narrative and thematic issues rather than linguistic characteristics and effects.

Not only in relation to translation, but across the spectrum of fundamental issues, such as history, composition and interpretation, it is my aim throughout the book to make scholarly work on each of the texts available to my readers. My approach is to combine the most useful and persuasive expert opinion currently available, with my own first-hand reading, in order to provide a series of interpretative introductions. It is not difficult to find introductory (as well as more advanced) books, websites and articles on any of these texts – in the case of the biblical texts and the *Odyssey*, they are available in bewildering numbers – but I am not aware of any other work which offers introductions to all of them in one place. While I am not conversant with Sumerian cuneiform, ancient Hebrew or Greek, medieval Welsh, nor Middle English, I have studied these texts in translation for many years, and hope what I have learned may be of use to new and more experienced readers alike.

Chapter by chapter

Before considering the ancient literary works themselves, two preliminary chapters provide an interpretative framework by exploring the complex and much-debated matter of the place of myth in the modern world. Chapter 1 examines the question of definition, outlining some of the most influential approaches to the subject. Mythopoeic thought emerged from worlds unlike our own in crucial ways: before the rise of science and the development of democratic forms of government, and before the formation of modern attitudes to the self and its place in society. This creates what I have termed 'cognitive distance': while we can recognize myths, we can never fully appreciate how they were understood by their creators and earliest users. To modern minds, they can appear to propagate prejudicial and discriminatory values, and to encode defunct ideas about the world, so they have often been treated with suspicion or even contempt. The suspicious approaches of nineteenth- and twentieth-century thinkers are discussed, before turning to the work of French philosopher Paul Ricoeur, who argued that although myths are potentially dangerous, they can offer modern people insights into issues such as free will and the nature of evil.

Perhaps the most contentious and far-reaching issue in the study of myth's relation to modernity is its status as a prescientific discourse. Chapter 2 deals with this relationship. Often considered an outmoded way of thinking, myth was long represented as striving for truths about the nature of the cosmos, and the place of humans within it, which science has finally revealed. This view is subjected to questioning, and confronted with the fact that, as Karl Popper argued, science necessarily began with myth. Drawing on the work of contemporary scholars Gregory Schrempp and Jason Josephson-Storm, modernity is shown to be characterized by an ongoing dependence upon myth, both philosophically and as a means of communication. This does not mean that myth and science are identical nor that they share the same cultural functions. Key differences between them are explored, before being illustrated in two ancient mythological texts: the Babylonian creation story *Enuma Elish* and the book of Genesis.

The first ancient text to be examined in detail is the oldest known extended literary composition: *The Epic of Gilgamesh*, dating from around 4,000 years ago. Its plot is outlined, its historical context described and key textual issues laid out before the mythological significance of its geographical setting is considered. Environmental factors shaped the characters and relationships of the gods and the roles they play in Gilgamesh's story. Once this mythological context is in place, the chapter turns to the epic's exploration of human limits expressed in the relationship between Gilgamesh, Enkidu and the city walls, the opposition between forest and city, the story of the Great Flood and the powerful metaphor of decaying loaves of bread. Human mortality forms one of the central themes of the narrative, but it is no less concerned with the nature of the divide between civilization and its others: forest and wilderness. The opening and closing of the poem draw attention to the city walls, suggesting a parallel between civic structure and narrative order as marking out the boundaries of human experience.

Narrative order might be considered both hallmark and theme of the biblical book, Genesis. Focussing on the relationship between the mythopoeic first chapters and the realist tales which follow, Chapter 4 opens with considerations of the book's genre and scope, moving on to outline the most important theories of composition. Key myths – Creation, Flood and the tower of Babel – are read as critical reworkings of their Mesopotamian precursors, and the chapter concludes with a discussion of exile as typifying human existence. The book was designed to foster a sense of national identity rooted in divine will and inseparable from a universal purpose. With consummate skill, the writers/editors of Genesis yoked its myths of Creation, Fall, Flood and exile to the stories of Israel's founding fathers, weaving complex narrative patterns which reveal the universal in the individual and vice versa.

If the book of Job appears to focus on a single individual, it too has universal concerns: chaos, order, justice and retribution. After outlining Job's story and examining some aspects of its origin, translation and generic identity, Chapter 5 moves on to consider the manifold interpretative difficulties it presents. Throughout its lengthy debate, the book uses the rhetoric of trial and justice to interrogate the suffering of innocent people. Protesting his innocence, Job demands that Yahweh confront him face to face to explain why he is being punished so severely when he has done nothing wrong. Yahweh eventually makes an appearance, ending Job's suffering and closing the argument, but the conclusions reached are self-contradictory. Although the story offers the reader a kind of closure, this remains in tension with the fact that the moral and religious questions have no satisfactory answers. A deeply troubling and uniquely daring composition, Job works ancient polytheistic combat mythology into its depiction of a monotheistic cosmos, to suggest that chaos is never far beneath the ordered surface of Yahweh's world.

In trying to understand a cosmic order which seems to victimize him, Job is akin to Homer's Odysseus, who finds himself at odds with a god who wishes him ill. But in a polytheistic system, the issue is less troubling since if one god persecutes you another may come to your aid. In the *Odyssey*, Poseidon pursues the hero, while Athena defends him and pleads his case with Zeus and the Olympian court. Beginning with the texts, history and composition of Homer's epic, Chapter 6 moves on to look at setting, plot and mythological character, as well as the use of folktale. The story of the Cyclops (Polyphemus) was not original to Homer; it was a widespread tale, circulating in many variant forms, one of which was woven into the world of the poem. The intricacy of the tale's integration demonstrates Homeric narrative sophistication and complexity, and the interpretative discussion, here, focusses on the highly wrought nature of the epic's storytelling. Elaborate structuring, reflective of highly developed rational thought processes, has been argued to undermine the *Odyssey*'s mythological content, but examining patterns in the treatment of women, hospitality and food makes it evident that the social order reflected in the plot's architecture rests on solidly mythopoeic foundations.

Classical mythology persisted in Western culture, the Greek material preserved and transmuted in Roman traditions and passed on by imperial expansion. Even though Christianity became the official religion of Rome, stories of the gods, monsters and heroes survived, often being reimagined as the adventures of saints and champions of the faith. As the empire spread across, and then receded from, Europe, other mythologies competed and mingled with the Graeco-Roman. The uneasy process of Christianizing pagan stories is in view throughout Chapter 7. The focus is on the life of myth in the medieval period when it was recycled by the two most significant literary genres of the age: hagiography (lives of saints) and romance. The British post-Roman context is outlined before *The Life of St Cadoc* (*c.*1086) is introduced as a work of Christian propaganda, adapting Celtic mythology to the service of Christian teaching and church politics. Attention then turns to the Middle English romance *Sir Orfeo* (late thirteenth to early fourteenth century) and its Celtic-influenced reworking of the myth of Orpheus.

Medieval Romance remains a concern as Chapter 8 examines the Welsh stories sometimes said to represent the earliest traces of a distinct British mythology. Translated into English from medieval Welsh in the nineteenth century by Charlotte Guest, the *Mabinogion*'s eleven tales are described, and their relationship with the Arthurian tradition considered. The focus then narrows to the tales known as the 'Four Branches': 'Pwyll', 'Branwen', 'Manawydan' and 'Math'. Each is summarized, and issues of date and composition considered, including the question of why they are referred to as 'branches': Are they offshoots of a lost epic? Or remnants of a larger, long lost, body of narrative? Although the 'Four Branches' include unambiguous references to magic and the Otherworld, and some of the characters may well have begun life as gods, to describe them as mythological is controversial. Celtic culture and mythology are much disputed, some scholars denying the plausibility of claims to its presence or influence in Britain. Key interventions in the debate are detailed as a means of introducing the supernatural and (possibly) divine elements of the Four Branches. With this critical background in view, the structure and themes of the cycle are explored in relation to the Norman context, conventions of medieval romance and the reinvention of mythology as a conduit for Christian moral doctrine.

It may seem strange to some readers that I move from the medieval focus of Chapters 7 and 8 to contemporary culture, without including a chapter on the intervening early modern period. My reasons for doing so have to do with the nature of the book as I have conceived of it. Despite proceeding in chronological order, this is not a history of mythology in Western literature. Had that been my project, I would have included Roman writers such as Virgil and Ovid, and would, perhaps, have devoted a chapter to the earliest English translations of Homer, the King James Bible of 1611, the uses of mythology in Shakespeare, and Milton's reimagining of the Fall in *Paradise Lost*. But my intention here is to offer an introduction to specific texts from the ancient world and to their underlying mythologies. It so happens that the latest of these, the *Mabinogion*, did not appear until the eleventh or twelfth century and so that is where my journey through the ancient world ends. What happened to mythology in the post-medieval age is, of course, profoundly interesting, and I have tried to offer some account of it in Chapter 2.

The final chapter surveys the role of myth in contemporary culture, focussing on fiction and cinema. It borrows its title 'Myth Today' from an essay by Roland Barthes, which forms part of his famous book, *Mythologies* (English translation, 1972). I criticize his identification of myth with bourgeois ideology for its failure to engage with the scope and cultural functions of stories in and from the ancient world, as well as for certain logical inconsistencies. Nonetheless, his insistence on myth's conservative (or even regressive) power is taken seriously as a challenge for anyone reading, reusing and reinterpreting ancient texts today. Literary and cinematic uses of myth are extremely popular, borrowing plots, characters and situations to create fictions in a variety of forms and genres. A few examples of novels and films based on mythology are considered in the light of Barthes' insistence on the 'immobilizing' effect of myth (its power to resist political progress), finding that not all of them are as conservative as his analysis might lead us to believe: myth is used as much to critique as to bolster contemporary values. Its continued importance lies in its potential to make us think, and think again, about our world, our stories and ourselves.

PART I

MYTH DECODED

CHAPTER 1
DEFINING AND INTERPRETING MYTH

The problem of definition

Myth is extremely difficult to define. So wide-ranging and divergent are opinions regarding its precise nature that some scholars are led to view the problem as incapable of any satisfactory resolution: 'myth', Eric Csapo writes, 'does not lend itself to a clear definition of any sort' (2005: 7). Csapo's scepticism is understandable; people have been trying for centuries to clarify the issue, yet no consensus has been reached.

Just about every modern approach to the subject has deep historical roots – stretching back to at least the seventeenth century – but the field became increasingly fragmented towards the end of the nineteenth century (Feldman and Richardson 1972: xxii). Since that time, many divergent attempts have been made to identify the fundamental characteristics of the mode. Max Müller (1823–1900) saw myth as deriving from metaphorical descriptions of nature, especially the movements of the sun, which were misunderstood as literal by later generations. E. B. Tylor (1832–1917) placed the belief that natural phenomena are indwelt by living spirits (animism) at the centre of his descriptions, while Jane Harrison (1850–1928) defined myth in terms of its relation to ritual. For James Frazer (1854–1941) myth focussed on fertility. Bronislaw Malinowski (1884–1942) gave myth a primarily social function as repository of moral and spiritual values, codifying the beliefs of a culture, while Sigmund Freud (1856–1939) insisted on their psychological significance as the societal equivalent of dreams, providing a privileged source of information about the unconscious. Ernst Cassirer (1874–1945) characterized myth as a necessary but limited and transient form of consciousness which had to be overcome if human knowledge was to progress and become fully scientific.

Joseph Campbell indicates the scope of modern attempts to come to terms with an ancient and elusive discourse, adding to his brief account of Frazer's and Müller's approaches further neat summations of how myth has been characterized

> as a repository of allegorical instruction, to shape the individual to his group (Durkheim); as a group dream, symptomatic of archetypal urges within the depths of the human psyche (Jung); as the traditional vehicle of man's profoundest metaphysical insights (Coomaraswamy); and as God's Revelation to His Children (the Church). Mythology is all of these.
>
> *(Campbell 1949: 382)*

As Campbell's catalogue of critical positions suggests, one of the difficulties facing the student of mythology is that it has been understood to be pertinent to an array of different disciplines, each with its own interests, concerns and analytical conventions. Each has left its fingerprints across the scene, making assessment of the evidence a challenging, if not impossible, task. Charles Long observes: 'The study of myth and mythical thinking may form a part of several disciplines, covering the areas of theology, philosophy, psychology, ethnology, and anthropology. It is, however, in the area of the history of religion that the interpretation of myth poses the most crucial problem' (Long 1963: 1). Whether or not Long is right to make the history of religion myth's chief discursive locus, we could add to his list the fields of philology, archaeology and literary studies.

Such an assortment of approaches indicates both the rich diversity of specialized enquiry and the range of surviving myths – the sheer breadth of their purview. There are myths about the origins of the world, the rising and setting of the sun, the moon and stars, oceans, rivers, mountains, cities, wars, language, places, names, fire, music, animals, crops, rain, floods, rainbows, storms, diseases, death. Myths take in the whole of the natural world and every kind of human experience. Not only so, but we cannot be sure that early myth-producing societies had anything in common with each other, and myth is likely to be as diverse as the societies in which it arose. Thus, when scholars attempt to relate myth to certain natural or cultural phenomena, there are always counter examples which resist any definition based on the identification of generic markers or functional characteristics. Laurence Coupe writes:

> Though fertility myths are often linked with a ritual, not all myths are linked with a ritual; though fertility and creation myths are about gods, not all myths are about gods . . . though fertility, creation and most hero myths take place outside of historical time, deliverance myth involves the fusion of myth and history, and some hero myths (the story of Odysseus, for example) have their roots in historical events (the Trojan War). Exceptions to, and contradictions of, any particular paradigm are endless.
>
> *(Coupe 2009: 6–7)*

The difficulties encountered by anyone seeking to understand myth, then, are manifold. Nevertheless, there are some important aspects of the question, which, once appreciated, can help us negotiate the perilous terrain, however hesitant or cautious our steps might need to be.

In the modern era, following the rise of science to the position of dominant explanatory mode in Western cultures, we tend to use the term 'myth' to refer to a story, belief or statement which is obviously false. We will explore in the next chapter the extent to which presumptions underlying such a tendency have been, and continue to be, challenged. For now, we might simply observe that to function as a myth a story must be believed to be true within a particular culture or society. This, perhaps, is what distinguishes myth from allegory, legend, fairytale, folktale and other traditional or established story types.[1] In this sense, myth has its own peculiar kind of root system, as

Mary Magoulick observes: 'Myths are symbolic tales of the distant past (often primordial times) that concern cosmogony and cosmology (the origin and nature of the universe), may be connected to belief systems or rituals, and may serve to direct social action and values' (Magoulick n.d.: n.p.). The circumspect character of Magoulick's description – its repetition of 'may' – indicates the extent to which modern interpreters have learned to tread rather carefully when it comes to approaching the fraught business of definition. Nonetheless, she offers the enquiring reader a few helpful waymarks, not only in identifying some of the chief concerns and implications often associated with myth but also by pointing to their function of directing social action and values – a point to which I will return shortly.

Whether or not myths had such a function in their most ancient forms and contexts, modern understandings have certainly reflected societal norms and expectations. The cultural codes and values embedded in the earliest stories and in the uses to which they have been put are made particularly obvious by the representation of women in myths and in the discourse about them. Introducing *The Woman's Companion to Mythology*, Riane Eisler marks the dawning awareness among scholars of myth's contribution to the establishment and maintenance of patriarchy: 'Today many of us are becoming aware that such myths have served to legitimize male control – be it in the family or the state. We are also becoming aware that most works on mythology ignore this and even beyond this, offer no explanation for why they focus primarily on male rather than female mythological figures' (Eisler 1992: ix). Eisler's remarks indicate not only the potential danger of mythology as a culturally regressive force but also its malleability: its almost infinite adaptability to interpretative causes. Such semantic plasticity is both the joy and the peril of engaging with myth: a welcome and a warning to those who wish to work with it.

In the same book, noting that women have begun to make inroads into the male-defined interior of the world of myth, its editor, Carolyne Larrington, observes: 'Meanings and emphases can change, and can be reclaimed and reinterpreted over time; moreover, the "original" meaning of a myth is simply one among many' (1992: xiii). The idea that the meanings of myths change is crucial to the endeavour of unpicking the various ideological webs in which they have been caught, whether patriarchal, imperialist, racist or totalitarian. But, in my view, this needs to be pushed a little further by insisting that myths *do not have* 'original' meanings. By which I mean both that we cannot recover either texts or contexts of myths in their most ancient forms, and that, even if we could, they would come with no guarantee that we understood them as did the societies which generated them. This is because myths will always confront us, as modern people, with a cognitive distance which we can never overcome.

The problem of interpretation: Cognitive distance

Although myth survives in modern cultures in a variety of forms, human relationships with nature in technologically advanced societies are no longer determined by myth;

rather, they are dependent upon science. I will have cause to qualify this observation in the following chapter, but, broadly speaking, I think it is safe to say that modern worldviews are, on the whole, necessarily remote from those of prescientific cultures. Take, for example, the way we think about disease. When we fall ill, we do not (typically) make offerings or appeals to deities, perform healing rituals or exorcize demons; we look to medical and surgical practitioners to prescribe treatments based on scientific principles of research, experimentation and testing.

Even if we know little about, or have no interest in it, our lives are shaped by, our thoughts coloured by and our worldview informed by science. This is examined in more detail in the next chapter, but here I want to note that the divergence between modernity and mythopoeic culture creates the problem of cognitive distance: the remoteness of the prescientific past and our inability to re-enter the world as it was when myths emerged.

The way we think has, necessarily, been shaped by our cultural history. Even what we think of as 'nature' – how we view, use, imagine, relate to the natural world – is specific to our time and place in human civilization. Although we are, in a sense, products of nature, we tend to think of human activity as somehow outside of it. We oppose 'nature' to 'culture'. When we speak of 'culture', we mean something like the sum of human customs, achievements, attitudes, beliefs and practices. Any glance at history makes obvious the fact that culture changes over time, and the most cursory appreciation of human geography makes plain that it differs widely from place to place. Each of us derives our understanding of the world around us from our culture, even if we owe aspects of our development to more than one cultural context. Since there is no neutral standpoint from which to view nature, we can never completely escape our formative traditions, values and customs even if our heritage is an eclectic mix of diverse influences. Nature is necessarily viewed from within a framework of beliefs and ideas or set of socially constructed perceptions, and therefore has no universal, fixed or stable meaning. What is meant by nature will be determined by our time in history, our place in the world and our social and educational background. I am aware, for example, that my own relationship with nature has been shaped by what little I know of scientific research in biology, botany, zoology and environmental studies. It is no less a product of my reading of works by William Wordsworth and other Romantic writers, TV nature programmes such as David Attenborough's documentaries, stories of space exploration and the imperative to cut carbon emissions. I am not always conscious of all or any of these influences when I am out walking with my dog, any more than I am aware of the shaping power of the Christian beliefs in which I was raised, and yet, if I stop to think about the river, the woods, the birds or the clouds, those animating spirits will be whispering in the grass all around me. I cannot escape them even if I want to. In fact, the very desire to do so would probably be attributable to their influence on my sense of myself as a thinking individual.

For most modern people, then, the world we live in is explained by, or felt to be within the purview of, science: everything from the origin of the universe to a sore throat, potentially, has a scientific explanation. We can imagine how it might have been to live in a world where none of these explanations was available, but we cannot know for sure, and we cannot experience such a world. Where science observes natural, physical laws at work in storms, earthquakes, floods, famine, disease and so on, myth typically sees the encounter with non-human will and intelligence: gods, angels, devils, spirits, fairies, ghosts, giants and so on. Inhuman forces were sometimes beneficent and sometimes malign: they could destroy you or they could send you plentiful crops, fertile livestock, health and stability. So, they seemed to have personalities, and your quality of life, even your life itself, could depend upon how they were disposed towards you. However familiar we become with the stories in which such beings appear, and however vividly our imaginations might respond to the worldbuilding devices of modern scholars, novelists, filmmakers and game designers, we can only ever read mythological texts from a modern viewpoint. As we have already seen, this has led to a great variety of interpretations, not only of the stories but of myth itself – of what it is and how it functioned in the ancient world.

Although we cannot define myth with any certainty or clarity, nor re-enter the world it evokes, we can recognize mythological stories as such and consider their characteristics. As John Gentile argues, the difficulties involved in defining myth, and the controversies which have long attended its study, do not have to be a bar to engagement; such openness can be a source of fruitful encounters: 'Myth – as a term, as a concept, and as a field of study – is multivalent and ambiguous, and like its many narratives, holds together binary opposites that enrich its study and enliven its discussion' (Gentile 2011: 85).

Identifying myths

If we cannot with any certainty say exactly what myth is, can we at least identify individual examples of the form? Mircea Eliade contended that '[e]very myth shows how a reality came into existence, whether it be the total reality, the cosmos, or only a fragment – an island, a species of plant, a human institution' (Eliade 1963: 97). Of course, not everyone would agree with Eliade that all myths are about origins, but I think everyone would agree that ancient origin stories are always myths. Again, many would disagree with Jane Harrison's assertion that 'myth arose out of, or rather together with the ritual, not the ritual out of the myth', but few would deny that many myths were associated with ritual (Harrison 1912: 13).

The ancient Babylonian creation epic *Enuma Elish* is an example of a mythological tale which was probably closely related to ritual performance. It tells the story of how the god Marduk defeated the monstrous Tiamat – a figure representing precreation chaos. After killing her, he 'split her into two like a dried fish', using one-half of her body to form the heavens, the other the earth. 'Some scholars asserted that the Akitu [Babylonian New Year Festival] included a re-enactment of Tiamat's defeat by Marduk, an event that was explicitly mentioned during the festival when Enuma Elish, the Babylonian epic of Marduk the creator, was recited' (Sommer 2000: 82). Even though we cannot define myth with any certainty, we can identify stories such as this as mythological on a number of grounds: it is an ancient cosmogonic story (relating the origins of the cosmos); it takes us back to a primordial time; it may well have been associated with rituals.

As I mentioned earlier, Mary Magoulick's tentative definition of myth characterizes it not only as concerned with the distant past, cosmogony, cosmology, belief systems or rituals, but also notes that it 'may serve to direct social action and values'. While it is difficult to say what social values might have been attached to the story of Marduk and Tiamat, some creation myths suggest just such implications. In the Sioux creation myth from North America, for example, the present world is said to have replaced an earlier creation in which people behaved in a way displeasing to the Creating Power. The implication of this seems to be that humans are required to live in a way which pleases the Creator, or he will start over again with a new world. The Creator's act of fashioning an unspoiled earth involves his calling upon the assistance of a loon, an otter, a beaver and a turtle, which clearly indicates an underlying value system enshrining a reverence for non-human life. Animals seem to be closer to the Creator than humans: they are partners in the worldbuilding process. 'For tens of thousands of years, Native people have cultivated their symbiotic relationship with the animal world, and these relationships demonstrate a unique centralized status that animals have for many tribal cultures' (Deer and Murphy 2017: 703–4).

The Apatani myth of Kujum-Chantu (northeast India) associates the creation of the world with an act of generosity on the part of the earth-mother figure. Realizing that if she ever stood up all the people living on her body would fall off and die, she sacrifices herself and, in doing so, gives her flesh to provide humans with a diverse and fertile place to live. This perhaps suggests what kind of moral values underpinned the society which gave rise to the myth: not only the reverencing of motherhood, generosity and self-sacrifice but also the valuing of the earth and its resources as the body of the mother.

Such gender values are very often written into myths. By contrast with the story of Kujum-Chantu, the story of creation in the *Enuma Elish* depicts a male hero (Marduk) slaying a female figure (Tiamat) who represents chaos. The Creation myth in the *Popol Vuh* (Guatemala) is likewise dominated by male figures – the 'forefathers'. A strong Christian/biblical influence is notable in its text: 'This water should be removed, emptied out for the formation of the earth's own plate and platform. . . . And then the earth arose because of them, it was simply their word that brought it forth' (Tedlock 1996: 65). The author of the *Popol Vuh*, probably writing in the sixteenth century, was working from some earlier written source, but by the time of composition, Christianity, with its male creator God, was a powerful presence in the regions occupied by the Mayan civilization.

The Finnish origin story from the *Kalevala* tells of female figures being present at the beginning of the world: the 'water mother' and a female duck. The duck can find no solid ground on which to land and make a nest, and so the water mother raises her knees above the surface to provide a firm location. The duck lays its eggs and from them the world is hatched. In contrast to Tiamat, the Finnish water mother is a benign figure who has something in common with Kujum-Chantu, at least inasmuch as she uses her body to make dry land.

Whether or not the values which we can read into these ancient tales – moral, spiritual, social, environmental – were part of their meaning for the cultures in which they emerged, can never be much more than speculation. On the other hand, the fact that they seem, even to modern readers, to be value-laden and to invest cosmogonic and cosmological processes with social significance is surely part of what makes them identifiable as myths. But such a recognition should also be a spur to suspicion. By which I mean that the symbolic potential of myths to encode social values enables us to see in them the traces of certain power relations – between gods and humans, male and female, insiders and outsiders, the rejected and the accepted. Those relations might be interpreted in prejudicial terms; they might be used to bolster regressive ideologies, or to prop up delusory worldviews.

Versions of suspicion

As we examine ancient texts through the following chapters, it will be obvious that the worldviews they encode differ from those of Western science-orientated cultures. These stories include the presence of supernatural beings, the personification of natural phenomena, rigid, divinely sanctioned, and mostly patriarchal social orders, belief in the efficacy of ritual practices, and fixed ideological formations which shape beliefs about social organization, religion and nature. We may well regard such notions as highly questionable, or, at least, as very unlike our experience of, and attitude towards, the world. It is certainly true of most modern scholarly approaches to myth that they are underpinned by a profound critical suspicion.

Eric Csapo points out that myths not only reflect ancient belief systems but can be understood to have played a crucial part in creating and sustaining those systems: 'Most ancient myths survive because they operate at the highest ideological level: they participate in the creation of a unifying general ideology' (Csapo 2005: 301). Such an ideology would, without doubt, have expressed the interests of those holding power in whatever culture produced it. Ordinary people in the ancient world would, generally, have been unable to assert their individual or collective will, impose themselves on social structures, or participate in establishing the order to which they belonged. Myths served to naturalize and eternalize that order and their position within it.

One form of modern suspicion directed at myth, then, is political: it scrutinizes the distribution of socio-economic power in the stories. In Marxist thought, for example, all human activity is embedded in history, and this means that all human activity is also bound up with social conditions. On this account, myths necessarily reflect the social context from which they arose. Although myths appear to deal with the impossible, the preternatural, the unfamiliar and the inhuman, they disguise real-world conditions in ways which blind ordinary people to the reality of their situation. Myths dress up human power relations in supernatural guises so that the ruling classes can claim to derive their power from a higher authority.

Myth appears to be ahistorical (outside of history) and to relate to what we might call the 'transcendent' or the 'spiritual'. From a Marxist perspective, nothing human can be ahistorical, so myths had ideological functions (rather than spiritual ones), serving the interests of the powerful. Exploitation and control are masked by myths of divine order, reward, cosmic purpose and predestined conclusions. In *The Epic of Gilgamesh*, for example, the hero is a powerful tyrant:

> The young men of Uruk became dejected in their private quarters.
> Gilgamesh would not leave any son alone for his father.
> Day and Night his behaviour was overbearing.
> He was the shepherd
> He was their shepherd yet
> Powerful, superb, knowledgeable and expert,
> Gilgamesh would not leave young girls alone,
> The daughters of warriors, the brides of young men.
>
> *(Dalley 2000: 52)*

Gilgamesh is the son of a goddess and favoured by the sun deity, Shamash. The gods gave him his great strength, suggesting that power and oppression are sanctioned by divine will. He is characterized not only as an oppressor of his own people but also as their shepherd, as if the two were faces of one coin rather than mutually exclusive qualities. Thus, neither his right nor fitness to rule are questioned despite his manifest misuse of his position. The people of Uruk cannot by any means resist him; they can only seek help from the gods. So, the constitution of human power relations is masked by being rooted in an absolute and irresistible cosmic regime. Since the gods of ancient Mesopotamia tended to be associated with natural phenomena (the sun, storms, fresh water), systems of control which appealed to their wills and actions could well have taken on the appearance of a natural, and therefore unalterable, order of things. In a layered dissimulation, the cultural is confused with the natural, the political with the spiritual, the human with the divine. Such is the work of ideology as exposed by modern critical suspicion.

As is evident in the case of Gilgamesh and in the mythologies of the ancient Near East more generally (and is no less apparent in ancient Greek culture), the overarching cosmic order which legitimates human power is typically patriarchal. Feminist approaches to the study of myth seek to expose the prejudicial representations of female figures in mythology and its interpretations, as Carolyne Larrington observes:

> Within the study of mythology, female figures have too often been viewed reductively, purely in terms of their sexual function and thus confined in a catch-all category labelled fertility. . . . Women need to know the myths which have determined both how we see ourselves and how society regards us.
>
> *(Larrington 1992: x)*

> Historically women have been disbarred from the means to fix their myths in literary form, to give them a distinctively female perspective.
>
> *(Larrington 1992: xiii)*

Feminist scholars have used a variety of critical approaches to re-read myths in terms of their representations of political, social and sexual conflict between men and women in the ancient and the modern world. Their conclusions are sometimes shaped by controversial reconstructions of two major topics: the treatment and position of women in ancient Greece and the theme of rape.

The question of women's status in ancient Greek society has been, and continues to be, much debated. Interpreting the evidence is difficult, and fraught with issues of scholarly perspective and political commitment. As Marilyn Katz points out, the matter was raised by the work of classical scholar A. W. Gomme in 1925 and reiterated by H. D. F. Kitto in 1951. These two highly influential accounts, although by no means straightforwardly promoting a rigid position, responded to, and fed into, a kind of orthodoxy. A convention emerged that societies of ancient Greek city-states were, across the board, contemptuous of women, committed to their seclusion, neglectful of their education, determined to constrain their movement and designed to limit their participation in public matters.

From the second half of the nineteenth century on, this creed was challenged, not least because the sources on which it was based represent male points of view and treat women as a unified category without taking heed of class, individual or local differences (Katz 1992: 72–82). Nonetheless, as far as it is possible to tell, women seem to have been subordinate to men in most ways, and their freedoms severely curtailed: 'Often secluded within the private household, or *oikos,* women were also excluded from the public areas of endeavour valued by their culture, such as politics, law, commerce, and art. Sources are unanimous in their approbation of this ideal of seclusion' (Goff 2004: 1).

In a sense, it is precisely such gender oppression which drives resistance to the idea that women's experience should be characterized as falling entirely within narrowly drawn bounds. Just because the culture was steeped in prejudicial values and practices, it does not mean women always acquiesced, nor that their seeming silence and obscurity should be accepted rather than investigated. The hiding away of women's lives by assumptions based on their marginalization has been reversed by scholars such as Mary Lefkowitz and Maureen Fant, who have collected a great deal of material which sheds light on women's lot in ancient Greece, bringing them out of the shadowy recesses of patriarchal history. Similarly, Barbara Goff's work reveals their activity beyond the home, especially in contexts related to ritual and cult activity. Complicating the picture in this way serves to disrupt a male-dominated discourse.

When it comes to the theme of rape, Greek and the Roman cultures tended to depict gods such as Aphrodite, Eros or Dionysus as inspiring lust and passion, often with the direst consequences for human and divine beings alike. The flip side of this emphasis on libido was an interest in sexual abstinence, epitomized by figures such as Artemis, the virginal Greek goddess of hunting. Such passions were often, but not always, gendered so that men were associated with lust, women with chastity. Stories of rapacious abduction such as Zeus' taking of Europa, Callisto, Antiope and others are layered in terms of their cultural significance, having social as well as religious implications. Sexual predation by the gods may be motivated by simple lust or driven by some longer-term goal such as selecting a mother for a divine child with a specific destiny. The woman may or may not consent to such treatment. The same myth, then, might be fraught with conflicting themes of attraction, violence, ambition, pride, fate and redemption. But whatever the symbolic complexities of the stories, the fact that Zeus, Poseidon, Hades and Dionysus were all guilty of assaults on human women gives the impression of the normalization (if not the deification) of rape. Little wonder that the topic has attracted a good deal of critical attention and that feminist thinkers have worked to rebalance the interpretation of classical mythology. Jane Caputi draws attention to the ongoing critical project:

> Throughout this century [ie the twentieth century], feminist thinkers have continued to expose the patriarchal bias of mythographers (past and present) and the ways that these entrenched mythic symbols and paradigms construct and maintain phallocentric reality. Simultaneously . . . feminist thinkers actively reinterpret ancient myth, focusing attention on female divinities, supernaturals and powers that have been repressed and silenced.
>
> *(Caputi 1992: 423)*

Some of the most powerful feminist critiques of mythology have been, as Caputi says, *reinterpretations*, many of which have taken the form of creative works. Perhaps the best-known example is Margaret Atwood's retelling of parts of the *Odyssey* from Penelope's viewpoint in *The Penelopiad* (2005), but there were nineteenth-century precursors such as Letitia Landon's 'Calypso Watching the Ocean' (1836), and Augusta Webster's 'Circe' (1870). Even further back, Aemelia Lanyer's poem 'Eve's Apology in Defence of Women' (1611) reinterpreted the myth of the Fall in the book of Genesis, mounting a powerful argument against its misogynistic interpretation in Christian tradition.

These imaginative responses to specific myths draw attention to their psychological aspects, ascribing agency and complexity to underdeveloped figures. Landon's 'Calypso' explores the isolation, grief and hopelessness of the abandoned goddess in a world which cuts her adrift once the male hero is out of the picture. Webster's Circe longs for love and an end to the stifling familiarity of her surroundings, but her island is peopled by beasts she can hardly believe to be men. Lanyer's Eve is motivated by a thirst for knowledge and her love for Adam. Simultaneously creative and critical, the poems encourage their readers to see in their originary myths the lineaments of human, especially female, desire, emotion and psychological depth.

Although in some ways far removed from such re-imaginings, modern psychological approaches to myth have proved enduring and influential. In their intensity, strangeness and obscurity myths bear comparison with dreams: 'Insofar as myths are products of fantasy they are, like dreams, products of relaxed repression. Insofar as myths are products of primitive cultures, they are also products of relatively unrepressed minds. Myths are therefore a privileged source of information about the unconscious' (Csapo 2005: 93). Although Sigmund Freud – that well-known interpreter of dreams – used myths in forming his theories about human psychology, his influence on modern understandings of myth has been minimal. The work of Carl Jung (1875–1961), on the other hand, has seemed persuasive to many people. Jung saw myths as emerging from the unconscious and containing abiding truths about human existence. He distinguished his approach from Freud's by insisting that not all fantasies and dreams can be reduced to, or derived from, individual, personal experience. The similarities between them, and among myths, are the projections of what he called the 'collective unconscious': the region of the human mind – common to all and distinct from individual consciousness – in which ancestral memory is stored.

Similar characters, themes and images appear in many myths from different cultures, independently of one another. Thus, Jung observed that within the collective unconscious there are what he calls *archetypes*. An archetype is a person or cultural role such as the mother, father, wise old man, trickster, hero, companion, double, scapegoat, outsider, which are recognizable across diverse mythological formations. For example, wherever she appears, the mother figure displays caring qualities: she is reliable, sympathetic and compassionate. This is consistent from one culture to another and remains constant through time. Archetypes are often present as characters in myths, and this makes myths the most potent resource in uncovering the unconscious.

Even though myths are rich in archetypal symbols, they cannot offer an unequivocal account of unconscious processes since the meanings carried by the archetypes exceed those any particular myth can communicate. This can be compared with an imaginary modern novel, including a character called, say, Isis, or Athena or Jesus: whatever happens to that character in the novel, the plot could not possibly exhaust the potential for the reader to draw their own inferences based on stories, images, beliefs and ideas which preceded and helped to fashion – consciously or otherwise – the novelist's choice. As Robert Segal puts it: 'no myth can fully convey the meaning invested in it by the archetypes it conveys' (Segal 1999: 72).

Jung considered the symbols occurring in myths to be comparable with those appearing in dreams. Unlike Freud, he was not content to think of dreams and fantasies as purely the products of personal experience or individual desires, precisely because they share a repertoire of archetypal images with mythology. In this sense, myths 'steer one away from a Freudian diagnosis' (Segal 1999: 70).

For Jung and other psychoanalytical thinkers, myth can be explained by human psychology, and human psychology can be brought to light by the dream-like stories and images typical of mythological representations. But that leaves out of account the extent to which psychology and social structures are shaped by language. Like all stories, myths are produced and reproduced in spoken and written forms, so they are necessarily constituted linguistically. Since that is the case, understanding their composition and functions might be a matter of treating them as made up of components which can be assembled in any number of ways, much as a sentence is composed of words with limitless potential for recombination: 'If there is a meaning to be found in mythology, this cannot reside in the isolated elements which enter into the composition of a myth, but only in the way those elements are combined. Myth, like the rest of language, is made up of constituent units' (Lévi-Strauss 1955: 431).

Structuralism, as practised by Claude Lévi-Strauss (1908–2009), developed from the study of language, especially from the work of Swiss linguist Ferdinand de Saussure

(1857–1913). It treats all human phenomena in terms of structures or systems derived from that of language. Language is structured by binary oppositions: that is by a system of choices between opposed meanings (up/down; light/dark; living/dead; good/evil etc.). All human activity is structured in this way since all human activity depends upon, or derives its meaning from, language. Just as language is constituted of units which are combined according to certain rules and conventions, so are myths. The building blocks of language are phonemes (units of sound) and morphemes (units of form), and so, on this model, Lévi-Strauss described myths as made up of 'mythemes', each of which is a single event or circumstance in the story. 'Once you've found the mythemes . . . and laid them out in Lévi-Strauss' pattern, you can interpret them in an almost infinite number of ways' (Klages).

Linguistic units form opposing pairs which provide the basic structure, and so myths might be thought of as operating with certain key binary distinctions: the sacred *versus* the profane, the human *versus* the inhuman, chaos *versus* order, this world *versus* Otherworld. Lévi-Strauss argued that 'mythical thought always works from the awareness of oppositions towards their progressive mediation', and that 'the purpose of myth is to provide a logical model capable of overcoming a contradiction' (Lévi-Strauss 1955: 440, 443). If that is the case, then we might read myths as proposing bridging phenomena which mediate between perceived oppositions: demigods who mingle the human with the inhuman; shamans who move between this world and another; prophets who bring the divine perspective to human affairs; gods who overcome chaos and establish cosmic order; once-ordinary places which become sacred because of some incident or process; omens which function in the human world as signs sent from the divine realm. Of course, as Alan Dundes points out, 'binary opposition is in no way peculiar to myth', and so we might conclude, as he does, that noting its presence in any number of mythological tales 'tells us precious little about the nature of myth in particular' (Dundes 1997: 47). Having said that, the ubiquity of bridging phenomena in ancient narratives is a significant detail, if neither exclusive to, nor definitive of, mythopoeic thought.

For approaches which are suspicious of myths, whether on the basis of class, psychology, gender or linguistic patterning, the ancient stories misrepresent the world in various ways because the ancients were ignorant of many things science and cultural progress have taught us. Geomythology, on the other hand (while, in common with other modern discourses, it rejects mythopoeic understanding of the world), examines myths for their revelatory potential. Its interest is not in supernatural entities, spiritual visions or moral values, but in what myths might have to tell us about geological events in the distant past. 'The geomythologist seeks to find the real geologic event underlying a myth or legend to which it has given rise; thus he helps convert mythology back into history. . . . It is the sudden – especially the catastrophic geologic events such as earthquakes, volcanic eruptions, and floods that make the most profound impression on those who live through them' (Vitaliano 1968: 5–6). To 'convert mythology back into history' implies, of course, that myths – at least some myths – arose out of real events. Momentous geological or meteorological upheavals would, naturally, have been memorialized in stories of inhuman forces and the actions of beings with superhuman capabilities. In a world before science, such events implied the presence of gods who could wield or command the otherwise inexplicable movements of cosmic energies.

Beyond suspicion

Suspicion, then, in the form of a sceptical attitude towards the supernatural, the divine, the demonic and the otherworldly, is endemic in modernity's response to myths. But it is not necessarily the last word on the matter. French philosopher Paul Ricoeur (1913–2005) accepted the need for the suspicion with which myth is treated by modern critical thinkers, but his analysis takes such a disposition as its point of departure rather than its conclusion.

Left unchecked, myth has the potential to present us with false and unrealistic pictures of the world and of ourselves. If we did not interrogate myths for their ideological content, then we would be vulnerable to their influence without knowing it. To understand why this matters one has only to think of the uses to which myth has been put: the Nazis used Nordic myths to justify their claims to racial and cultural superiority and the extermination of those they considered unfit. Patriarchy (the system of male dominance) has employed myths like that of Adam and Eve to insist on the superiority of men and the inferiority of women. European imperialism employed myths of kingdom, race and salvation to justify subjugation and occupation, the theft of natural resources and the oppression of conquered peoples.

For Ricoeur, important as suspicion is, there is another dimension which should be considered. He argues that there is a positive pole to myth without consideration of which we lose a vital aspect of cultural critique. Myth has something to offer the modern interpreter which is not fully accounted for in modern critical readings. Handled with due care, it can be a powerful tool in the study of cultural productions. That much is clear from the persistence of myth in contemporary works in a range of media. So, what we need to construct or formulate might be thought of as a double reading of myth which is both suspicious and attentive.

In *The Conflict of Interpretations* (1974), Ricoeur discusses myths concerned with the origin of evil, dividing them into two groups: those depicting it as having a primordial existence and those tracing its beginnings to a bad choice made by early humans. In the first type, evil stems from the chaos which came before the creation of the ordered world; in the second type, it arose out of the free will humans had to choose between obeying and disobeying the god or gods.

In the Babylonian creation epic *Enuma Elish*, good and evil are implicit in the battle between the god Marduk and the monstrous Tiamat. As the embodiment of chaos, Tiamat represents the presence of evil in the very fabric of the cosmos made from her body. By contrast, the myth of the Fall in Genesis is usually understood to attribute its presence in the world to Adam and Eve's choice to disobey god's direct command not to eat of the tree of the knowledge of good and evil. In the contrast between these two stories, then, we can see the distinction Ricoeur is making.

But Ricoeur argues that, in fact, the story of the Fall presents us with a more complicated picture than is generally acknowledged. The two divergent ways of understanding the origin of evil are interwoven in the biblical narrative, and this fact opens the possibility of reading the myth both suspiciously and attentively. In order to make clear how the myth of the Fall in Genesis interweaves these two versions, Ricoeur first points to what he calls 'the instant of the Fall' (Ricoeur 1974: 295). By this, he means the moment of choice – the point at which Eve eats the fruit. That moment, taken in isolation, presents evil as arising with a human decision. But this is not the whole story, for there are other participants in the narrative: God, who issues the command; the serpent who tempts Eve; Adam who follows Eve's example. There is also more than one episode: Gen. 2.8-9 shows God planting a garden in the middle of which grow the trees of life and of the knowledge of good and evil; God forbids the man to eat the fruit of the latter, on pain of death, in Gen. 2.16-17; finally, in Gen. 3.1-7, the serpent convinces the woman to eat the forbidden fruit and she persuades the man to join her.

The number of participants in the story, and the fact that the Fall is a drawn-out process, suggests that it is neither merely an event nor simply a matter of choice or decision. The tree of the knowledge of good and evil was in the garden before the humans were placed there, so evil as something which can be known and chosen must predate their existence. The serpent is a presence which seduces the humans to choose badly, standing 'for the tradition of evil more ancient than man himself' (Ricoeur 1974: 295). Thus the myth encodes two divergent accounts: the serpent represents evil as always already there and the human couple represent evil as the product of human choice, will and action.

Ricoeur's reading is both suspicious of, and attentive to, the myth. It is suspicious inasmuch as it does not accept the myth on its own terms: it does not depend for its meaning upon the existence of God, nor of talking serpents; it does not treat the issue of evil as a matter of inhuman influence (in the sense of demonic forces); it makes no judgement about the value (cultural or theological) of obedience; it does not treat the text as sacred but approaches it critically. On the other hand, it allows us to think about the myth in terms of our own experience, because it raises the issue of existential freedom. If we are attentive to the myth, it offers us the opportunity to understand evil as always there to be chosen, and yet to see it as emerging from human choices. Adam and Eve stand for freedom, choice and responsibility, while the serpent stands for pre-existing conditions which constrain, influence or limit individual choice. The myth can thus be shown to encode both sides of the argument about free will, without offering any easy way to resolve the tension between them.

Another creation myth, found in the Babylonian *Epic of Atrahasis*, offers a picture of the human condition which has both similarities to, and striking differences from, that found in Genesis. It tells of humans being created as drudges, fashioned by the gods to do the work the gods themselves are tired of doing. For 3,600 years, the elder gods (Annunaki) have made the younger gods (Igigi) do all the heavy labour involved in making the earth, and, after digging the beds for the Tigris and Euphrates rivers, the young gods finally rebel. In response Enki (or Ea), the god of wisdom, suggests the gods should fashion a new kind of being – humans – to do the hard work. One of the gods, We-Ilu (also known as Ilawela or Geshtu) referred to as the god 'who had the inspiration', offers himself as a sacrifice and is killed. The goddess Nintu (the mother goddess, also known as Ninhursag) adds his flesh, blood and intelligence to clay and creates seven male and seven female human beings.

There are many ways in which we might approach the story suspiciously. A Marxist perspective would prompt us to consider the relationship between power and labour in the myth. The division between the elder and younger gods suggests that a human social order – which distinguishes between labourers and a privileged elite who enjoy unbroken leisure – is being ascribed to the gods. This would make the political order a cosmic reality with divine endorsement rather than a product of human economic relations serving the interest of the powerful. It would also render these social arrangements timeless, disguising their historical and cultural specificity.

Taking a feminist approach might lead us to consider the role of the mother goddess. She has three names in the poem: Belet-ili, Mami and Nintu. Even though she is tasked with creating humans here, giving her a significant role for which she is praised and called 'Mistress of all the gods', she is made subservient to the male god Enki. She bows to his authority, saying: 'It is not for me to do it; the task is Enki's. He it is that cleanses all, let him provide me the clay so I can do the making.' This ascription of her creative function to a secondary status may have contributed to the process by which the goddess was diminished in later texts, and deprived of her role as creator. Tablet VI of the *Enuma Elish* (around 500 years later than *Atrahasis*) denies her a part in the fashioning of humans, attributing it to Ea (the Akkadian name for Enki):

> Qingu is the one who instigated warfare,
> Who made Tiamat rebel and set battle in motion.
> They bound him, holding him before Ea,
> They inflicted the penalty on him and severed his blood-vessels.
> From his blood he (Ea) created mankind,
> On whom he imposed the service of the gods, and set the gods free.
>
> *(Lambert 2013: VI, 29–34)*

Tikva Frymer-Kensky describes the erosion of the role of female deities, even with regard to traditionally motherly or creative processes, as 'the marginalization of goddesses' (Frymer-Kensky 1992: 70–80).

But what, if anything, might a myth like this one tell us about the collective unconscious? That depends upon how we understand the comparative roles within the story. In Jungian terms, we have to view those roles as symbolic rather than reading the story literally. The symbolic figures and actions in myths are, Jung insists, necessarily archetypes (recurring figures with timeless value), but identifying those archetypes will always be a matter of interpretation. Myths are the symbolic manifestation of archetypes, but their symbolism is elusive and multivalent. There are clearly certain roles at work in the myth which might be understood as Jungian archetypes: the mother figure (Belet-ili), father (the Annuna gods), the hero (Ea/Enlil) and the scapegoat (Aw-ilu). Humanity appears out of the conflict between these figures, which might indicate the extent to which the collective unconscious characterizes the human as shaped by these determinative roles. At the heart of the myth is the act of sacrifice necessary to the creation of humans. For Jung, the sacrifice archetype is related to the forming of adult identity. It expresses the transition from carefree and leisurely dependence on the mother to self-reliance and responsibility: 'One must give up the retrospective longing which only wants to resuscitate the torpid bliss and effortlessness of childhood' (Jung 1967: 414). The young gods appear to be suffering from precisely such a 'retrospective longing', thus the sacrifice which returns them to the 'effortlessness of childhood' becomes the means by which humanity moves in the opposite direction: to be defined by a laborious existence.

Having identified aspects of the myth about which we might be suspicious, a Ricoeurian reading would lead us to look for ways in which being attentive to it can be productive. In the myth humanity is represented as shaped for drudgery. This might be taken to indicate the psychology of labour: that it is our natural condition, but also that it is felt to be an imposition. Without work, people can lack direction or a sense of value; and yet work can make us miserable. We might read the myth to indicate that labour both defines and limits us; it can represent both the highest and the lowest extremes of human life.

The conflicted relationship we have with work indicates something of our complex nature: we have evolved from simpler life forms, but we aspire to transcendence. We can read this into the myth's representation of the sacrificed god. The spirit of Aw-ilu is said to survive his slaughter: 'From the flesh of the god the spirit remained. It would make the living know its sign.' While it is not entirely clear what this implies, we might construct it as the projection of our higher instincts, ambitions and desire for self-fulfilment onto a divine forebear. Humanity is represented as a mixture of clay and divine spirit, and, however we understand divinity, that might strengthen our sense of self-worth and prompt us to transcend our earthbound origins, reminding us that even the drudge has dreams. Although humans are, here, fashioned to be nothing but the slaves of the gods, it was surely the misery of much human labour which gave rise to the myth's characterization of resentment and conflict between the leisured elite and the put-upon grafters.

The double reading of myth, then, while it does not furnish us with a definition of that disputed term, has the advantage of re-animating ancient stories in the present without making us prey to their darker potentialities. Knowing how to handle myths is, perhaps, more important than knowing precisely what they are. In Book 11 of his *Confessions*, Saint Augustine wrote: 'What, then, is time? I know well enough what it is, provided that nobody asks me; but if I am asked what it is and try to explain, I am baffled' (Pine-Coffin 1961: 264). As time for Augustine, myth for me: I know pretty much what it is until called upon to offer an explanation. As this chapter has shown, a satisfactory definition has proved elusive for a very long time, and the debate looks set to continue.

It may be that a widely accepted account of myth will always elude us because it is a term which exists in the gap between the ancient and the modern, itself a product of what I have called cognitive distance. Myth, after all, is a word used by modern people for a prehistoric discourse. When the ancient Egyptians told of Ra's nightly journey in the solar barque and his battle with the serpent Apophis in the waters of the underworld, they did not think of it as a myth. They might have thought it literally true or considered it an allegory for the human struggle against chaos or understood it as no more than a picturesque way of speaking of nightfall and dawn. Or maybe they thought of it in some other way too remote from modern sensibilities to occur to us now. We call it a myth; we do not know what they called it, or even if they had a name for it.

While my concern in this book is not to elaborate any new definition or theory of myth, I want to offer a minimal description of it which makes clear my approach to the texts discussed. My aim, here, is to explore ancient stories, and try to make sense of them as a modern person in a science-infused, post-Christian culture, and I wish to do so with the Ricoeurian poles of suspicion and attention in view. In doing so, I will draw on a wide range of expert opinion from a number of different theoretical perspectives, but always bearing in mind that, for the purposes of this study, a myth is a story which demands both suspicion and attention, but can be contained by neither.

Note

1. On the relationship between myth, legend and folktale, see Hansen (2002: 1–25).

CHAPTER 2
MYTH AND SCIENCE

Myth as prescientific explanation

In *The Grand Design* (2010) the celebrated theoretical physicists Stephen Hawking and Leonard Mlodinow make a point of contrasting science and myth. Their second chapter begins with a reference to the story of Sköll and Hati – the wolves from Norse mythology who chase, and eventually catch up with, the sun and moon. They interpret the tale as a primitive attempt to account for eclipses and note that other cultures produced similar stories. Another myth follows – one told by the Klamath people of Oregon – in which the eruption of the Mount Mazama volcano in about 5600 BCE is memorialized. According to Hawking and Mlodinow, the story, involving conflict between the chief of the Below World and the Klamath chief, over the latter's daughter, 'faithfully matches every geological detail of the event but adds a bit of drama by portraying a human as the cause of the catastrophe' (Hawking and Mlodinow 2010: 16).

The point of citing these stories is to reveal the inadequacies of mythological explanation by contrast with the power of science to uncover the truth:

> Ignorance of nature's ways led people in ancient times to invent gods to lord it over every aspect of human life. . . . When the gods were pleased, mankind was treated to good weather, peace and freedom from natural disaster and disease. When they were displeased, there came drought, war, pestilence, and epidemics. Since the connection of cause and effect in nature was invisible to their eyes, these gods appeared inscrutable, and people at their mercy.
>
> *(Hawking and Mlodinow 2010: 17)*

Such assertions reveal that, though brilliant scientists and great communicators, Hawking and Mlodinow understand little about myth. Their implicit characterization of the gods as being the same throughout every pantheon and consistent across every ancient culture is highly misleading, as is their reading of the stories they cite. The depiction of Sköll and Hati in pursuit of the sun and moon may have been prompted by observation of eclipses, but to imagine it was no more than a fanciful way of explaining the associated phenomena is to make a number of unwarranted assumptions. First, it ignores the connection between the story and the onset of Ragnarök (the death of the gods and the end of the world order) – a detail implying it was far from being conceived as a simple account of how eclipses come about; second, it takes for granted that such ancient stories can be fully and unproblematically grasped by modern people whose worldview is necessarily extremely remote from that of the original tellers of the tale; third, it reduces myth to a primitive and naïve form of science. In the case of the Klamath story, Hawking and Mlodinow treat the human dimension as an afterthought – 'adding a bit of drama' – apparently ignorant of the fact that myth is inherently dramatic and involves humans in every aspect of the natural world. The story was clearly not told as a straightforward causal explanation of an eruption; it bespeaks the intimate involvement of the people with the land – their bond with it – and the natural forces that shape it.

Hawking and Mlodinow assume that the stories they cite are very obviously mistaken about the world in ways which science has made all too clear. The conviction that myths encode a set of obsolete approaches and conclusions, and the belief that we can both fully understand and easily disprove their claims, are aspects of a long-lived and widespread, but misguided, response to their depictions of natural phenomena. The two scientists are, in fact, expressing an attitude which has been around since at least the nineteenth century. But modern scholarship in the field has rejected the simplistic and patronizing view of ancient cultures implied by such readings, in favour of acknowledging that the temporal and cultural gap between ancient and modern ways of responding to the world may be unbridgeable: 'Much of the thought of primitive peoples is difficult, sometimes almost impossible, for us to understand, in that we cannot follow their reasoning because the underlying assumptions on which they are based, while taken for granted by them, are totally alien to us' (Horton and Finnegan 1973: 251–2).

The alienation a modern person is likely to feel in reading ancient texts is the effect of what I referred to in the previous chapter as 'cognitive distance': what Horton and Finnegan call the 'underlying assumptions' of the earliest known cultures are inevitably far removed from those which underpin cultures shaped by science. Perhaps most fundamentally, science teaches us to believe that whatever we encounter in the world has a physical explanation and is the product of natural laws operating independently of any will or guiding intelligence. We cannot read far into any text from the ancient world without coming across a very different understanding: that natural processes have supernatural causes, and that what ends in human experience begins with divine action. But even though the modes of explanation appear to be contradictory, it is possible to understand both as betraying unremitting drives to understand, account for, and even to control the human environment. In this sense, ancient dispositions can have a recognizable character, if not a familiar discursive context.

There are a number of divergent ways of understanding this apparent similarity of purpose: we might imagine, as Hawking and Mlodinow appear to have done, that myths and the narratives shaped by them are out-of-date textbooks propagating outmoded beliefs. Or, we might conclude that science grew out of the explanatory ambitions of myth but in rejecting its worldview forgot (or wilfully buried) its social meanings and cultural functions. Again, we might acknowledge that the modern age, for all its investment in scientific understanding, has, despite its best efforts, never made a clean break with its mythopoeic roots. For many contemporary scholars, the last of these options has proved most fruitful, and it is now widely accepted that myth cannot be dismissed as a failed attempt to do what science has finally achieved. As we shall see, scientific humanity can neither dispense with myth nor claim, realistically, to have outgrown it. The work of many scholars demonstrates that the relationship between myth and science is not as straightforward as has often been portrayed, especially by scientists.

In common with modern science, some of the earliest texts we know of demonstrate an imaginative fascination with how it all began. As anyone who has heard of the 'big bang' knows, the birth of the universe continues to be the subject of an undiminished interest for humans. There are creation myths from all around the world, and just about every ancient culture had its own version of what happened to bring the world into existence. For some, it emerged from a 'cosmic egg', while for others it was formed by the dredging up of mud from the bed of a primordial ocean. A 'parent' figure features in some stories, giving her body to provide a place for humans and animals to live. In some mythologies, the world was called into being out of nothing by a supremely powerful deity; others viewed the creator as being more like a potter or blacksmith, fashioning the world from pre-existing materials. Yet another kind of creation myth involved the defeat of a chaos monster whose body was dismembered to form the earth, sea and sky.

Because of the prevalence among them of origination themes, myths are sometimes thought of as falling into two broad categories: cosmogonic and anthropological. Cosmogonic myths are those which describe the origin and nature of the cosmos, for example, the story of the creation in the first chapter of Genesis. Typically, these are set at the beginning of time and usually feature gods and/or the first humans. Anthropological myths account for the emergence of human meanings, values, beliefs and practices. For example, the story of the Fall in Genesis 3 might be thought to depict the origins of painful childbirth, patriarchy, the wearing of clothes and nomadic lifestyles.

Whether or not our early forebears really told such stories as a prescientific mode of explanation which made sense of the world for people whose understanding of nature relied on personifications of seemingly animated phenomena, that is pretty much how they have tended to be understood by modernity. Viewing it in this way does not necessarily lead to the disparaging of myth as a defunct and discredited discourse, but it does prompt the positing of an impermeable barrier between myth and science. Stella Villarmea writes: 'Myth is a first attempt to understand the world and the place of human beings within it. . . . It contains a "cosmogony" or a narration about origins that identifies natural facts with divine agents and that includes supernatural facts' (Villarmea 2001: 3). Since myths account for the origin and nature of the world by appeal to the action of deities, and the performance of supernatural or magical feats, they have often been contrasted with the empirical revelation of natural laws and processes, such as Isaac Newton's discovery of gravity, Charles Darwin's detection of evolution by natural selection or Edwin Hubble's observation of an expanding universe.

Robert Segal notes that throughout the nineteenth century, 'myth was taken to be the "primitive" counterpart to science which was assumed to be wholly modern. Science rendered myth not merely redundant but outright incompatible, so that moderns, who by definition are scientific, had to reject myth' (Segal 2004: 3). Reason, especially in its scientific mode, was considered to have declared myth beyond the pale: an inutile and outmoded form of expression. For many people, even today, myth and science are understood to be mutually exclusive: science, the argument goes, has proved myths false and shown their cosmologies to be mistaken. From such a perspective, modern people can look back at their ancient ancestors with a degree of smugness, confident of knowing more and better, and treating myth almost as one might a child's drawing: charming, maybe even intriguing, but hardly accurate. The drawing would be likely to tell you more about the child than about the subject of their artistic efforts, myth more about the primitive mindset than about the cosmos.

That this is neither a realistic nor a just assessment became increasingly evident during the twentieth century, as science was revealed to be both continuous with and dependent upon mythological discourse in a number of significant ways. At its simplest, this is a matter of replacing one kind of story with another, as Roger Briggs suggests:

> Ancient myths were the highest truths, originating from the most revered sages and prophets. Yet today, the word 'myth' is taken to mean falsehood – the very opposite of truth. What happened? The short answer is, science happened. . . . The origin story that science can now tell is our new creation myth. It is the story of all people, and all living things, and the universe itself. It awakens us to whole new possibilities for humanity, and inspires us to create a better world.
>
> *(Briggs 2013: n.p.)*

To refer to the big bang theory (or its contemporary competitors) as 'our new creation myth' is provocative but not altogether unreasonable. If we think of today's leading scientists as our 'most revered sages and prophets' and their work as 'the highest truths' according to current knowledge, then the parallel is not too far-fetched. And if, indeed, the story science tells us of 'the universe itself' has the salutary effect on our imaginations Briggs describes, then its cultural function may be similar to that performed by myth in ancient societies.

But the issue is a more complex one than this suggests, for three reasons: first, because science did not emerge from nowhere, and its roots are necessarily sunk in mythological soil; second, because scientific modernity tends to define itself in opposition to myth (and opposition is always necessarily dependence – we can't know what light is unless we also know what darkness is); third, because the communication of science continues to depend upon images, metaphors and ideas drawn from mythological sources.

Science out of myth

Francis Bacon (1561–1626), a man often considered to have formulated key aspects of modern scientific method, did so by distinguishing the new approach to learning from traditional ways of thinking. In *The Wisdom of the Ancients* (1609), he examined mythological figures and stories as allegories or parables from which could be extracted enduring lessons about the world and human experience. In his preface to the book, he claims to see 'certain mysteries and allegories' beneath ancient myths. Contrasting his approach with religious perspectives, he observes that religion 'doth sometimes delight in such veils and shadows', suggesting that his interpretation will remove the masks and bring underlying meanings to light (Bacon 1886: 14). What myths rendered in figural form Bacon's reading will make literal. Peter Pesic describes Bacon's agenda as delivering 'crucial messages concerning what experiment should be . . . he used a rich variety of rhetorical figures to express his vision; especially, he turned to ancient myth as a storehouse of potent images that he reinterpreted to illustrate his meaning' (Pesic 1999: 81). Chapter XI of *The Wisdom of the Ancients,* for example, takes the myth of Orpheus – the consummate musician who, by playing his harp, charmed the god of the underworld into releasing his wife, Eurydice – as a metaphorical representation of philosophical and scientific endeavour:

> Orpheus's music is of two sorts, the one appeasing the infernal powers, the other attracting beasts and trees. The first may be fitly applied to natural philosophy, the second to moral or civil discipline. The most noble work of natural philosophy is the restitution and renovation of things corruptible; the other, as a lesser degree of it, the preservation of bodies in their estate, detaining them from dissolution and putrefaction. And if this gift may be in mortals, certainly it can be done by no other means than by the due and exquisite temper of nature, as by the melody and delicate touch of an instrument.
>
> *(Bacon 1886: 58)*

The fact that Orpheus set out to rescue his wife from death is compared with scientific interest in 'restitution and renovation of things corruptible' and 'preservation of bodies'. The only way such aims can be realized is by understanding and refining natural processes. The phrase 'delicate touch of an instrument' implicitly compares the dextrous musicianship of Orpheus with the fine-grained observation and careful experimentation of the new scientific practice. When the ancients depicted the preservation of Eurydice's life as brought about by a skilful musical performance, they were encoding the possibility that science might one day 'play' nature no less effectively. Orpheus' musicianship had the potential to reverse the depredations of nature; similarly, science might one day be able to master its laws and command its processes.

Turning to the stories of the distant past had twin advantages for Bacon: on the one hand, it tied the humanist concerns of the period (its interest in the literature, art and thought of classical antiquity) to the cause of science, while, on the other hand, offering a repertoire of object lessons which helped make clear some of the unfamiliar ideas of the new learning. Rightly used, myths could help to 'lead the understanding of man by an easy and gentle passage through all novel and abstruse inventions which any way differ from common received opinions' (Bacon 1886: 18–19).

In Bacon's turn to mythology, there is a recognition, albeit a tacit one, that science necessarily built on older understandings of the world. It was not founded on air: it had preformed ground on which to construct its new laboratory. The mythmakers, philosophers and poets of antiquity had set out a vision of the cosmos which would give shape to scientific enquiry, if only by giving them ideas to question and belief systems to unpick.

The great twentieth-century philosopher of science Karl Popper (1902–1994) argued 'that the only logical technique which is an integral part of scientific method is that of the deductive testing of theories which are not themselves the product of any logical operation' (Thornton 2021: n.p.). Deductive reasoning is the scientific method which starts out with a statement, hypothesis or theory, and then tests it to reach a specific, logical conclusion. Obviously, this demands that the investigator has a theory to test: to make deduction possible in the first place, there had to be some kind of pre-existing hypothesis subject to rigorous scrutiny. As Popper made clear in *Conjectures and Refutations* (1965), this implies that science had to take myth as its starting point:

> A critical attitude needs for its raw material, as it were, theories or beliefs which are held more or less dogmatically. Thus science must begin with myths, and with the criticism of myths; neither with the collection of observations, nor with the invention of experiments, but with the critical discussion of myths, and of magical techniques and practices.
>
> *(Popper 1965: 66)*

A similar point has been made more recently by Jean-Michel Maldamé: 'Scientific reasoning cannot be "self-founding": it bases itself on that which partially evades reason, on intuitions or postulates. . . . Notwithstanding the difference existing between scientific and mythological discourse, it cannot be denied that myth may even have had a fundamental role in the development of scientific thought' (Maldamé 2002: n.p.).

If we take cosmology (the origins and structure of the universe) as an example, it is possible to trace a line of descent from Greek mythology through the works of Plato and Aristotle to the system elaborated by Ptolemy (100–170 CE) sometime around 150 CE. In *Timaeus*, Plato depicted the cosmos as the creation of a figure known as the Demiurge (one of the gods) who, working from an eternal model, imposed order on pre-existing chaos. For Plato (427–347 BCE), the Earth was at the centre of the cosmos, with the other heavenly bodies circling it. Aristotle (384–322 BCE) too considered the Earth to be the unmoving centre around which the sun, moon, planets and stars rotated. Ptolemy, in order to account for movements of the planets which could not be explained by Aristotle's picture, developed a system of mathematical contrivances to reflect the observed motion of each heavenly body. His characterization of the universe as comprising concentric spheres, each with its own motion, survived in European culture until the Renaissance when it was superseded by the observations of Copernicus and Galileo.

As Luc Brisson has argued, the difference between scientific and mythological discourse, can itself be traced to antiquity, especially to the thought of Plato. Not content to accept nature as depicted in mythology, Plato characterized the latter as a mode of thought inferior to philosophy. He saw myths as stories aimed principally at children, and as appealing to the lowest part of the human soul – the part he associated with physical appetites. Philosophy – the love of wisdom – on the other hand, obeyed the dictates of reason. Myth was 'unverifiable discourse', for Plato, and as such, it was not to be trusted (Brisson 2004: 15–28). And yet, just as Bacon would do in the seventeenth century, Plato had to characterize his own practice in terms of its relation to the world he found depicted in myth.

In Plato's wake, the interpretation of myth developed mainly through the use of allegory, and this allowed it to survive the emergence of philosophy and Christianity. Brisson traces the lineage of the allegorical mode from antiquity to the Renaissance, showing how adaptable and resilient the ancient stories and images proved. This was not just a matter of the emotive or imaginative power of a good yarn; it was also because myths demand to be decoded, unveiled or parsed according to the needs of the time: 'Regardless of the context in which a myth is communicated, its receiver is seeking less a textual or literary critique than an interpretation, which . . . makes it possible to adapt the myth to the context of its performance – whence the enduring success of "allegory" through the centuries' (Brisson 2004: 114).

Allegorical readings could turn gods into stars, constellations and planets; into virtues, vices and moral precepts; into philosophical and even scientific principles. They could make the ancient tales stand for historical processes, patterns of conflict and resolution, or form parallels to biblical figures and sacred events. For Francis Bacon, as for the Roman writer Plutarch, it was the very absurdity of things appearing in myths which made it necessary to look for obscure or deep-laid meanings. Myths could be made reasonable, and so kept from oblivion, by recasting them as ciphers of whatever superseded them, be it philosophy, Christianity or science.

Absurd or not, mythological renderings of the natural world formed the foundations on which its detractors, revisers and re-interpreters erected their post-mythological systems of thought and belief. Stella Villarmea argues that reason itself – the mode of thought which looks for sufficient ground to accept or dismiss any proposition, and underpins philosophical argument – is not opposed to myth, but shares with it a history and lineage:

> There is a historical continuity between myth and reason. For example, the first physics and cosmologies developed in Greece (by the Naturalists or Milesians) tried to escape myth and individual gods, but they still interpreted the causes of movement and stability as animated powers, similar in many respects to divine powers. Thus, there will always be traces of myth in philosophical and scientific constructions in Ancient Greece, where logical reasoning and mythical reasoning helped each other.
>
> *(Villarmea 2001: 4)*

Reason and science, then, were born the rebellious children of myth, and so, inevitably, carry its genes in their blood. The work of Gregory Schrempp and Jason Josephson-Storm reveals the extent to which this might be considered a material factor even in contemporary scientific thought.

Science, myth and modernity

According to Milton Scarborough, modern, scientific culture seeks to dispense with myth as 'associated with what is primitive, past, subjective, and untrue – namely, all the things that modernity hopes to outdistance' (Scarborough 1994: 30). The work of a number of contemporary scholars (including Scarbrough himself) shows just how wide of the mark such a perception is. In *The Ancient Mythology of Modern Science* (2012a), Gregory Schrempp demonstrates that in their search for inspiring ways of communicating with non-specialist readers, writers of popular science invariably return to and repeat images and patterns characteristic of traditional mythological views of the cosmos, to the effect that 'popular science writing provides a primary arena for the creation of contemporary mythology' (Schrempp 2012a: 3). This is not to characterize science as a kind of myth-replacement service, in which new stories are put for old, nor to reject science as helplessly weighed down with various forms of cultural baggage (such as gender, class or disciplinary ambition) which keep it from pursuing objective knowledge. Nor yet is it a simple rejection of the other extreme: the 'vision of science as a progressive, culture-transcending venture that promises final, pan-human validity' (Schrempp 2012a: 4). Schrempp's argument is, rather, a matter of uncovering a persistent self-contradiction in the communication of science to non-specialists: 'popular science writers decry even while trying to exploit, myth' (2012a: 5). He sees in the work he discusses a will 'to go beyond mere findings and, through a myriad of extrapolative devices, to venture into visions that aspire to grandeur and something like wisdom – the inclination, in other words, to mythologize' (Schrempp 2012a: 21).

Driving the mythologizing impetus, Schrempp indicates, is a need to provide 'compensatory visions'. He borrows and adapts this term from the work of the anthropologist Ruth Benedict as a framework within which to anatomize the popular science offer. Writers in the genre often allude to the Copernican revolution as the signal moment at which humans had to give up their naïve view of themselves and their world being at the centre of the universe. This is characterized as both loss and gain: the loss of innocence (a myth of the Fall, effectively), and the gaining of knowledge. Since science has forced us to forego our pre-Copernican view, and with it our cherished cosmic supremacy, its apologists feel the need to offer some kind of recompense. This, Schrempp argues, takes a variety of forms. As a consequence of our chastened view of ourselves, the popular scientific rhetoric would seek to persuade us, we come closer to truth and to evolutionary and cultural maturity, we are encouraged to wonder at the scale, scope and prodigies of the universe, we see a new ground for old (moral) values in the authority of scientific discourse, and we find that an expanded sense of kinship offers us a secure place in the cosmos. We are thus compensated for the privations imposed on us by Copernicus, Darwin and all those who have pulled the cosmic rug out from under our once privileged feet (Schrempp 2012a: 224–31).

Why, then, Schrempp asks, do writers of popular science continue to mythologize, while decrying myth? There are, he suggests, many reasons: to impress readers and gain a reputation as a communicator, to promote science and 'earnest convictions' and even to throw 'a sop to the masses'. But, perhaps the most telling reason, for Schrempp, is that 'there are some things that myth still does best and for which as yet we have found no alternative' (2012a: 232).

It might be argued that we have found no alternative for what myth does because it is definitive of the way we think of and relate to the world, at least in the sense that even at our most modern, scientific and rational, the magical, the mysterious and the supernatural retain their grip on our imaginations. This is the story told by Jason Josephson-Storm in *The Myth of Disenchantment* (2017) – a rich and complex study which unpicks the enduring philosophical and sociological oppositions between science and religion, science and superstition, science and magic and science and myth.

Following the diagnosis by German political economist and sociologist Max Weber (1864–1920), modernity has often been characterized as an era of disenchantment and the loss of myth. Scientific discoveries such as gravity, the laws of planetary motion and natural selection led Western cultures to imagine a universe more like a machine than an organism, and natural forces removed from modern perceptions of the cosmos the need for life – whether divine, demonic, angelic or spiritual. From the late eighteenth century on, processes of industrialization and urbanization deepened the sense of living in a mechanized and dehumanizing world. Weber wrote of a process of cultural intellectualization and rationalization by which the mysterious forces that once dominated our understanding were exorcized, so that we can now, in principle, 'control everything by means of calculation. That in turn means the disenchantment of the world . . . we need no longer have recourse to magic in order to control the spirits or pray to them. Instead technology and calculation achieve our ends' (Weber 2004: 12–13).

Josephson-Storm shows how the widespread insistence that modernity is characterized by Weberian disenchantment is at odds with the intellectual and cultural history of Europe and America. At every turn, whether in scientific, philosophical or sociological thought, magic, the supernatural and the inexplicable have been in the background – in the lives of the pioneers and revolutionaries and in the wider social milieu – undimmed by even the most thoroughgoing rationalist agendas. He shows us Giordano Bruno as a magician who was long seen as a martyr in the cause of science, Francis Bacon's self-representation as alchemist and prophet, Isaac Newton studying magic and alchemy, Max Weber toying with mysticism and longing for the emergence of a prophetic voice, Sigmund Freud drawn to occult phenomena, Marie Curie attending a séance and Robert Oppenheimer (father of the atomic bomb) reading eastern mystical texts. As the modernist era dawned – allegedly steeped in disenchantment – it did so in tandem with a wealth of spiritual, esoteric and magical movements such as theosophy, spiritualism and the occultist Order of the Golden Dawn. Today, in a world dominated by science and technology, Josephson-Storm notes, survey after survey reveals that 'the majority of Americans are at least open to the idea of ghosts and psychic powers' (2017: 24). The picture is similar in the UK: 'belief in ghosts, guardian angels, and telepathy [is] comparably widespread in Great Britain and Northern Ireland' (Josephson-Storm 2017: 30).

Josephson-Storm's argument is not aimed at the denigration of science, nor does it set out to promote mysticism, magic or supernaturalist beliefs. The case he makes is that the representation of modernity as an age which has outgrown, transcended or dispensed with myth is misleading. I am necessarily oversimplifying a lengthy, complicated and self-critical investigation, but not, I think, misrepresenting the book, when I say that it demonstrates the extent to which scientific modernity is not only everywhere confronted with its counterculture, but is, and always was, dependent upon that very counterculture for its existence. Like Schrempp, Josephson-Storm concludes that 'we can never fully escape myth' (2017: 316); the rise of modernity demonstrates this, not least because in the very act of trying to escape, it created its own 'myth of disenchantment'.

Key differences between myth and science

While we should bear in mind the evidence and arguments which show science and myth are not mutually exclusive, nor entirely separate, there are some significant distinctions to be made between the two discourses. 'A key difference is that information about the universe presented in myths is not testable, whereas science is designed to be tested repeatedly. Science also depends on cumulative, frequently updated knowledge, whereas myth is based on passed down stories and beliefs' (Magoulick n.d.: n.p.). This is an important consideration, not least because science is definitively the pursuit of knowledge through observation and experimentation and is, therefore, necessarily open to the new and the emergent. But even though, unlike science, myth is not defined by empirical progress, it is not static since it must be responsive to expanding knowledge and changing perceptions if it is to retain its cultural pertinence: 'Myths begin precisely as models of reality, which gradually change by degrees, becoming increasingly complex. As human beings become interested in ever more comprehensive spheres of phenomena, they strive to introduce new concepts into their systems of opinions, reshaping, supplementing, and transforming the mythological model of the world' (Chernyshova 2004: 346).

Such a process of evolution can be seen in ancient Near Eastern accounts of creation. The Sumerian tale of unchallenged separation of heaven from earth by An (the sky god) and Enlil (god of air) morphed into the more complex Babylonian combat myth in which Marduk formed heaven and earth from the body of the personified primeval ocean – Tiamat. The book of Genesis revised the myth again to depict the process as the work of a single deity with no one either to aid or confront him. Exactly what prompted these revisions is not clear, but conflict over water supplies was a constant feature of ancient Mesopotamian life, so perhaps it is no surprise that a mythology developed which depicted creation as a battle to control water. Whatever the stimuli, the myth changed over time, probably in response to cultural and/or environmental factors.

Magoulick's description needs qualifying in another way, too: in relation to the question of beliefs. While it is manifestly the case that myth involves 'passed down stories', the extent to which beliefs are passed down with them is debatable. In the final chapter, we will consider the place of myth in contemporary culture, but in this context it can be observed that myth most certainly *has* a place in contemporary culture, and this is not necessarily a matter of 'belief'. Novels, poetry, drama, films, TV shows and games all draw on 'passed down stories' which we recognize as myths, but they do not demand or entail any belief on the part of the storytellers or their audiences, in gods, supernatural events or superhuman powers. To a great extent, in the modern world, myths have been severed from the belief systems which gave rise to them. Whether or not that means they no longer, strictly speaking, function as myths depends on what we think a myth is, and, as the previous chapter made clear, this is a complicated and probably irresolvable issue.

But if we think of myths as products of prescientific cultures, it needs to be acknowledged that science approaches nature in a way far removed from ancient practice. Anthony Aveni makes the point: 'For people who tell their myths to relate events they experience to beliefs and practices in their lives, myths are truth. . . . The language of myth, however, is different from the abstract mathematical and geometrical reasoned language of science. Its narrative consists of poetry and imagery' (Aveni 2019: n.p.). Aveni's formulation assumes that narrative and poetry are intrinsic to myth rather than describing the iterative forms in which the stories have come down to us. This seems to me uncertain since it is likely that many myths existed long before their appearance in epic poems and narrative cycles. As Gregory Schrempp argues, myth may be rooted in 'structural conceptions' rather than in narrative, poetry or imagery. Which is to say that 'ways of structuring the cosmos (e.g., as a large village, or as an encompassing kin-group)' may have been more important to the founding of mythologies than any particular mode of expression (Schrempp 2012a: 16). Such conceptions must have been given shape and currency by being expressed, but the specific forms in which they emerged and were first propagated cannot now be recovered.

Given these provisos, the contrast between stories and abstraction is a useful one. If some have understood this distinction as one which opposes false and true pictures of the universe, others have interpreted it as more a matter of divergent interests and unassimilable agendas:

> Mythical stories are a way of preserving collective memories that can be checked neither by the storyteller nor by the listener. Their function is not to explain what happened at the beginning of the world but to establish the basis of social or religious order, to impart a set of moral values. Myths can also be interpreted in many different ways. Science, on the other hand, aims to discover what really happened in historical terms by means of theories supported by observation.
>
> *(Luminet 2016: 502–3)*

Luminet's perception that myths 'establish the basis of social or religious order, to impart a set of moral values', indicates that they are stories which neither propagate nor communicate knowledge for its own sake. A mythological universe is fraught with meaning and purpose; myths invest natural phenomena with life, intelligence, will and design. Whatever they have to say about the world, its origins, its shape, its contents and its destiny, they do so with a social and moral agenda which invites, or even demands, participation in the energy and impetus of the whole. Members of the society for whom and among whom the myth is fashioned are implicated in its worldview and invested in whatever religious beliefs and practices might be associated with it. Science, on the other hand, avoids the questions of meaning, raison d'être, goal; as Leon Kass notes, its discoveries and inventions have been the product of its eschewal of theology, philosophy and the search for wisdom in favour of 'securing knowledge of how things move and work' (Kass 2006: 5).

Science, then, stands back from the world: it attempts to treat natural phenomena as objects. It does not participate in nature, but examines, observes, explains it, setting up a distance between observer and observed.

> Scientific objectivity is a characteristic of scientific claims, methods and results. It expresses the idea that the claims, methods and results of science are not, or should not be influenced by particular perspectives, value commitments, community bias or personal interests, to name a few relevant factors. Objectivity is often considered as an ideal for scientific inquiry, as a good reason for valuing scientific knowledge, and as the basis of the authority of science in society.
>
> *(Reiss and Sprenger 2020: n.p.)*

As far as we can tell, for the prescientific mind, humanity was, by contrast, essentially social, interconnected and interdependent, and the social was, in turn, embedded in the natural world. In mythopoeic cultures, humanity appears to be neither a disinterested observer nor a passive sufferer of the processes and events of nature. People are involved in continuous interaction with the inhuman forces all around them.

Ancient myths, then, in their originary settings were not likely to have been recounted as a means of conveying information like a science textbook. Myth was dramatic: it had participants with certain specific roles which made the invention of rituals both possible and necessary as symbolic re-enactments of key happenings. Re-enactment of the mythic stories was a form of engagement in the cosmic conflict between the forces of order and the forces of chaos.

Objectivity is a principal point of divergence between science and myth which makes analysis possible. That is to say: an observer can analyse only what appears distinct and detached from themselves. Analysis is the breaking down of things into their components or constituent elements. Scientific progress is marked by an ever-intensifying gaze into the inmost workings of matter, the discovery of ever finer detail in natural phenomena, whether we think of the periodic table of elements, the identifying of protons, neutrons, electrons and quarks or the search for the Higgs boson particle. Adopting analysis as its primary direction, science begins with the whole and assiduously seeks out the parts of which it is composed. Myth, on the other hand, moves in the opposite direction: it is synthetic inasmuch as it views the world holistically, taking everything human, subhuman and superhuman to be embedded in a cosmic order. To understand a sunrise, a river, a storm or a person is not to anatomize their material composition, but to know how each fits into the overarching set of relationships fixed by gods, nature or eternal necessity.

Enuma Elish and Genesis

Some of these points can be illustrated by appeal to ancient texts which reveal aspects of the mythological formations underlying them. Composed no later than the twelfth century BCE, *Enuma Elish* – the Babylonian creation story – is written on seven clay tablets and continues for a little over 1,000 lines. The title, meaning 'when above', is taken from the opening words of the poem, and the first lines take us back to the dawn of time, before anything had emerged from the pre-existing chaos: 'When the heavens above did not exist, / And earth beneath had not come into being' (Lambert 2013: I, 1–2). The first six tablets tell the creation story, while the seventh is devoted to praising the creator. Many gods are involved in the story which concerns a great conflict between the parents (the god Apsu and the goddess Tiamat) and their children. In the decisive battle, the god Marduk defeats his mother (Tiamat) to become the supreme god. He then proceeds to create the world and humans.

In the epic we encounter certain primordial deities: Apsu (fresh water) who circled the earth and mingled with his consort Tiamat (a personification of primordial chaos and the salt sea); these two were parents to the gods. Among the other most important deities were Anu (the sky god) and Nudimmud (god of wisdom, magic and incantations, also known as Ea and Enki), who resided in the ocean under the earth. Naming and describing the roles of the members of the pantheon, the poem is the main source of knowledge about Mesopotamian cosmology. It gives us an account of the origin and shape of the cosmos, beginning with gods who represent elements or forces of nature. The epic is less about creation itself than it is about Marduk as the champion of the gods and the creator of the earth and the heavens, its main purpose being to account for his elevation from one of many Babylonian gods, to the head of the entire pantheon – an honour explained by his victory over Tiamat.

After killing Tiamat, Marduk dismembers her body and uses the parts to form the heavens and the oceans:

> He split her into two like a dried fish:
> One half of her he set up and stretched out as the heavens.
> He stretched the skin and appointed a watch
> With the instruction not to let her waters escape.
>
> *(Lambert 2013: IV, ll.137–40)*

Tablet V reveals that, as well as depicting Marduk as the creator, and singing his praises, the epic is designed to celebrate Babylon as the city of that most powerful of gods, strengthening its claim to dominance and supremacy among the cities of the region:

When you come up from the Apsû to make a decision
This will be your resting place before the assembly.
When you descend from heaven to make a decision
This will be your resting place before the assembly.
I shall call its name 'Babylon, The Homes of the Great Gods'.

(Lambert 2013: V, ll.125–9)

As the divine residence fashioned by Marduk himself, Babylon's power and status were asserted: it was a city of unrivalled pedigree and importance.

If the epic is considered in terms of an interest in the relationship between myth and science, the combat between Marduk and Tiamat conforms to Gregory Schrempp's description of myth: 'Most traditional mythologies offer astute (for their time) observations about nature. It would be more accurate to define the "mythic" as a readiness to parlay [transform] the best empirical understanding of the cosmos (of whatever time and place) into aesthetically and morally compelling visions' (Schrempp 2012b: n.p.). Underlying the story of Marduk and Tiamat are the observations that water encircles the earth and that freshwater and saltwater mingle where streams and rivers reach the sea – thus Apsu and Tiamat exchange bodily fluids, becoming the parents of the gods. It also recognizes that water is crucial to the emergence and sustenance of life, and that control over it is a matter of existential significance.

Since the story is not simply a creation myth but also represents the glorification of Marduk and the city of Babylon, we can see that it illustrates Jean-Pierre Luminet's argument that myths have a cultural function unlike that of science: 'Their function is not to explain what happened at the beginning of the world but to establish the basis of social or religious order, to impart a set of moral values.' By making Marduk the supreme god, the story establishes a social and religious order, while also serving a political purpose in characterizing Babylon as the chief city of the region (and the world). Clearly, the myth is designed to be participatory: its original users would have seen it as being about them as Babylonians: *their* city and *their* origins. Such a story promotes not only a kind of civic pride but also a sense that the city and its citizens are embedded in a cosmic order established by divine will and power.

The account of the world's creation in *Enuma Elish* has much in common with the first two chapters of Genesis in that the latter associates the act of creation with dividing the primordial waters much as Marduk divides the body of Tiamat. Marduk uses one-half of Tiamat's body to make the sky and the other half to make the sea, and, similarly, God divides the waters above the 'firmament' from those below.

Like its predecessor, the creation story in Genesis establishes certain religious values. For example, it places all the creative power in the hands of a single god who is above and beyond the natural world, and who sets norms and boundaries for human behaviour. At the end of six days' labour, the deity rests, laying down a rhythm for human life, the vestige of which is still with us in the form of the weekend. While for most Westerners this is now more a social than a religious convention, it was not always so, and the seventh day (*shabbat*) remains a cultic observance within Judaism. As the account of creation moves seamlessly into the story of the Fall, further norms emerge: power is placed in the hands of men and secondary status is imposed on women; the wearing of clothes takes on a moral value; hard labour becomes the dominant characteristic of human life. The Fall might also be taken to encode the ancient conflict between agriculture and nomadic herding in the story of the garden and banishment from it.

As well as illustrating the points made by Schrempp and Luminet, *Enuma Elish* and the more familiar creation myth recorded in Genesis reinforce the point made by Anthony Aveni: '[t]he language of myth . . . is different from the abstract mathematical and geometrical reasoned language of science. Its narrative consists of poetry and imagery' (2019: n.p.). Although it might be argued that 'poetry and imagery' are not necessarily definitive of myth, the imagery of the Garden of Eden, the trees of life and of the knowledge of good and evil, the image of the serpent and of the angel with the flaming sword are powerful poetic renderings of how the world came to be and why it is the way it is. Much like the *Enuma Elish*, the vision includes observation of the natural world: the multiplicity of animal species, the danger presented by serpents, the pain of childbearing, universal mortality, the culture-shaping power of means and modes of food production. But it combines observation with storytelling. As Schrempp argues of myth in general, this account of origins transforms an understanding of the world based on observation into a memorable and value-laden narrative.

Conclusion

Since there is no single, fixed definition of myth, the precise relationship between myth and science is impossible to determine. This is evident from the different ideas about the relationship encountered in modern scholarship. In a scientific culture, we no longer need myth as an explanatory discourse in quite the way they may well have done in the ancient world, but it remains significant for modern people, even playing a part in the representation of scientific ideas.

The creative energies which produced pre-literate accounts of the cosmos are no less a part of modern than of ancient consciousness. However incomplete its information and however limited its investigative resources, the human mind is capable of drawing firm and sometimes stubborn conclusions about the world. As a species, we seem to find ignorance and obscurity unendurable and tend to invent what we cannot know so that our deepest uncertainties can be laid to rest. Where there is insufficient information about any phenomenon, knowledge of a different phenomenon or region of interest can be modified to supply the lack. One version of how ancient myths came into being is that people 'considered the whole surrounding world to be analogous to what was already known and mastered, and nature appeared in everything to be similar to human society' (Chernyshova 2004: 348). This is not altogether different from the way science proceeds. Modern knowledge is neither complete nor absolute, and so science has proved unable to eliminate the mythmaking impulse which Schrempp reveals in its contemporary discourse, not only as 'compensatory vision' but as analogous thinking designed to fill gaps in our information. As Tatiana

Chernyshova points out, there are many examples of science supplementing knowledge with its own stories based on analogy: 'The astronomer Pickering,[1] for example, observing certain changes in the moonscapes, explained them as the migration of insects. Herschel[2] thought sunspots to be breaches in a cloud cover. The story of the discovery of Martian canals[3] is well known – they were perceived as analogous to irrigation systems' (Chernyshova 2004: 349).

It may be that human knowledge is definitively analogical – as dependent upon metaphor, allegory and parable as on observation and experiment. This is certainly the impression created by biological sciences in which the identification of genera and species depends upon comparative form and the measuring of similarities. Such family resemblances make possible the creation of categories in every discipline, whether we think of the groups into which the periodic table of elements is divided or the genres by which we classify literary texts. In ancient times, the gods were often similarly arranged in families based on how their relationships appeared among the natural phenomena they controlled or personified. If, as Luc Brisson argues, myth was kept alive through the rise of Christianity and the burgeoning of scientific method by means of allegorical interpretation, then maybe that is because such comparative thinking has always been necessary to our understanding of the world. The making of myth by analogy suggested a mode of interpretation which could also remake it in line with new information.

Analogy-making is as crucial to the creation of stories as it is to the formation of conceptual knowledge, as important to concrete as to abstract thinking. When we read a story, we understand characters, events and plots by comparison with what our experience tells us about people, action and occurrences in the real world. Even fictions at the furthest remove from that experience (fantasy, sci-fi, gothic) depend upon the reader being able to recognize familiar features in the imaginary world, without which what they encounter in the pages of a novel could make no sense. The acts of imagination by which observations are turned into stories, and by which stories are read and recognized as transformations of one world into another, translate abstraction into experience, and vice versa, by means of analogy.

The fact that we have taken myth into our fictions as well as into our science suggests that it is indispensable, precisely because it involves analogy-making which relates ideas, observations and concepts to experience and feeling. It is a mode of understanding to which we turn instinctively when we need to bridge the gap between material encounters and abstract thought. C. S. Lewis explains:

> Human intellect is incurably abstract. Pure mathematics is the type of successful thought. Yet the only realities we experience are concrete – this pain, this pleasure, this dog, this man. . . . The more lucidly we think, the more we are cut off: the more deeply we enter into reality, the less we can think. You cannot study pleasure in the moment of the nuptial embrace, nor repentance while repenting, nor analyse the nature of humour while roaring with laughter. . . . Of this tragic dilemma myth is the partial solution. In the enjoyment of a great myth we come nearest to experiencing as a concrete what can otherwise be understood only as an abstraction.
>
> *(Lewis 1961: xx)*

A similar perception appears in Francis Bacon's *The Advancement of Learning* (1605), in which he writes of the imagination as a kind of ambassador between reason (or understanding) and affection (or will): 'For sense sendeth over to imagination before reason have judged, and reason sendeth over to imagination before the decree can be acted. For imagination ever precedeth voluntary motion.' He turns to myth to furnish his discourse with a suitable analogy, comparing the imagination with Janus – the Roman double-faced god of gateways and transitions: 'for the face towards reason hath the print of truth, but the face towards action hath the print of good' (Bacon 1974: 116). Reason and sense, abstract and concrete, science and myth: two faces, one god.

Notes

1. William Henry Pickering (1858–1938) was an American astronomer who discovered Phoebe, the ninth moon of Saturn, and predicted a planet beyond Neptune.
2. William Herschel (1738–1822) was a British-German scientist who discovered Uranus, along with two of its moons, and two of the moons of Saturn.
3. In 1877, Giovanni Virginio Schiaparelli (1835–1910), director of the Brera Observatory in Milan, began mapping and naming areas on Mars. He saw channels on Mars and called them 'canali'. Canali means channels, but it was mistranslated into 'canals' implying intelligent life on Mars. In 1894, Percival Lowell, a wealthy astronomer from Boston, made his first observations of Mars from a private observatory that he built in Flagstaff, Arizona (Lowell Observatory). He decided that the canals were real and ultimately mapped hundreds of them. Lowell believed that the straight lines were artificial canals created by intelligent Martians and were built to carry water from the polar caps to the equatorial regions (NASA. https://www.nasa.gov/audience/forstudents/postsecondary/features/F_Canali_and_First_Martians.html, 13 April 2009).

PART II
MYTH NARRATED

INTRODUCTION TO PART II

As we have seen, myth is subject to a wide range of definitions and interpretative approaches. The study of literature, too, has been marked by prodigious diversity and (sometimes heated) conflict. Historical contexts, biographical resonances, formal and generic characteristics, linguistic composition, geographical settings and political implications have each given rise to schools and factions. Thus, when it comes to literature which incorporates, draws upon or emerges from myth, the difficulties involved in establishing an explanatory framework are multiplied. My approach to this problem is pragmatic: I draw on as wide a range as possible of translations, interpretations and critical responses without attempting to assimilate them to any specific theoretical model.

Although I have not allowed allegiance to any school of either literary studies or myth criticism to dictate my practice, I have tried to remain true to a few guiding principles. First, as already made clear, I take seriously Paul Ricoeur's insistence on the need to combine suspicion with attentiveness. It will be evident to my readers that in approaching ancient works I take modern suspicion as my starting point. My interpretations are informed by the rejection of totalitarian, authoritarian, patriarchal and racist values, as well as scepticism about the reality of supernatural, divine or transcendent forces. On the other hand, I argue that the outmoded presumptions of ancient stories are just one side of the coin. I set out, for example, to not only alert my reader to Gilgamesh's tyranny and the epic's cosmic pretensions but also encourage appreciation of the story's sober judgements about human limitations and the power of social bonds. Similarly, the oppressiveness and brutality of Homeric culture are exposed, but the development of highly sophisticated narrative representation, more capable than earlier modes of dealing with the complexities of life, is venerated. I have aimed to strike just such a balance in relation to each of the texts discussed in this book.

Second, I have endeavoured to do justice both with and to these long-lived works. By which I mean that, without exception, the texts under scrutiny here include elements which are prejudicial and potentially oppressive to some classes of people. The patriarchs depicted in Genesis are occasionally misogynistic; they own slaves and, on at least one occasion, accept child sacrifice as a means of communicating with their deity. Odysseus and his men steal, destroy, maim and kill with little compunction. Such horrors are everywhere in ancient stories, and I do not think we should let their inhumanity go unchallenged or excuse them as being 'of their time'. I have tried to make sure that my reading acknowledges, and is sensitive to, the victims and their suffering. But doing justice *to* the texts as well as *with* them means ensuring that, wherever possible, they are allowed to speak rather than having modern ideas, attitudes, beliefs – whether mine or another's – imposed upon them. This is not a matter of pretending that we have untroubled access to a long-gone world, or can inhabit the consciousness of ancient writers, but of exposing where and how modern readings are necessarily speculative, limited, gapped or tendential.

Critical discourse, whether in literary studies or any other branch of the humanities, tends to be oppositional and confrontational. It often proceeds by showing where previous approaches have been wrong, or inadequate, or might stand in need of revision. My third and final principle is that I have sought to resist, or at least to limit the jurisdiction of, that convention: I set out to gather, assimilate and synthesize rather than picking fights. This does not mean I shy away from disagreement where it seems necessary. On the contrary, as I resisted Hawking and Mlodinov in Chapter 2, I argue against Adorno and Horkheimer in Chapter 6, and I challenge Roland Barthes in Chapter 9. But, as a rule, I have looked for whatever offered insight, illumination and explanation, and made it my goal to aid broad understanding rather than fighting any corner.

Or, to represent my project in terms of its underlying aims, if I have a corner to fight it is not a matter of battling for or against any set of interpretative conventions: it is to advocate the ongoing relevance of some of humanity's earliest stories despite their investment in questionable worldviews. Nor is it the texts alone that I wish to celebrate. I think it important to honour their curators too. Brilliant scholarship has rescued and preserved these works, uncovered their secrets, kept them alive against the odds. We owe a huge debt to those who have learned the ancient languages, assiduously studied the oldest texts, patiently pieced together the fragments and doggedly followed the most difficult clues. Those who have devoted their highly developed critical faculties to bringing to light and making sense of these vanished worlds have enabled us, in the words of John Keats, to travel 'in the realms of gold' and, at times, to feel 'like some watcher of the skies / When a new planet swims into his ken' ('On First Looking into Chapman's Homer', 1817). Each of the texts discussed in the following four chapters is, in a sense, planetary: each is a world, a diverse terrain, a site of adventure and discovery. Exploration is not only dangerous but also revelatory and unforgettable. If I have communicated something of the excitement attending the quest, then I have succeeded in my purpose.

CHAPTER 3
THE EPIC OF GILGAMESH

The story and its hero

Despite its relatively recent discovery – the first parts to be translated appeared in 1873 – *The Epic of Gilgamesh* is the oldest known extended literary work.[1] It is a long poem, or sequence of poems, narrating a series of episodes in the life of the eponymous hero. Gilgamesh is a king and demigod associated with the ancient Sumerian city of Uruk. A tyrant whose superhuman strength and divine bloodline make him peerless and unchallengeable, his people call on the gods to grant them respite from his appetites for physical combat and sexual predation. The gods respond by creating Enkidu – a wild figure more animal than human – who is a physical match for the king. When the two meet, the inevitable fight issues in a stalemate, and an unbreakable bond is formed between them.

Together Gilgamesh and Enkidu venture into the cedar forest to find and kill its demonic guardian, Humbaba, before confronting the massive, destructive Bull of Heaven. Some of the gods, unhappy at these bloodletting exploits, demand recompense, and Enkidu is condemned to death. Heartbroken at the loss of his companion and newly aware of his own mortality, Gilgamesh sets out on a quest for everlasting life. His journey takes him to a remote region, reachable only by prolonged and perilous travel, where Utnapishtim and his wife reside. This secluded pair were granted immortality for their role in building a boat to preserve life when the gods sent the Great Flood to wipe out humanity. After narrating the tale of the deluge, Utnapishtim tells Gilgamesh that he will never be given the same divine gift since the world will never again be subject to such devastating judgement. However, he reveals to the hero the existence of a plant which can restore his youth if Gilgamesh can retrieve it from the ocean bed. He does so, only for the plant to be stolen by a snake while Gilgamesh is bathing. The weary hero returns to Uruk a wiser man who recognizes that the only things to live on after his inevitable death will be his name and the walls of the city with which he is identified.

The Gilgamesh tradition seems to reach back to a time when history shades into legend: to the age of the archaic Sumerian civilization. The Sumerians were the first literate inhabitants of ancient Mesopotamia (modern-day Iraq). The earliest texts of relevance to the epic were found at a place called Nippur, and these are in the language of the Sumerians. They were pressed into clay tablets with wedge-cut implements in a script known as cuneiform.[2]

Whether or not there ever was a historical Gilgamesh is uncertain, though Irving Finkel – an authority on ancient Mesopotamia – is in no doubt about it: 'Gilgamesh, we can be sure, was a real man', he writes, 'an early king of Uruk who founded a short-lived dynasty at the beginning of the historical period' (Finkel 2014: 82). His name appears in more than one ancient source: the 'History of Tummul' – a document dating from the early second millennium BCE – tells of Gilgamesh rebuilding the shrine of the goddess Ninlil in Nippur, and a later tradition deified him as a judge in the underworld. In the Sumerian King List, he is named as the fifth king of Uruk after the flood. Composed sometime around the beginning of the second millennium BCE, the list catalogues cities in Sumer and neighbouring regions, their rulers, and the length of their reigns. Thought to be semi-historical, it does not actually prove the existence of the epic's hero, as Jeffrey Tigay points out: '[t]he adventures of Gilgamesh mentioned in the Sumerian stories and the Akkadian epic are so overlaid with legendary and mythical motifs that one can only speculate about their possible historical basis' (1997: 41).[3] As is often the case in mythopoeic cultures, there seems to be no sharp divide in the Gilgamesh tradition between history and legend.

The text

There is no definitive text of *Gilgamesh*, and there may never be. As Michael Schmidt puts it: 'the poem will never stabilise. It abounds in contested readings . . . additional material that readjusts the poem keeps surfacing in archaeological digs, museum collections, and even on the black market in antiquities' (Schmidt 2019: 30). Andrew George – one of the leading experts on the poem – declares it to be 'riddled with holes' (George 1999: xv). The standard version (so named to distinguish it from the Old Babylonian version and various other fragments) is based on the Akkadian cycle known to Babylonians and Assyrians of the first millennium BCE, with some material taken from older texts to fill significant gaps (George 1999: xv).

It is possible that tales of Gilgamesh had been put into writing as early as 2500 BCE, though this is not certain. If this was the case, and if Gilgamesh were a historical figure alive between 2700 and 2500, then there cannot have been a long-lived oral tradition underlying the stories. The earliest known compositions regarding Gilgamesh are Sumerian tales assumed to have been composed about 500 years after his death (sometime after 2100 BCE). At least seven separate Sumerian compositions about Gilgamesh are known, four of which are steeped in Mesopotamian mythology. These four were drawn on in various ways in the composition of the Akkadian epic, which was written in the Old Babylonian Period (2000–1600 BCE) by an author (or editor) who bound together plots and motifs from three or four of the Sumerian tales, using Gilgamesh's concern with death and his futile desire to overcome it as the central unifying theme. Enkidu's demise triggers the hero's desperate search for Utnapishtim and the secret of his immortality. The flood hero's story existed in Sumerian, but originally had nothing to do with the tales about Gilgamesh (Tigay 1997: 42).

By the Middle Babylonian Period (1600-1000 BCE) the epic was widely known in Akkadian and in Hittite and Hurrian translations. By the end of this period, it had reached a form which seems to have become standard throughout Mesopotamia. Andrew George outlines the long-drawn-out process by which the Babylonian narrative poem we now know as *The Epic of Gilgamesh* was formed. The earliest known manuscripts of the entire epic are Old Babylonian and can be dated to about the eighteenth century BCE. Subsequently, over centuries, many versions were produced well beyond its region of origin, appearing in Syria, Anatolia and Palestine. Eventually, towards the end of the second millennium, an attempt was made to standardize the text (George 2012: 227). A man by the name of Sin-leqi-unninni, associated with a version of the epic probably dating from the Middle Babylonian Period, is attributed with authorship in a catalogue of cuneiform literature dating from around 1000 BCE. Exactly what his contribution was to the latest versions is not known.

The author, authors or compiler of the epic drew widely on Mesopotamian literary tradition to produce a work which is an agglomeration of diverse materials. Alongside the Sumerian tales, it uses hymnic form (a composition written in praise of a god or gods) in the opening and ending passages, and in the description of Gilgamesh. As Tzvi Abush notes, this is a birthmark of the epic mode: '[a]s a literary form, the epic draws upon and grows out of songs of lament and songs of praise' (Abusch 2001: 615). The passage describing the creation of Enkidu was derived from myths accounting for the origins of human beings, while myths of primitive human life may well underlie the description of his bestial existence prior to humanization. Gilgamesh's oppression of the people of Uruk is likely to have been modelled on folklore or on accounts of older royal practices, while Ishtar's sexual propositioning of Gilgamesh is based on sacred marriage texts and rituals.[4] The flood story is taken from *Atrahasis* – an Akkadian narrative poem dating from *c.*1800–1700 BCE.

Geographical setting

The physical geography of a region cannot but have an impact on the myths that arise among its inhabitants. As Dorothy Vitaliano says, 'man has always sought to explain his natural environment' (Vitaliano 2007: 1). Prior to the rise of science, such explanation inevitably took mythological form. The people of ancient Mesopotamia were confronted with an environment which could be frighteningly inhospitable. Thorkild Jacobsen offers a graphic account of the challenging conditions:

> The Tigris and Euphrates are not like the Nile; they may rise unpredictably and fitfully, breaking man's dykes and submerging his crops. There are scorching winds which smother man in dust, threaten to suffocate him; there are torrential rains which turn all firm ground into a sea of mud and rob man of his freedom of movement: all travel bogs down.
>
> *(Jacobsen 1949: 138–9)*

As well as floods, droughts and dust storms, the region is prone to earthquakes. Modern-day Iran straddles the Eurasian and Arabian tectonic plates and so tremors are frequent in that part of the world, and sometimes devastating. The arrival of the Bull of Heaven in Tablet VI perhaps evokes just such a geological upheaval:

> When it reached the land of Uruk,
> it dried up the woods, the reed-beds and the marshes,
> down it went to the river, lowered the level by seven full cubits.
> As the Bull of Heaven snorted a pit opened up,
> one hundred men of Uruk fell down it.
>
> *(George 1999: VI, ll.116–20)*

The snorting of the monstrous bull may well be an evocation of the rumble of shaking buildings as the ground is torn open. Ripple effects from earthquakes can be a cause of permanent change to a landscape, often resulting in alterations to the courses and levels of rivers and lakes in the affected zone.

Nature's tendency to throw such things at you without hope of resistance or redress is underlined by the words of Utnapishtim towards the end of the epic: 'Dragonflies drift on the river, / Their faces look upon the face of the Sun, / (But then) suddenly there is nothing (Dalley 2000: XI, vi). Figures of natural ephemerality, the dragonflies represent not only Gilgamesh's mortality but the brevity of all human life and the inevitability of loss. The image is a wonderfully succinct expression of a profound paradox, indicating the unendingness of natural cycles as a reminder of human transitoriness. Andrew George observes that 'like the insect, men too have only a brief share of time alive on earth. The image gains poignancy and depth from its allusion to the Babylonian flood story' (George 2012: 238). It evokes, perhaps, the horror of human bodies floating on the water and the fragility of life in the face of cataclysmic events.

If such a view of humanity's inconsequential place in the cosmos seems pessimistic by comparison with ancient Egyptian hopes for an afterlife, or the Greek celebration of heroic exploits under the tutelage of the 'deathless ones' (gods), or even the secure bond forged between humans and Yahweh in Genesis, it has to be understood as a reflection of real-world conditions. Little wonder that the epic begins and ends with a celebration of the walls of Uruk; they, after all, were the best defence against the depredations of an often-hostile environment.

Personification of environmental forces is evident in the gods of *The Epic of Gilgamesh*.[5] Highly unpredictable and capricious, their characters appear to be related to the physical geography and meteorology of the region: they can be friendly, helpful and solicitous but are equally likely to be querulous, vindictive and destructive. They send Enkidu to relieve the oppression in Uruk, and they assist the heroic pair against Humbaba, but they also cause disasters: they release the Bull of Heaven, and they send the flood. In this sense, they seem to personify the forces that one day facilitate, and another day destroy, human efforts.

The gods

As was often the case in the ancient world, the mythology underlying *Gilgamesh* tends to associate the gods with natural phenomena. The father of the gods was the sky god An (or Anu). Originally, he was one with Ki (the earth) and their child was Enlil – god of the air. Enlil begot the moon (Nanna, or Sin) who in turn begot the sun (Utu, or Shamash) and Inanna (or Ishtar) goddess of both love and war. Eventually Enlil became the chief god, and Anu became less significant. Enlil was the patron deity of the city of Nippur, and in *Gilgamesh* he is a turbulent and inconsistent figure: it was he who ordered the deluge to destroy humanity, causing friction among the gods. The mother goddess (Belet-ili, or Aruru), angry at the slaughter of her progeny, forbids Enlil from partaking in the sacrifice offered by Utnapishtim after the waters recede.

The conflict between Enlil and humans is counterpointed in the epic by the depiction of Shamash as sympathetic towards, and helpful to, Gilgamesh. An important presence in the narrative, Shamash is characterized as kindly, just, and all-seeing. He had a place in the Sumerian pantheon as a kind of judge to whom mortals could appeal for fair play. Ninsun – Gilgamesh's mother, herself a minor goddess – appeals to him when she is seeking success for her son in his quest to kill Humbaba (Tablet III), and her prayers are answered in specific terms in Tablet V (compare Tablet V, lines 135-45, with Tablet III, lines 85-95). Shamash's closeness to human concerns is implied when Enlil turns on him in reply to Shamash's charge that the death of Enkidu is unjust: 'Then Enlil became angry at Shamash, saying: "(It is you who are responsible) because you travelled daily with them as their friend!"' (Kovacs 1989: VII, ll.10–12). Enlil clearly despises the cosy relationship, suggesting that Shamash demeans his divine nature in consorting with his inferiors.

Ishtar, too, plays a significant role in the narrative, and, like Enlil, is depicted as a hostile figure. When she tries to persuade Gilgamesh to become her lover in Tablet VI, he responds by detailing the fates of her previous conquests, all of whom have come to harm as a result of her treatment. Angry at Gilgamesh's rejection of her, it is she who calls for the Bull of Heaven to be released. The goddess of war and of sexual love, her character is equivocal: she is both lovely and dangerous. In *Gilgamesh* she appears only in her predatory and aggressive aspects. In other ancient Mesopotamian texts, such as the hymns of Enheduanna, she is viewed very differently. An Akkadian princess, priestess and poet, Enheduanna is the earliest named author we know of. Many of her poems are hymns to Ishtar (known by the Akkadians as Inanna). In Temple Hymn 26, for example, Ishtar is described as 'great' and 'pure' and said to make 'the firmament beautiful / all on her own' (Meador 2009: 170).

The worshipful tone of the hymns, in which Ishtar/Inanna is depicted as 'Lady of Largest Heart' and 'Bearer of Happiness', reveal a side to the goddess not mentioned in *Gilgamesh* (Meador 2000: 117–36). For David Damrosch, the episode in which Ishtar propositions and is refused by Gilgamesh 'doubles the adventure against Humbaba', inasmuch as it signifies the hero's failure to accept human limits (Damrosch 2006: 217). He lacks the wisdom to treat the goddess with due respect, because he has yet to understand his own comparative finitude and guilt. He recites the instances of Ishtar's sexual predation and violence, forgetting that he has been guilty of precisely those crimes.

The only other god who plays a significant part in the epic is Ea (or Enki, or Nudimmud), the god of wisdom and of fresh water. He is mostly seen as a very clever, broadly benign being. He is sometimes thought of as a son of the sky god Anu. In Tablet XI he is the god who saves the life of Utnapishtim by forewarning him of the planned deluge and instructing him to build a boat.

Sumerian mythology also included gods of the underworld. Ereshkigal, who became queen of the underworld, is sometimes seen as the elder sister of Ishtar. There was ambiguity and even contradiction about the underworld. Its name was 'Kur', which also meant 'mountain' and 'foreign land'. Enkidu visits it in a dream and describes it as 'the house where those who stay are deprived of light, / where dust is their food, and clay their bread' (Dalley 2000: VII, iv). In the underworld we also find the Anunnaki, whose nature is not very well understood. In Sumerian texts, Anunna (Akkadian: Anunnaki, Anunnaku) are the highest gods, but the term can also be used to indicate the pantheon of a particular city or city-state, such as the Anunna of Eridu and of Lagash. It is not clear how many (or which) gods are included in the category, but one of their main functions appears to have been apportioning fates. At times, Sumerian sources associate the Anunna with the netherworld (Brisch 2016: n.p.).

Although the gods play an integral role in the story, *The Epic of Gilgamesh* is not an essentially religious work. There is no evidence that it was recited as part of any ritual performance. As a consequence of being unanchored in any such clearly defined cultural context, it has been understood in a variety of different ways. Among others, Thorkild Jacobsen has read it as a 'story of growing up', William Moran as a celebration of human values and an acceptance of human limitations, Susan Ackerman as an account of female liminality in the epic's 'rites of passage', and Tzvi Abusch as a tale of conflict between the hero as man, king and god. At this distance, it is probably impossible to tell what motivated the composition of the cycle or what functions it had for its original audience. Even its categorization as an 'epic' is misleading since it predates the epic form (associated primarily with Homeric models), possibly by more than 1,500 years.

Whatever the nature of its origins and earliest reception, its influence was almost certainly very widespread. Some scholars have argued that the Homeric epics show evidence of familiarity with it. Jonathon Riley, for example, claims that 'the *Odyssey* may take much of its overall structure from *The Epic of Gilgamesh*' (2013: 1), while David Damrosch expresses the opinion that '[h]earing *Gilgamesh* performed, it is likely that the Homeric poets found themes they could adapt to their own purposes' (2006: 212). Parts of the Hebrew Bible (especially the book of Genesis) bear the imprint of some of its stories and their underlying mythology. There is evidence that its influence came down through Mediterranean culture into legends of the medieval period, into the romances, and might underlie elements of Celtic mythology (such as the centrality of quest narratives).

Human limits

As is suggested by the roles played by gods and monsters in its episodes, *Gilgamesh* deals with the relationship between the human and those things which define it by marking out its territory, by fixing its limits and determining what might lie beyond them. It deals, in other words, with the boundary between the human and the inhuman. David Damrosch observes that 'an exploration of the limits of culture . . . in contrast to the world of nature' is 'one of the epic's great themes' (Damrosch 2006: 200). These oppositions are entangled with related binaries such as life *versus* death, order *versus* chaos, and city *versus* forest. Lévi-Strauss' analysis of myth in terms of binary structures is helpful here: 'Mythical thought always works from the awareness of oppositions towards their progressive mediation . . . the purpose of myth is to provide a logical model capable of overcoming a contradiction' (Lévi-Strauss 1955: 440, 443).

Perhaps the most obvious way in which the epic mediates oppositions is in the depiction of the hero as two-thirds god, one-third human, making Gilgamesh the earliest example of the god-man – a category which would later include Hercules, Achilles, Jesus and Superman. He connects the human with the divine and embodies the power of the state. In later Sumerian and in Old Babylonian writings, we find the assertion that 'kingship was let down from heaven', implying that the monarch's power has a divine source and is therefore unchallengeable. *Gilgamesh* makes clear that the people of Uruk cannot resist the oppressive behaviour of their king; they can only appeal to the gods for help. This is a direct consequence of his semi-divine status, of the fact that he bridges the divine–human divide.

Enkidu's appearance as a kind of anti-Gilgamesh rebalances the order overthrown by the tyrant's excessive behaviour. He is created by the gods to preserve the civilized state and to provide a counterweight to oppressive power: Gilgamesh might be said to represent overweening order, and Enkidu the opposite – wildness, nature and disorder.

The solution to Gilgamesh's tyranny, then, depends on the intervention of the gods. Because he embodies human-divine power like no other figure in early literature – the coalescence of the human and the divine in the figure of the king – he is the personification of irresistible force. On the other hand, he also embodies order, civilization, culture, as opposed to chaos and nature. As king of Uruk, he *is* the city in human form, an understanding made evident in his identification with the city walls at the opening and close of the epic. That symbolic identity suggests the belief that there was a divine dimension to the very existence of civilized order: 'Climb Uruk's wall and walk back and forth! / Survey its foundations, examine the brickwork! / Were its bricks not fired in an oven? / Did the seven sages not lay its foundations?' (George 1999: I, 18–21). The 'seven sages' (*Apkallu*) were semi-divine beings associated with water and with the founding of human civilization. According to James Davila, before the flood they guided humanity through its early progress, revealing more and more knowledge as time went on (Davila 1995: 200). So, there is an intimate connection between human and inhuman at work here. The city is construed as a bounded space between the superhuman (gods) and the subhuman (nature). Since Gilgamesh, being part god and part man, forms a bridge between the divine and the human, it is highly significant that he is depicted as a builder and is identified with the walls of the city.

On the other side of the human enclave, Enkidu forms a bridge between human and subhuman: he is created not in the city but in the wilderness, outside the city walls: 'Aruru washed her hands, she pinched off some clay, and threw it into the wilderness. / In the wilderness she created valiant Enkidu' (Kovacs 1989: I, ll.83–4). Just as Gilgamesh is part man and part god, so Enkidu is part man, part beast, depicted as covered in hair, eating grass and 'jostling at the watering hole with the animals' (Kovacs 1989: I, ll.86–92). Gradually, he moves towards civilization, beginning with his sexual encounter with Shamhat, who is sent out specifically to seduce him and initiate his transformation into a man: 'He was sated with her charms. / But when he turned his attention to his animals, / the gazelles saw Enkidu and darted off, / the wild animals distanced themselves from his body' (Kovacs 1989: I, ll.177–80).

Enkidu's estrangement from the animal kingdom is followed by his being clothed: 'She stripped, and clothed him in part of her garment' (George 1999: II, from Pennsylvania tablet, l. 70). Once clothed, he is given bread and ale: processed food and drink replacing grass and water (George 1999: Pennsylvania tablet, ll.100–1). The final stage of his humanization is the removal of his animal hair: 'The barber groomed his body so hairy, / anointed with oil he turned into a man' (George 1999: Pennsylvania tablet, ll.108–9).[6] Once fully human, Enkidu can enter the city.

Lodged between the chaos of nature (the wild) and the realm of the gods, the city is subject to the two forces – divine and the natural – both of which can be threatening and destructive. Since Gilgamesh is part god, while Enkidu is part beast, each mediates between the city and one of its opposites in a unified cosmic order. Thus, the bond between them forms a protective ring around civilization so that, together, they represent an embodiment of the city walls, and it is this bond which both prompts and enables their defeat of Humbaba, who embodies chaos: 'The identification of Humbaba as evil, along with his position in the wild, indicates in fact that we have here an example of a very common motif in the Near Eastern hero story: the fight between the hero as agent of order and a monster representing chaos, disorder' (Van Nortwick 1996: 21).

Just as they define the relationship between the human and that which lies beyond it in both directions, Gilgamesh and Enkidu undertake complementary journeys expressive of their bridging functions. Van Nortwick observes that Enkidu moves from wildness to civilization, while Gilgamesh moves from civilization to wildness. The balance struck by these journeys is definitive of the city. As we have seen, Enkidu's journey from beast to human has a number of stages: encounter with hunters, human sexual experience, putting on clothes, eating prepared or processed food, grooming and entry into the city. Gilgamesh's journey forms a mirror image: encounter with Enkidu, refusal of sex with a goddess (Ishtar), re-clothing in animal skins, eating wild (non-prepared) food (raw animal flesh), refusal to bathe and entry into the wilderness.

Once Gilgamesh has completed his descent into a subhuman condition, he makes the return journey. Symbolic washing and re-clothing mark the turning point:

And he washed in water his filthy hair, as clean as possible.
He threw away his skins, and the sea carried them off.
His body was soaked until it was fresh.
He put a new headband on his head.
He wore a robe as a proud garment.

(Dalley 2000: XI, v)

Clearly, these phases echo some of those through which Enkidu passed on the way to becoming human. At the end of his return journey, Gilgamesh looks at the city walls with a new understanding of what they represent: they define him, just as they do civilization. He is now able to be identified with the walls more completely, compensating for Enkidu's death by absorbing the experience of wildness, and so unifying the two inhuman extremes. He becomes a living symbol of the city as bastion against both chaos and unchecked power.

The forest

Given the extent to which the mythological and narrative focus of the epic is on the city walls definitive of human space, separating it from the wilderness, the first adventure of the newly bonded pair – their encounter with the forest – has profound implications. Benjamin Foster observes that throughout the epic images of material culture are used approvingly, while those comparing human or divine characteristics with nature are broadly negative, 'suggesting that poets were inclined to glorify civilization over natural phenomena' (1996: xvii). Nature might be seen to be at its most menacing, most remote, and most alien in the forest, and Robert Pogue Harrison argues that for ancient people forests represented the dark other of civilization, its fearful and threatening shadow. Gilgamesh, as a representative of the city and of civilized life, confronts the forest, personified as the monstrous Humbaba (or Huwawa).

Drawing on the work of the Italian philosopher Giambattista Vico (1668–1744), Harrison suggests a number of reasons why forests took on the character of demonic regions. Perhaps most fundamentally, they represented the absence of the sky, of heaven, of light. Divinity was often identified with the sky, the sun and stars, the very things hidden from view by the forest canopy (Harrison 1992: 6). Not only do the trees hide the sky, but they also compromise our sense of time by cutting us off from the marking of its passage by heavenly bodies. They seem timeless in the sense that trees can live for hundreds of years: 'Precisely because they lie beyond its horizon of linear time forests can easily confuse the psychology of human orientation' (Harrison 1992: 8). Since forests form what Harrison refers to as 'an obstacle to visibility', they represent a bar to progress, both literally (inasmuch as you cannot build a city in a forest without first making a clearing), and metaphorically (they make it impossible see the world clearly). They appear, then, to obscure what human knowledge and science bring to light (Harrison 1992: 10). In the ancient Mesopotamia of Sumerian civilization, forests would also have been associated with a kind of foreignness since the region included none. Hostile and dangerous environments, they were the very antithesis of civilization, and so the intimate connection between Gilgamesh and the city wall makes the forest episode particularly significant. The journey to the forest and the killing of its guardian are integral to the depiction of Gilgamesh as wall-builder and embodiment of the city.

The absence of forests from the region meant that timber of suitable quality for building could be acquired only by facing hardship and danger, by confronting and conquering the fearful terrain. Expeditions to the mountains to cut down cedars were perilous, not least because the forests were often inhabited by tribes prepared to defend their territory, 'but a leader could derive considerable fame from a successful expedition' (Harrison 1992: 17). This would have contributed both to the mythology of the forest and to the value of the city as its light-filled other. Two ancient Mesopotamian kings were said to have undertaken such expeditions: Sargon the Great (first ruler of the Akkadian empire) and Gudea of Lagash. Conquering the forests feeds into a belief that civilization is the definitively human space beyond which lie the intolerable dispersion and darkness of regions which had to be conquered in order for the city to be built. The defeat of Humbaba is a mythological rendering of the emergence of a new way life beyond the reach of all things wild.

The story of Humbaba's violent demise appears in Tablet V of the epic. In common with the other tablets, the text has many gaps or lacunae which can make it difficult to follow. The episode has the heroes venture warily into the forest, weapons drawn. Humbaba confronts them, accusing Enkidu of treachery for siding with humans against him. Gilgamesh and Humbaba close in combat, and Shamash sends thirteen winds to hamper and batter Humbaba until he is overpowered. The demon pleads for his life, while Enkidu urges Gilgamesh to finish him off before the gods take notice and intervene. Humbaba curses his attackers and is despatched. The victorious pair begin felling the huge cedar trees and transporting them back to Uruk.

Andrew George's book helpfully supplies the reader with an alternate version of the episode's conclusion from an Old Babylonian tablet, in which we can read of Enkidu's plan to build a great door from the plundered timber. The image of the door has a particular resonance since it suggests that the defeat of Humbaba is what makes the city possible: civilization is predicated upon the destruction of the forest. It seems significant, too, that what Enkidu wants to build is a *temple* door. The door is both what allows access and what shuts out. The temple, of course, is the sacred space where humans communicate with the gods, and so its door marks the threshold or boundary between the human and the divine. The conquering of the forest is, perhaps, what enables access to the divine, and this would fit well with the idea discussed by Harrison: that the forests were feared because they threatened to seal humans off from the gods. Using timber from the forest for a door both memorializes the primordial darkness which hid the gods from view and celebrates the removal of the obstacle every time the door is opened. We might add that the temple which Enkidu wishes to adorn with his magnificent door is devoted to Enlil – the supreme god in the Sumerian pantheon. Enlil was sometimes associated with the air and the wind, so, again, access to him may well have been associated with cutting down trees.

In the confrontation between Humbaba and his attackers, Enkidu's wild origins are referred to, the forest demon calling him 'son of a fish' and reminding him of his animal past (V, ll.78–80). Because he was once uncivilized (in its root meaning – not of the city) Enkidu is seen by Humbaba as a traitor in siding with the human cause: 'Now in treachery you bring before me Gilgamesh, / and stand there, Enkidu, like a warlike stranger!' (George 1999: V, 91–2). The mythological implication of this is that the combat is one which pits civilization against the wild. This is not just a fight between heroes and monsters; rather, it is a kind of primordial struggle between chaos and order. Gilgamesh and Humbaba represent these two poles, while Enkidu represents the shift from primordial wildness and dispersion to the fully human condition of life within walls.

During the confrontation, Humbaba threatens that he will kill Gilgamesh and feed his flesh to the birds. As Harrison observes (following Vico) burial of the dead is one of the markers of human civilization which 'defined the boundary of its place of belonging, rooting itself quite literally in the soil, or *humus*, where ancestral fathers lived underground. Humanity is bound to these funeral rites' (Harrison 1992: 7). So when Humbaba threatens to feed Gilgamesh to the wild birds, he is aligned, once again, with everything civilization is designed to overcome. His action would dehumanize Gilgamesh by removing him from one of the fundamental institutions of human civilization.

That this is a battle of cosmic significance, and one transcending the immediate circumstances is indicated by the scale of the destruction unleashed by the confrontation: 'At the heels of their feet the earth burst asunder, / they shattered as they whirled Mounts Sirion and Lebanon' (George 1999: V, ll.133–4). The Old Babylonian version from Ishchali puts it even more graphically: 'He slew the ogre, the forest's guardian, / at whose yell were sundered the peaks of Sirion and Lebanon, / the mountains did quake, / all the hillsides did tremble' (George 1999: Ishchali, 30–3). In this version, it is not the stamping feet which split the mountains; it is the cry of the defeated ogre. Either way, the killing of Humbaba is also the overcoming of the wild more generally: the natural environment feels the force of human domination, and this is depicted as a kind of earthquake.

While the emphasis is on the heroism of Gilgamesh and Enkidu and the literally earth-shaking significance of their victory, the role of the gods is crucial. Shamash in particular plays a key role in the battle, rousing thirteen winds which buffet and immobilize Humbaba. The number of winds evoked by Shamash is probably a reflection of the ancient Mesopotamian environment, but the fact that a god intervenes in the human cause is an important consideration. If the confrontation between Gilgamesh and Humbaba reflects a mythopoeic understanding of the primordial shift from wildness to civilization, then it suggests that civilization is, at least in part, the work of the gods.

Shamash, of course, is the sun god, so it should be no surprise that the defeat of the forest guardian is due to his intervention. Ruth Horry helps to make the connection: 'As the sun fills the entire sky with light, Šamaš oversaw everything that occurred during the daytime. He thus became the god of truth, judgements and justice. Šamaš also played a role in treaties, oaths and business transactions, as he could see through deceit and duplicity' (Horry 2013: n.p.). Shamash, whose light fills the city – unlike the forest – presided over so many aspects of civilized life that his role in the defeat of Humbaba supports the interpretation of the episode as an ancient combat myth related to the establishment of the world's oldest known cities. It also supports the idea that the city was understood as the antithesis of the forest.

And yet, despite (or perhaps because of) the profound opposition between them, city and forest are intimately related: timber becomes part of the fabric of the city, and the cutting down of trees is symbolic of the civilized rituals of death. Harrison depicts Gilgamesh as deeply affected by the sight of mortuary practices in which the bodies of the dead were floated down the river (Harrison 1992: 16). When Gilgamesh and Enkidu return from the forest, they bring home its timber in a similar manner, and the image of buoyant logs looks forward to the moment in Tablet XI when Utnapishtim's reference to the dragonfly on the surface of the water will prompt meditation on the brevity of human life and the inevitability of death. This pattern of images connects the epic's first adventure with its last and serves to make human mortality not only the focus of Gilgamesh's quest to find Utnapishtim but also the epic's abiding theme. The Great Flood is the ultimate expression of human finitude: it places us in the hands of capricious deities who command irresistible natural forces. Hearing about the Deluge, Gilgamesh comes to see that humans can be cut down and floated away as easily as trees.

The Great Flood

The flood narrative in *Gilgamesh* is based on the myth of Atrahasis which is, in turn, based on an older account known as the *Eridu Genesis*: a Sumerian text relating the oldest known Mesopotamian version of the Great Flood. The *Eridu Genesis* dates from *c.*2300 BCE in its written form, but its underlying oral tradition is thought to be much older. There may well be a direct line of descent from the *Eridu Genesis,* to *Atrahasis*, to *Gilgamesh*, to the biblical story of Noah.

The man chosen to survive the flood and preserve life on earth in the earliest version of the tale is Ziusudra, king of the city of Shuruppak, a lustration priest (conducting purification rituals) and a seer (Jacobsen 1981: 522). The Sumerian flood story begins with the creation of the world by the gods An, Enlil, Enki and Ninhursaga. After humans and animals are created, the gods, especially Ninhursaga (mother goddess), herd them into cities, the first of which was Eridu.

Following this section of the narration a few lines are missing; they probably explained why the gods decided to destroy humanity. In the later *Atrahasis* story, the reason is that people become too numerous and too loud, disturbing Enlil's rest. *Atrahasis* depicts Enlil sending a drought, then a plague and then a famine to decrease the population and reduce the noise, but each time, Enki (god of wisdom and friend of humanity) tells the people what they should do to reverse Enlil's plagues. The story continues with all the gods swearing an oath, presumably that they will not interfere in the decision of An and

Enlil to destroy humanity. Since it seems likely that Enki, along with all the other gods, has taken the oath not to interfere with the flood, he cannot warn Ziusudra directly and so speaks to a wall, knowing that Ziusudra on the other side of it will hear him. At this point, there are more lines missing which would (probably) have detailed Ziusudra's construction of a large boat into which he took many animals. The narrative resumes with a depiction of the flood, which continues for seven days and seven nights. Ziusudra makes a hole in the side of the boat, and Utu (Shamash), in the form of the sun's rays, enters. Ziusudra makes a sacrifice to the god but what happens afterwards is lost. In the end, An and Enlil seem to have repented of their genocidal decision and, grateful that Ziusudra has preserved their creations, grant him eternal life in the land of Dilmun (a kind of paradise). Based on fragments of the tablet, it appears that the story continued after this seeming conclusion for another thirty-nine lines, but the content is lost.

Stephanie Dalley, among others, sees the Sumerian flood story as the original version of all such stories which occur in mythologies from all over the world: 'All these flood stories may be explained as deriving from the one Mesopotamian original, used in traveller's tales for over two thousand years, along the great caravan routes of Western Asia: translated, embroidered, and adapted according to local tastes to give a myriad of divergent versions' (Dalley 2000: 7).

Thorkild Jacobsen suggests that the flood myth proved so enduring and popular because it is not really a story of an all-embracing catastrophe, so much as it is about surviving such an event and making the world anew. The import of the story is that humanity pulled through a one-off disaster which taught the gods that they must, in future, behave differently towards the world under their power. For those who witnessed the destruction, recounting the story was a matter of hope and reassurance in the face of a natural order which could turn against humans to such devastating effect (Jacobsen 1981: 527).

Probably prompted by actual events, or at least by environmental factors, the Babylonian deluge epic had its origins in an independent myth. Its inclusion in *Gilgamesh* serves to draw attention to certain theological and philosophical themes such as human finitude, divine justice and the relationship between them (Fisher 1970: 393–5). Forming the climax to the epic's action, it draws together the thematic strands which have been threaded through the episodes – mortality and immortality, the familiar and the remote, quest and destiny. It might be said to serve a moral and religious purpose in *Gilgamesh*, prompting consideration of, among other things, the fraught relationship between human life, limits and aspirations, and the character of the gods.

The story is recounted as the culmination of Gilgamesh's quest both because the action of the gods in bringing the flood raises questions about their wisdom and moral probity and because Utnapishtim is the only human to have been granted immortality. According to Liesbeth Altes, in the aftermath of the cataclysm the gods are revealed to share with humans a 'striving for rationality' as they learn the value of restraint. The goddess Belet-ili laments her ill-considered support of the gods' decision to drown the world, and the text reveals the regrets of the other gods, too, for an action which proved too extreme. They come to see that they have failed in their duty to protect humankind, and to set an example of moderation. 'Hence the importance of the code of conduct which is then formulated, with moderation and rational behavior as prominent values. These are precisely the values that Utnapishtim holds up for Gilgamesh' (Altes 2007: 192).

Altes, in common with Andrew George, links this moment in the story with a shift of focus from individual to social. George considers that, in depicting a man obsessed with his own mortality coming to see the folly of his quest for everlasting life, the epic 'subordinates the concerns of man the individual to those of man the collective' (George 2012: 235). As George observes, the poem begins with praise for the hero and ends with an encomium on the city.

But the movement from the individual to the collective is crucial to the flood episode specifically, as well as to the narrative as a whole, and applies to the gods as much as to humans. In sending the flood, the gods were acting in their own short-term interests with no thought of the consequences; this is evident from the upbraiding of Enlil by Ea in the aftermath of the devastation: 'How, how could you bring about a Flood without consideration? / Charge the violation to the violator, / Charge the offense to the offender' (Kovacs 1989: XI, ll.180–2). The words echo Belet-ili's expression of dismay at Enlil's action: 'he lacked counsel and brought on the Deluge, / and delivered my people into destruction' (George 1999: XI, ll.159–60). The assembly of the gods has been divided by the flood and its consequences, but only by acting in concert can they restore order. Their final act in the episode is an agreement to bestow immortality on Utnapishtim and his wife – a symbolic reversal of the carnage and an acknowledgement that the flood was an error of judgement. What one god – Enlil – instigated is remediated by the collective response. The gods, then, must learn the wisdom of collective decisions, and how to act justly, revealing the extent to which the mythological formation underlying *Gilgamesh* was shaped by the terrifying unpredictability of the environment. Such environmental concerns are encoded in the depiction of mercurial and fallible deities who needed a lesson in rationality.

Bread, plant and snake

The episode which follows Utnapishtim's recounting of the flood story emphasizes Gilgamesh's mortality in such a way that he recognizes his own weakness, and by extension, the impossibility of human immortality. Utnapishtim challenges him to stay awake for six days and seven nights to show that he has the strength and stamina for interminable existence. He promptly falls asleep for the full length of time required of his wakefulness. On awaking, he tries to convince Utnapishtim and his wife that he has not slept long, but in order to prove to him the excessive duration of his slumber, Utnapishtim's wife has baked him a loaf of bread each day, and his attention is drawn to the distinctive stage of decay in each one. Bread, of course, is what sustains human life, and it becomes a metaphor, too, for the ageing and decay of the human body.

The fact that Gilgamesh tries to deceive his way into immortality by lying about how long he slept underlines his unworthiness to be rewarded in the way that Utnapishtim has been. We know he is lying rather than just not realizing how long he has slept, because Utnapishtim warned his wife in advance: 'Man is deceitful, he will deceive you' (George 1999: XI, 219). Hence the need for the loaves. So Gilgamesh is neither strong enough nor honest enough to be given the gift of immortality. This is reinforced by the final episode in which Utnapishtim tells Gilgamesh of a plant which can reverse the effects of ageing. Gilgamesh acquires the plant, but it is stolen from him by a snake while he bathes.

The narration of the hero's return journey repeats the lines: 'At twenty leagues they ate their ration. /At thirty leagues they stopped for the night' (Dalley 2000: XI, vi). It is during one of these breaks that Gilgamesh bathes and the plant is lost. The need to eat, rest and bathe emphasizes once more the weakness and limitations of human flesh. It is neither an accident nor the judgement of the gods which deprives Gilgamesh of his immortality; it is human finitude writ large in the semi-divine hero.

On consuming the plant, the snake immediately sheds its skin, suggesting that its life has been renewed. At this point Gilgamesh not only concedes defeat but acknowledges that in his determination to find the plant, he has made his journey home more difficult and perilous: 'Now the high waters are coursing twenty leagues distant, / As I was opening the conduit (?) I turned my equipment over into it (?). / What can I find (to serve) as a marker (?) for me ? / I will turn back (from the journey by sea) and leave the boat by the shore!' (Kovacs 1989: XI, 306–9). Although it is not quite clear (to me, at least) what these lines mean, they seem to suggest that during his attempt to recover the plant from the ocean bed, the tide has turned, and left Gilgamesh unsure where he is in relation to his boat.[7] It may even suggest that the boat has been carried off by the rising water. The episode underlines the foolishness of Gilgamesh's quest, his all-too-human weakness and, again, his unsuitability to be rewarded with everlasting life. And so he heads for home a wiser man.

The epic ends with attention being drawn once more to the walls of Uruk. But, as Andrew George makes clear, the emphasis of the closing lines is rather different from those at the beginning. Returning to Uruk with the boatman Urshanabi (banished by Utnapishtim for ferrying Gilgamesh over the Waters of Death), Gilgamesh urges him to look not only at the walls themselves but at what they enclose. If the opening lines associate the walls with Gilgamesh, and hint that they will be a lasting memorial to him, the closing lines make the city more important than its king. This, ultimately, is what the hero's journey has shown him. He once treated the city as his playground and its people as his to command and control for his personal gratification. Chastened by confrontation with his own finitude and made wiser by those he has encountered on his travels, he now knows that the city is what endures, and that it is greater than any one individual. George writes: 'The Uruk that Gilgamesh urges Ur-shanabi to look upon is divided into four: city, date-grove, clay-pit and temple. These terms do not describe the city topographically; they organize its contents thematically. For me they symbolized four fundamental activities of human existence: raising of family, production of food, manufacturing, and intellectual and spiritual life' (George 2012: 234).

The walls of the city remind us that human limits have been set by the gods, but that those boundaries are not so much individual as they are intrinsic to humanity and the activities which define it. Two thousand or so years later, the Greek philosopher Aristotle would describe a human as a 'political animal': that is, as one who lives in a *polis* or city. He might have learned as much from *Gilgamesh*: a story in which the city defines what it means to be human by marking the boundaries of our existence. But the epic was drawing on an older tradition with regard to cities: in the *Eridu Genesis*, they are a gift to humanity from the gods:

Nintur was paying attention:

Let me bethink myself of my humankind,
(all) forgotten as they are;
and mindful of mine, Nintur's, creatures
let me bring them back,
let me lead the people back from their trails.

May they come and build cities and cult-places,
that I may cool myself in their shade;
may they lay the bricks for the cult-cities
in pure spots, and
may they found places for divination
in pure spots!

(Jacobsen 1981: 515)

Nintur is the mother goddess also known as Ninhursaga and Belet-illi, and her speech reveals a view of the city as the rightful place of humans. Gilgamesh's return, then, restores the proper order. Along with the city came divinely sanctioned kingship, and, as a king, this is where Gilgamesh belongs. His responsibility is to lead his people, a responsibility he has neglected in favour of a foolhardy quest for something which does not belong to humanity. The limits of human life have thus been made clear. These limitations are indicated earlier in the tablet, when Utnapishtim and his wife are removed from human society on becoming immortal:

'Until now Utnapishtim was mortal,
But henceforth Utnapishtim and his woman shall be as we gods are.
Utnapishtim shall dwell far off at the mouth of the rivers.'
They took me, made me dwell far off, at the mouth of the rivers.

(Dalley 2000: XI, iv)

The deathless couple do not belong inside the city walls but far beyond the precincts of human habitation because they have become like the gods in their immortality.

The epic narrative

In its narrative complexity, its interlocking thematic concerns and the skilful linking of its episodes, *Gilgamesh* creates the impression of being a literary composition even if one with oral traditions and mythological cycles underlying it. Benjamin Foster has little doubt that it was literary rather than oral in origin: 'There is no evidence that *The Epic of Gilgamesh* began as an oral narrative performed by bards or reciters and only later coalesced as a literary text. In fact, the poem as we now have it shows many signs of having been a formal literary work composed and perhaps performed for well-educated people' (Foster 1996: xiv).

Liesbeth Altes, among others, has shown that its composer or compiler mobilized a range of sophisticated narrative techniques, weaving a variety of diverse sources into a richly patterned whole. She is surely right to assert that 'narratives work on the basis of shared knowledge between teller and audience. It is a thrilling experience to read a narrative like the Gilgamesh Epic from such remote times and find oneself moved by it' (Altes 2007: 185). As she implies, modern readers are not among the audience sharing knowledge with the teller. Such audiences are, obviously, long gone, and yet the epic still has the power to move. Perhaps that is one meaning of myth.

Interleaving myths and legends with hymns and chronicles, the epic forges them into a story which begins and ends with the city and its imposing walls, as if those material boundaries stood as a figure for the shaping power of narrative as much as for the ordered world of civilization. It might be read as a representation of the city as definitive of human life, bounded by the walls which brought to an end the primordial dispersion, creating both culture and society in the process. On this account, it offers us a means of interpreting the function of narrative as an exploration of the limits of human experience. Tzvi Abusch writes: 'The Epic explores many issues; it surely provides a Mesopotamian formulation of human predicaments and options. Most of all, the work grapples with issues of an existential nature. It talks about the powerful human drive to achieve, the value of friendship, the experience of loss, the inevitability of death' (Abusch 2001: 614).

Here, as in so many ancient texts, the narrative which foregrounds enduring aspects of human experience and desire appears to emerge as an expression of the will to impose order on that experience. *Gilgamesh,* as a story about coming to terms with death, reveals mortality to be the enabling condition of the sense-making narrative process, for without ends there are no narrative structures. As we will see when we look at Genesis, narrative creates order and defines humanity no less than do the walls of the city.

Notes

1. A fascinating account of the discovery, translation and cultural impact of the epic can be found in Cregan-Reid (2013).
2. For a detailed introduction to cuneiform writing, see Finkel and Taylor (2015).

3. 'Akkadian was the principal language of ancient Mesopotamia (approximately corresponding to modern Iraq). It was spoken by the Assyrians in the north and the Babylonians in the south and survived as a written language until the 1st century AD.' https://www.orinst.ox.ac.uk/akkadian#/ See also Rubio (2005: 90–2).
4. In *The Treasures of Darkness*, Thorkild Jacobsen describes the Mesopotamian form of sacred marriage thus: 'In the rite he [the ruler] took on the identity of Dumuzi-Amaushumgalanna and married the goddess Inanna, or Ishtar. Their union magically ensured fertility and plenty for all. As shown by the famous Uruk vase on which the rite is pictured, it was celebrated in that city as early as Protoliterate times' (1976: 209).
5. On the ancient environment of the region, see Cordova (2005).
6. David Damrosch sees Enkidu's transformation as a parallel to the story of the Fall in Genesis: it is a story of 'knowledge achieved at the price of the earthly Paradise'. One of the key differences between the two stories is that the early Hebrews, as a seminomadic people, 'were profoundly suspicious of city culture', while for the Mesopotamians 'civilization was epitomized in city life' (2006: 201).
7. Kovacs says these lines are fragmentary, 'and the sense is not at all certain' (1989: 107 n.9).

Translations used in preparing this chapter

Dalley, S. (1989, 2000), *Myths from Mesopotamia: Creation, The Flood, Gilgamesh, and Others*, rev. edn, Oxford: Oxford University Press.
George, A. (1999), *The Epic of Gilgamesh: A New Translation*, London: Allen Lane.
Kovacs, M. G., trans. (1989), *The Epic of Gilgamesh*, Stanford, CA: Stanford University Press.
Mitchell, S. (2004), *Gilgamesh: A New English Version*, London: Profile Books.

CHAPTER 4
THE BOOK OF GENESIS

What kind of work?

The book of Genesis is part myth, part chronicle and part theological treatise. Among the most influential texts ever produced, its cultural impact has been incalculable. Whether we think of its myths of Creation and Fall, its depiction of the Garden of Eden, its account of the Great Flood, its story of the tower of Babel, or the sweeping narratives of the founding figures of Israel – Abraham, Isaac, Jacob and Joseph – the book tells some of the most memorable and enduring tales to emerge from antiquity. It has inspired religious devotion, prompted archaeological and historical enquiry, driven critical, linguistic, and philosophical endeavours and, for centuries, furnished rich materials for artists in every medium.

And yet, wide as its purview may be, its focus is, in a sense, narrow and specific. Leon Kass characterizes it as beginning with 'a comprehensive and universal panorama of the entire cosmic whole (chapter 1)', moving to 'naturalistic and universal portraits of human life (chapters 2-11)', before concluding with 'the emergence of a tiny and distinctive people, bearing a new and distinctive human way on earth (chapters 12-50)' (Kass 2006: 11). The 'distinctive people', of course, is the nation of Israel and its 'new way', in Kass' formulation, an order of being ideally characterized by righteousness in social relations and holiness in respect of the deity.

Genesis has come down to modern Western culture as part of the Holy Bible, an aura of divine sanction lending it authority and shaping its translation and interpretation. Contributing to the religious beliefs of Judaism, Christianity and Islam, it remains hedged around with a kind of residual mystique, even for those of no faith. But it has a history and lineage which connect it with a wider ancient context pre-dating the great monotheistic religions and the emergence of biblical culture. Ronald Hendel makes the point: 'We now have thousands of texts from Mesopotamia, Canaan, Egypt and other neighboring lands, and many shed light on the backgrounds of the Genesis narratives' (Hendel 2013: 25). He goes on to observe that Genesis grew out of a combination of stories and sources deriving from ancient folkloric traditions.

Scope and composition

There is nothing from the ancient Near East which is comparable with Genesis, neither in terms of the plurality Hendel alludes to nor its temporal scale. The *Epic of Atrahasis* –

more than 1,200 lines long – combines creation and flood myths in a continuous story which parallels just the first eight chapters (out of fifty). To its stories of human origins and primeval catastrophe, Genesis adds the lives of four generations of patriarchs, lived against the background of two different civilizations: the Mesopotamian and the Egyptian.

In summary, the book includes

- Creation and Fall (1–3);
- Adam and Eve's son Cain killing his brother Abel (4.1-16);
- Cain's descendants becoming the builders of civilization (4.17-26);
- The 'sons of God' having sex with mortal women (6.1-4);
- God sending a flood, but saving Noah and his family (6.5–8.22);
- Noah's descendants resettling the plain of Shinar (10.1-32);
- God's disruption of the plan to build a city with a tower reaching to heaven, his scattering of people and creation of multiple languages (11.1-9);
- The genealogy connecting Noah with Abraham (11.10-30);
- Abraham's family leaving Ur and settling in Haran (11.31-32);
- The narrative of Abraham's life (12.1–25.8);
- The narrative of the life of Abraham's son Isaac (up to the end of ch. 27);
- The narrative of Isaac's son Jacob (up to the end of ch. 36);
- The stories of Jacob's son Joseph, and the migration of the family into Egypt (37–50);
- The death of Joseph in Egypt.

By yoking the stories of a nation's founding to a primordial mythology, Genesis establishes a national identity which is at once cosmic and specific, furnishing Israel with a divine lineage linked to the very design and purpose of the world's creation.

Impressive as its scope might be, Genesis is but one part of a larger cycle of stories known collectively as the Pentateuch, for which it serves as a kind of prologue (Schmid 2012: 29). The composition of the Pentateuch (comprising Genesis, Exodus, Leviticus, Numbers and Deuteronomy – the first five books of the Bible) is a controversial issue. The Judaic and Christian traditions ascribed authorship to Moses, but no one knows for sure who wrote or compiled it.[1]

The text as we have it today is often thought to have been stitched together from various pre-existing sources, and there is no agreement about the age, or even the number, of those putative constituents. But if the textual history of the book is controversial, archaeology and ancient records furnish us with a timeline appropriate to the culture which produced it. Richard Friedman offers a historical anchor, noting that 'the first point at which we actually have sufficient evidence to begin to picture the life of the biblical community is the twelfth century BCE, the period when the Israelites became established in this region' (Friedman 1997: 35–6). Some of the materials recorded in Genesis, however, relate to earlier periods, and it is impossible to be precise about when they were first formulated.

Perhaps the most influential theory regarding the formation of the Pentateuch is the so-called Documentary Hypothesis, set out most persuasively in Julius Wellhausen's *The History of Israel* (1878). Wellhausen, drawing on the work of several earlier scholars, argued that the Pentateuch was based on four documents known as the Jahwist, Priestly, Deuteronomist and Elohist sources, often shortened to JEDP. Underlying this theory is the observation that there are in Genesis two versions of the creation myth, which seem to contradict each other (Gen. 1.1–2.4a and 2.4b-23), and two versions of how the flood came about, with different emphases (Gen. 6.5-8 and 6.9-13). The Pentateuch contains many such duplications and variations. The use of different names for God, particularly the references to El Shaddai, Elohim and Yahweh, also contribute to the impression that Genesis draws on more than one source.

Although contemporary scholars disagree with Wellhausen (and with each other) about the details of division, ascription, precedence and even the number of documents which went to the making of the Pentateuch, they mostly agree that some version of the Documentary Hypothesis best explains the repetitions, variations and contradictions found in its pages. This approach was given new impetus by Joel S. Baden's *The Composition of the Pentateuch* (2012), which offered a simplified version of the theory based on the argument that a single 'compiler', who added none of his own material, interwove four pre-existing sources. Insisting that the Documentary Hypothesis is 'a literary solution to a literary problem', Baden characterizes the compiler as focussed on narrative coherence rather than language, style or theology (2012: 249).

There are scholars who reject such an approach, Italian Jewish scholar Umberto Cassuto (1883–1951) being one of the first to do so. He argued that 'what had been construed as contradiction, repetition and variance were in fact literary tools succinctly conveying polyphonous meaning' (Berman 2017: xii). The supposed linguistic and stylistic traits indicative of separate documents were, Cassuto urged, common in Hebrew language and writing and were shared with other biblical and post-biblical Jewish literature. He contended, too, that the supposed divergence – whether grammatical or theological – within the narrative, when analysed in context and in connection with similar and related literatures from the ancient Near East, demonstrated unity and a consistent sense of purpose. Such features had been ignored, or not understood, by the proponents of the Documentary Hypothesis.

More recently, P. J. Wiseman developed what became known as the 'Tablet Theory' of composition. He maintained that the phrase, 'These are the generations of . . .' (KJV), used eleven times in Genesis 1–36, was 'the master-key' to understanding its structure. These eleven uses of the *toledot* phrase were, he maintained, markers in the text indicating breaks between eleven tablets on which primeval and patriarchal history had been originally recorded (Ball 2015: 97–8; Woudstra 1970: 184).

Robert Alter, who published his translation of Genesis in 1996, argues that the principles of narrative composition typical of the Pentateuch have been misread by generations of scholars influenced by classical and Western traditions. Deceived by a desire for clarity and consistency, they have missed the extent to which the narrative technique of the Hebrew Bible delights in the creation of enigmas and in 'leaving its audience guessing about motives and connections' (Alter 1996: xi). Its style is marked by parataxis (using parallel phrases linked by 'and') rather than by the employment of subordinate clauses (hypotaxis), and this is the expression of a worldview in which links between events have to be teased out, forged by interpretation (Alter 1996: xvii).

In such a work, narrative itself becomes interpretative inasmuch as it demands the artful appreciation of what Paul Ricoeur has called 'the hermeneutical [interpretative] problem of the collusion between the inevitable divine plan and the unpredictability of human contingency' (1990: 239). For Alter, then, the Documentary Hypothesis is of limited value for our understanding of Genesis, because it draws attention away from its 'powerful coherence as a literary work' and from its 'integrity as a book' (1996: xlii). This is neither to deny the strains and contradictions nor to assert the rights of a single authorial hand; rather, it is to acknowledge the text's value as a sophisticated and complex work of art, whatever its prehistory.

There have been many attempts, some extremely elaborate, to identify patterns in these narratives, whether based on the *toledot* divisions (the genealogical tables) or the outlining of multiple chiasmatic structures – forming rhetorical *x* shapes – in the narrative, by means of repetition and variation.[2] Genesis is a richly patterned artefact, and its purposeful narrative shape might be seen as the key to understanding its use of myths in relation to its more realistic stories. The events and episodes of the patriarchs' lives, traced back to primordial roots, are related with minimal detail, but are put together in such a way as to invite the reader to make connections necessary to (re)create the sense of underlying cosmic design.

National identity

The most obvious and simplest structural division is the one characterized by Robert Alter as between 'the Primeval History (chapters 1-11) and the Patriarchal Tales (chapters 12-50)' (Alter xliii). It is worth considering in some detail the chapters either side of this break to see how they suture the two portions, since this is the point at which the book conjoins myth and 'naturalistic portraits' by means of a brilliantly conceived piece of narrative engineering.

Chapter 11.1-9 tells the mythologically charged story of Babel's ambitious builders.[3] Babel is the name used here for Babylon, playing on an Akkadian word meaning 'gate of god' and a Hebrew word meaning 'confusion' (Alter 1996: 47). As already noted, Hendel observes that Genesis has to be understood within the 'larger matrix of ancient Near Eastern myth and epic', and that broader cultural background is very evident in the tale of the unfinished tower. Verse 2 reads: 'And as men migrated from the east, they found a plain in the land of Shinar and settled there' (RSV). Shinar is the biblical name for Sumer, so the setting of the story is Mesopotamia. This is made more obvious by what follows in v 3: 'And they said to one another, "Come, let us make bricks, and burn them thoroughly." And they had brick for stone, and bitumen for mortar' (RSV). We might remember that *The Epic of Gilgamesh* mentions the building of Uruk from fired bricks. The story in Gen. 11 clearly belongs to a culture familiar not only with ancient Mesopotamian building practices but also with a different method of construction: 'they had brick *for stone*' (emphasis added).[4]

There seems to be a memory, too, of the building of the first cities in Mesopotamia. We saw in the previous chapter that the text known as *Eridu Genesis* suggests city building was a distinctive feature of that region, and that cities were said to be a divine gift associated with the mother goddess Nintur. So, Gen. 11.1-9 looks back to the remote past, making clear that the culture which produced the story was related to, or descended from, ancient Sumerian culture. But the story also seeks to distance itself from that past by associating the building of the city with punitive judgement. If the gods of the city builders both inspired and approved the building, Yahweh looked on the venture as being somehow corrupt.

At the heart of the ancient city, the story goes, was a tower which was designed to reach heaven, and the motivation for building it was a matter of cultural cohesion and identity: 'And they said, Go to, let us build us a city and a tower, whose top may reach unto heaven, and let us make a name, lest we be scattered abroad upon the face of the whole earth' (11.4, RV). This is exactly what Yahweh's judgement undermines. The effect of his imposition is to scatter the people 'upon the face of all the earth' (11.9, RV) by introducing linguistic diversity: 'Let us go down, and there confound their language, that they may not understand one another's speech' (11.7, RV). The story begins with the observation that 'the whole earth had one language and few words' (11.1, RSV) and this is clearly a myth of the origin of multiple languages, but it is also a story of religious revolution and the rejection of the Sumerian/Babylonian gods. While in the *Eridu Genesis* Nintur gathers the scattered people into the city, Yahweh does exactly the opposite.

The tower at the heart of the city offers another clue to the religious significance of the story. The towers in Sumerian cities were ziggurats: sacred structures of which the earliest examples date from the third millennium BCE (Zamazalová 2015: n.p.). Although the precise nature of their role in beliefs and practices is not known, they were almost certainly connected with the religion of the ancient Mesopotamians, so Yahweh's intervention to stop the building is indicative of a rejection of that religion. As Nahum Sarna says, the city of Babylon was probably chosen as the scene for the story because it was closely associated with Marduk who had become the chief god of the region (Sarna 1966: 76). The story effectively collapses the period between the first cities in Mesopotamia and the Babylonian era, to suggest that the great construction project was never completed because Yahweh intervened to prevent it.

Yahweh's supremacy over the gods of Babylon is demonstrated in his thwarting of the tower-builders' plans, allowing the episode to form a key moment in the overarching story of national identity. Apart from establishing Yahweh's credentials as divine overlord, the events at Babel prepare the ground for distinguishing one nation from others; before that can happen there must be multiple peoples. In this sense, the story serves as a myth of origination, marking the point at which the people descended from Adam and Eve divided into linguistically and culturally diverse groups. Once it has been established that the will of Yahweh has brought about ethnic divergence, a distinctive nation can be born and nurtured.

The story of the tower and the scattering of the people of Babel is followed by a genealogical passage culminating with Abram – the man chosen as founder of the new nation. The chapter concludes by singling out his family at the moment they leave their home in Ur: 'Terah took Abram his son, and Lot the son of Haran, his son's son, and Sar'ai his daughter-in-law, his son Abram's wife; and they went forth with them from Ur of the Chaldees' (11.31 RV). There was an Ur to the southeast of Uruk (the city of Gilgamesh) on the Persian Gulf, but some scholars have suggested that Abram's original home was at Urfa, close to Turkey's Syrian border.[5] His place of origin might be uncertain, but whether or not he came from the same part of the region as Gilgamesh, the associations between the early chapters of Genesis and Mesopotamia are clear and are not confined to the Babel story. For example, ch. 10 includes the following verses: 'The sons of Ham: Cush, Egypt, Put, and Canaan . . . Cush became the father of Nimrod; he was the first on earth to be a mighty man. He was a mighty hunter before the LORD . . .[6] The beginning of his kingdom was Babel, Erech, and Accad, all of them in the land of Shinar' (10.6-10, RSV). Nimrod is said to be the builder or founder of the city of Erech – the biblical name for Uruk.[7] Some of the material found in Genesis, then, certainly belongs to the same world as that associated with *The Epic of Gilgamesh*, and much as the hero of that story is suspended between myth, history and legend, the relationship between the stories told in Genesis and actual people and real events is the object of ongoing study and speculation. Genesis probably contains material we would want to call historical, but even that historical material may be, at the same time, mythological. History neither excludes nor invalidates myth; as ch. 11 ends and ch. 12 begins, a silent shift takes place from one mode to the other.

Chapter 11 begins in Mesopotamia; ch. 12 ends in Egypt. Genesis tells the story of a people who emerge as a nation between these two great cultures which dominated the ancient Near East. Whatever prompted the migration from Ur, severing Abram and his descendants from their Mesopotamian roots, it became for the writers/compilers of Genesis a moment of national and religious importance. Nahum Sarna refers to it as 'a fateful movement inaugurating the birth of a new nation whose history and destiny are to acquire unique purpose' (Sarna 1966: 100).

Once the family has been taken from its Mesopotamian homeland, the story homes in on the one man who will found the chosen nation and on his descendants. There are three crucial moments in ch. 12 each of which is at the heart of the story told by the Pentateuch: Yahweh promises to make a nation of Abram's descendants (vv. 1-2); he promises those descendants their own land (vv. 6-7); Abram inaugurates the worship of Yahweh (v. 8). So, the text singles out Abram as the founding father of both the nation and the religion of Yahweh, and in doing so renders the two inseparable. Placing these fundamental developments between preceding events in Babylon and following events in Egypt, the text marks out a definitive cultural space.

Traditional Christian readings tend to stress Abram's faith as the reason for his divine election. On the grounds of faith alone, the story goes, he leaves behind everything he knows in order to pursue his divine destiny. But as David Gunn and Danna Fewell argue, the narrative is more equivocal than such interpretations imply. They observe that by the time God's call comes, Abram 'has already left his land and the place of his birth. . . . We might ask ourselves, how much faith does it take to do what one has already decided to do?' (Gunn and Fewell 1993: 91). Not only so, but ch. 12 depicts Abram as a man prepared to sacrifice his wife to save his own skin – a gesture he repeats in ch. 20 – as if he had no trust that Yahweh's promise might protect them both. For Gunn and Fewell, Abram, far from being the champion of religious devotion celebrated by Christian tradition, is a man of 'great contradiction' who havers 'between faith and unfaith, courage and cowardice', and whose motivation is ever unclear (1993: 90). Such is the quality of this narrative that the reader is left to decide on the nature of its heroes, and whether the divine plan proceeds because of human fortitude, or despite human finitude.

In 12.10 (RV) we read: 'And there was a famine in the land: and Abram went down into Egypt to sojourn there.' In Egypt, he tries to pass off his wife as his sister in order to protect himself from attack. This wife/sister trick happens three times in Genesis: Abram does it again in ch. 20, and his son Isaac repeats the deception in ch. 26. Some Bible critics have seen this as evidence that Genesis was produced by the weaving together of multiple source texts. As John Ronning puts it: 'For the source critic, this is a classic example of multiple versions of the same original story, demonstrating a multiplicity of sources' (Ronning 1991: 1). Whether or not these episodes reflect such a process of redaction, the telling of the story at this point serves a particular purpose in the ongoing narrative of the birth of the nation by divine will and intervention. Verses 15-17 read:

> And the princes of Pharaoh saw her [Sarai], and praised her to Pharaoh: and the woman was taken into Pharaoh's house. And he entreated Abram well for her sake: and he had sheep, and oxen, and he-asses, and menservants, and maidservants, and she-asses, and camels. And the LORD plagued Pharaoh and his house with great plagues because of Sarai, Abram's wife.
>
> *(11.15-17, RV)*

Despite the strangeness and apparent immorality of Abram's strategy, it works well for him: the Pharaoh lavishes gifts on him. At the same time, and by virtue of the same deception, the story effectively portrays Yahweh's power over the Egyptian people and, implicitly, his command of Egyptian gods.

As noted earlier, chs 11–12 take us from Mesopotamia to Egypt – the seats of the two dominant powers in the region. These two chapters effectively characterize Israel as distinct from, and superior to, both. It may have come out of Mesopotamia, and later been enslaved by Egypt (the latter story is told in the book of Exodus), but it could not be identified with either. Neither the apparent precedence of Mesopotamian culture nor seeming power of Egypt can be taken at face value since Yahweh proves himself more than a match for the gods of both. He is depicted as being unlike the pagan gods: he is not associated with any city, terrain or locality: he has power in Mesopotamia *and* in Egypt. The narrative is designed to imply that Yahweh outperforms rival deities, and the nation he raises from the seed of Abraham and Sarah is similarly peerless.

By moving from Mesopotamia to Egypt while at the same time transitioning from primeval myths to realistic narratives, the book performs a brilliant manoeuvre, the upshot of which is that the Mesopotamian past (including its mythology) is transcended, and the future of enslavement in, and delivery from, Egypt – yet to be narrated – is seen to rest not in the hands of the pharaohs or their patron deities, but in the supreme will of Yahweh. As ch. 12 follows ch. 11, he emerges from myth to enter history, and he does so by forging a nation in whose traditions he will be made known.

Mythology: Creation

The narrative of Genesis, then, might be said to create a myth on a grand scale: the myth of a divinely willed genealogical identity. But there is a qualitative difference between that overarching pattern of connected stories by means of which Israel is created, and the depictions of primeval events found in the first eleven chapters of the book. That difference is marked by a kind of mirroring: from ch. 12 on, and throughout the remainder of the Pentateuch, historical narrative takes on mythic significance, rooted in myths which take on historical significance. The first myth, of course, is that of the world's creation.

As already observed, there are two versions of the creation myth: the first runs from the opening of ch. 1 to halfway through the fourth verse of ch. 2. According to the Documentary Hypothesis, this account derives from the P source, the second version from J. The text clearly marks the division, drawing P's narrative to a close with the words: 'These are the generations of the heavens and of the earth when they were created' (2.4a, RSV). The second version begins immediately: 'In the day that the LORD God made the earth and the heavens' (2.4b, RSV).

Alter notes some key differences between the two accounts: the first employs, predominantly, parataxis, the second hypotaxis. The second tends to anthropomorphize the deity to a greater extent than the first; the deity is referred to as *Elohim* in the first and as *Yahweh Elohim* in the second (Alter 1996: 7). Other contrasts include the creation of male and female at the same time (1.27), as against the creation of the male first and the forming of the female at a later stage with a rib taken from the male (2.21-22); the placing of humans in a garden occurs in the second version but not the first; the act of creation is first effected through the calling of things into existence, whereas the second version has the deity fashion living beings out of the earth, giving Adam the job of naming them.

Aspects of the first version appear to have been derived from Mesopotamian creation myths. Exiled in Babylon, in the sixth century BCE, Hebrew people would probably have heard the *Enuma Elish* performed at each New Year festival.[8] The tale of Marduk's victory over Tiamat (discussed in Chapter 2 of this book) and his subsequent slicing of her body into two to use as his cosmic building materials, must have made a lasting impression.

An embodiment of primordial chaos, Tiamat's sundered form became the upper and the lower waters, the land emerging from the latter. The description of precreation chaos in Gen. 1.2 tells us that 'the earth was without form, and void; and darkness was upon the face of the deep' (KJV); the Hebrew word rendered here as 'deep' is *Tehom* – a word closely related to the name Tiamat. In 1.7, God separates the waters above the firmament from the waters below, and then forms dry land by 'gathering' the lower waters into seas (1.9). According to Samuel Noah Kramer, the Sumerian cosmogony from which Babylonian myths were ultimately derived depicted the origins of the world in similar terms: a mountain rose out of a primeval sea and Enlil (god of the air) split it apart to form heaven and earth (Kramer 1972: 40–1). But while the Mesopotamian myths personified the primeval waters in Apsu and Tiamat, Genesis represents them as inanimate and subject to the manipulation of the deity.

So, the similarities are clear, but, as Stephen Greenblatt explains in vivid terms, there are important contrasts to be made between Genesis and its forebears: 'Creation for the Hebrews was not a tangle of incest, conspiracy, and intergenerational bloodletting; it was the act of Yahweh and Yahweh alone. He did not grapple with a rival or impregnate a goddess. Indeed there was no one else in all the vastness at the beginning of things, no consort, no assistance, and no resistance' (Greenblatt 2017: 44). For Greenblatt, as for a number of other commentators, the reworking of Babylonian mythology represented a self-conscious rejection of the gods, monsters and personified natural phenomena that it also echoed. Those responsible for writing and redacting the text worked to distinguish their origins as well as their destiny from the culture of their oppressors and the despoilers of their homeland, and that meant mounting a tacit critique of their founding stories.

Israel's god, too, was different: unlike other creation mythologies from the ancient Near East, there is no theogony in Genesis. That is to say, the account of creation has nothing to say about the origins of the creator. Elohim is simply there, pre-existent, transcendent and in complete control of all cosmic processes. There is no Yahweh Elohim mythology, as Sarna puts it, at least inasmuch as there are no stories told about his origins, his life or his exploits, as there are about Enlil, Ea, Ishtar or the gods of Egypt and Greece (Sarna 1966: 3, 10). He is not a personification of any specific natural phenomenon; in the first version of the creation story, he appears to stand outside a natural world over the whole of which he has command. Earlier mythologies which resound through the narrative, then, are present as traces of their own overthrow: they make plain the supersession of the polytheistic past.

But the first of Genesis' creation stories is much more than a riposte to a spurned mythology; it is a new vision of cosmological structure, expressed in a sophisticated and complex narrative. Ronald Hendel shows that it uses textual patterns to suggest the order that it also describes, in a manner typical of the book as a whole. For example, the creation process takes six days: the first three are devoted to cosmic form, while days four to six see the filling of the world with flora and fauna. The two periods of three days are matched up in pairs so that the creation of light on day one is developed by that of the sun, moon and stars on day four; the forming of the heavens and separation of the waters on day two finds its echo in the fashioning on day five of the creatures that live in water and fly in the air; day six completes the pattern when the land created on day three is populated with appropriate creatures, including humans (Hendel 2013: 33–4). So, allude as it might to Babylonian precursors, this creation story '[i]n its elaborate symmetries, coherent structure, and majestic style . . . is unique in the ancient world' (Hendel 2013: 37).

The second version of creation is less obviously derived from Mesopotamian sources but does carry certain echoes of the older stories. When, for example, Yahweh Elohim shapes Adam from what the King James Version memorably calls the 'dust of the ground', he is following the example of the goddess Nintu (or Belet-ili) in *The Epic of Atrahasis* and *The Epic of Gilgamesh* (in which she is called Aruru). But the contrasts are readily apparent: the Mesopotamian gods make human beings as beasts of burden, fashioned to relieve them of the hard work entailed in shaping a hospitable environment. Humans were not part of the original plan so much as what Sarna refers to as 'a kind of afterthought' (Sarna 1966: 15). The biblical myth places humans, made in the divine image, centre stage, and the world is designed, above all, as a home for them rather than a playground for the gods. A new dignity is thus conferred on humanity, transforming it from a congeries of comparatively worthless drones at the mercy of capricious and unpredictable forces, to a noble, if fallen, bearer of divine light, invested with a distinct destiny unlike the lot of other creatures. Such a vision prepares the way for the depiction of the patriarchs as men singled out by the will of Yahweh to fulfil his purposes in giving rise to the unique nation.

Mythology: Flood

Despite the comparative nobility of Adam, Eve and their offspring, humanity's moral condition eventually earns the ire of its creator: he regrets his decision to make people and resolves to wash them away. Nowhere is the early part of Genesis closer to its Babylonian sources than in the story of the Great Flood sent to wipe out life on earth. Its account of Noah's boat-building rescue mission has close parallels in the Atrahasis and Gilgamesh traditions. The story of Utnapishtim in *The Epic of Gilgamesh* and its precursor in the *Epic of Atrahasis* both tell of a man who, warned by a god, builds a great boat, fills it with animals and rides out the god-sent cataclysm. According to *Atrahasis*, the flood was occasioned by Enlil's impatience with the racket caused by the sheer number of multiplying humans. He sends various plagues to reduce their numbers, but each time the god Enki thwarts his plans by offering the hero, Atrahasis, advice on how to ensure survival. Eventually, the flood is sent and Atrahasis, acting on Enki's advice, builds his floating zoo.

The fact that these stories would have been known to the writers of Genesis meant that inclusion of some version of the deluge was necessary if its rendering of primeval events was to supplant the older myths. The monotheistic tradition which dominated ancient Israelite culture and religion could neither reiterate the Mesopotamian polytheistic reasons for the flood's occurrence nor stick with the old explanation of how its goal of total annihilation was circumvented.[9] Having more than one god involved in the action made survival of the flood explicable by disagreement between deities: Enlil its instigator and Enki/Ea the defender of humanity. The story of Noah, by contrast, had to make Yahweh both the perpetrator of the flood and the agent of human survival. This meant changing the divine motivation for both deluge and rescue. Yahweh is depicted as acting out of moral outrage at human behaviour: 'And the LORD saw that the wickedness of man was great in the earth, and that every imagination of the thoughts of his heart was only evil continually' (6.5, RV). Conversely, the preservation of life is motivated by the goodness of a single individual: 'Noah was a just man and perfect in his generations: Noah walked with God' (6.9, RV).

Despite the theological divergence, there is an echo of *Atrahasis* in the lead-up to these observations: Genesis 6 begins with the multiplying of humans, as does the earlier story. While an expanding population alone sufficed to drive Enlil into murderous action, it could not be condemned or punished by Yahweh since he gave humans the express command to 'be fruitful and multiply' (1.28, RV). That command is reiterated to Noah after the flood (9.1), emphasizing the contrast with the Mesopotamian story. So, what is attributed to the caprice of unpredictable and amoral gods in *Atrahasis* is laid at the door of human corruption in Genesis. This is both a matter of making humans moral agents and of establishing a monotheistic order which depends upon Yahweh acting as a righteous judge rather than a whimsical killer.

Although human fallibility is woven into the text of Gen. 1–11 – whether we think of Adam and Eve's consumption of the forbidden fruit, Cain's murder of Abel or the overreaching of the Babel-builders – there is something decidedly odd about its flood story. While this has something to do with the paradox of identifying a world-destroying deity with the Creator who, at the end of his six-day labour, declares his handiwork to be good (1.31), it is made all the stranger by the first four verses of ch. 6:

> And it came to pass, when men began to multiply on the face of the ground, and daughters were born unto them, that the sons of God saw the daughters of men that they were fair; and they took them wives of all that they chose. And the Lord said, My spirit shall not strive with man for ever, for that he also is flesh: yet shall his days be an hundred and twenty years. The Nephilim were in the earth in those days, and also after that, when the sons of God came in unto the daughters of men, and they bare children to them: the same were the mighty men which were of old, the men of renown.
>
> *(6.1-4, RV)*

These four verses are notoriously difficult to make sense of. Robert Alter refers to them as 'obviously archaic and mythological', noting the similarity between the implied copulation of male gods with human women and aspects of Greek mythology (Alter 1996: 26). These mysterious figures – Nephilim, and 'sons of god' – and their deviant practices appear to be what tip Yahweh's anger into desperate regret and genocidal intent, but no one knows for sure who or what the Nephilim were, or if they are to be identified with the 'sons of God'. Alter comments: '[t]he only obvious meaning of this Hebrew term is "fallen ones" – perhaps, those who have come down from the realm of the gods; but the word might conceivably reflect an entirely different, un-Hebraic background' (Alter 1996: 27). 'Un-Hebraic' seems germane since such figures cannot easily be made to fit into a monotheistic worldview.

The passage raises some tricky questions for interpreters, as outlined by Loren Stuckenbruck: 'How are any of these groups involved in God's decision to punish evil by sending a flood (cf. 6.3, 5-7, 13)? Are "the sons of God" or their progeny somehow involved with the "great evil," "violence", and "corruption" upon the earth (vv. 5, 11-13), or is the deluge simply God's response to the escalation of human wickedness alone?' (Stuckenbruck 2000: 356). As is so often the case in the Pentateuch, the reader is left to make what connections they might. The presence of the Nephilim and the nature of their exploits appear to be intimately connected with what follows: the 'great wickedness' of humans is bound by narrative proximity to the birth of children who are part god and part human ('sons of god'). For all the puzzling qualities of the passage, its association of demigod-like figures with 'wickedness' fits a pattern in Genesis of Yahweh's condemnation of anything suggesting a blurring of the line between humanity and divinity. The curse visited upon Adam and Eve results from their falling for the serpent's temptation to be 'as gods, knowing good and evil' (3.5), and the builders of Babel threaten to become godlike in their abilities: 'now nothing will be restrained from them, which they have imagined to do' (11.6b, RSV). The common propensity of these transgressors might be understood as human hubris, while the agenda of the writers/compilers of the book appears to show the culpability of polytheistic beliefs.

As well as being a recasting of Mesopotamian stories, the account of the flood in Genesis is what Nahum Sarna calls 'a fusion of traditions' (1966: 43). As in the case of the creation story, chs 6–9 bring together two versions of events, which the Documentary Hypothesis would attribute to J and P, respectively. According to Hendel, two distinct introductions are preserved intact, the first in 6.5-8 (J) and the second in 6.9-13 (P). They cover much the same narrative terrain but encode subtle differences of emphasis. For J, God's response to the state of his world is emotional: 'And it repented the LORD that he had made man on the earth, and it grieved him at his heart' (6.6, RV). P's God is less anthropomorphic, and his view is less focussed on humanity: 'And the earth was corrupt before God, and the earth was filled with violence' (6.11 RV) (Hendel 2013: 18–22). There are other differences too. The P narrative has Noah take a pair of each species of animal into the ark (6.19), while J has him round up seven pairs of each 'clean' animal and one pair of 'unclean' animals.[10] Richard Friedman points out that P describes the flood as lasting for 370 days, while J makes it 40 days and nights; Noah sends out a raven in the P version, while J has him send out a dove (Friedman 1997: 51). It seems that the editor, faced with two different accounts, was little concerned with the precise details or with producing a smooth blend of divergent elements.

More important than the minutiae of what and how to the Genesis narrative in its composite form is the universal significance of the flood as a cosmic watershed: a remaking of the world. Noah is depicted as the new Adam and as a bridge between the age of myth and the historical time of the patriarchs. Typically of the Pentateuch, the connection is made by means of a genealogy which plots ten generations from Noah to Abram (11.10-32), recalling the ten generations from Adam to Noah listed in ch. 5. The parallel between Adam and Noah is indicated not just by the issuing to each of the command to be fruitful and multiply but also by the image of each stepping into a new-made world which has emerged from the waters of chaos. The language used of the deluge echoes that used in the creation narrative:

> The very word *mabbul*, translated 'Flood', is now recognized as having denoted originally the heavenly, or upper, part of the cosmic ocean. 'The fountains of the great deep' are none other than the primeval sea. . . . The two halves of the primordial waters of chaos which God separated as a primary stage in the creative process, were in danger of reuniting. To the Bible, the Flood is a cosmic catastrophe.
>
> *(Sarna 1966: 55)*

In line with the flood's universal implications, a new order begins to emerge as soon as the ark's inhabitants set foot on dry land. The first thing Noah does is build an altar and offer a sacrifice to Yahweh:

> And the LORD smelled a sweet savour; and the LORD said in his heart, I will not again curse the ground any more for man's sake; for the imagination of man's heart is evil from his youth; neither will I again smite any more every thing living, as I have done. While the earth remaineth, seedtime and harvest, and cold and heat, and summer and winter, and day and night shall not cease.
>
> *(8.21-22, KJV)*

Revolutionizing relations with the deity, Yahweh's promises are the antithesis of the behaviour of the unpredictable Babylonian gods. He commits himself to acting consistently from this point on and to putting in place a stable and universal order which has a moral foundation.

In a telling allusion to the story as told in *Gilgamesh*, Yahweh's covenantal utterance is prompted by the appealing smell of the sacrifice. When Utnapishtim makes his post-flood offering, the gods are drawn to the aroma: 'The gods did smell the savour sweet, / The gods gathered like flies around the man making sacrifice' (George 1999: XI, 161–2). In *Atrahasis*, it is suggested that, in the wake of the deluge, the gods regretted wiping out humans because they depended upon their sacrifices for sustenance. The image of them gathering like flies makes them seem undignified and parasitic. By contrast, Yahweh is not depicted as needing the sacrifice as food, but as responding to it emotionally and morally.

The new, postdiluvian order is markedly different from the original state of things. Adam and Eve were given plants to eat; at the beginning of ch. 9, animals are put on the menu. The revised diet is outlined alongside rules concerning human–animal relations, and bloodshed more generally:

> Every moving thing that liveth shall be meat for you; even as the green herb have I given you all things. But flesh with the life thereof, which is the blood thereof, shall ye not eat. And surely your blood of your lives will I require; at the hand of every beast will I require it, and at the hand of man; at the hand of every man's brother will I require the life of man. Whoso sheddeth man's blood, by man shall his blood be shed: for in the image of God made he man.
>
> *(9.2-6 KJV)*

The dietary shift is part of an ethical order in which rules regarding the shedding of human blood are codified. Reminders of Eden and Fall are carefully placed in Yahweh's speech: the 'green herb' element of the new diet takes us back to the garden while 'the hand of every man's brother' recalls Cain's murder of Abel. So, it seems that even though this is a new world it remains a fallen one in which human behaviour has to be policed. When Noah replaces Adam, it is not in a new Eden but in permanent exile beyond the sealed and sentried gates of the old one.

Mythology: Exile

Permanent exile sets the tone for the rest of the book. A pattern established in the primeval myths, it is carried through to the patriarchal stories and helps to unify Genesis' many episodes:

> The loss of home, of native place, and in some case, of family was such a traumatic experience in the life of Israel, that it became, in Israel's literature, the critical characteristic of the human condition. The expulsion from the garden in Genesis 3, the banishment of Cain in Genesis 4, the scattering of the builders of the tower of Babel in Genesis 11, and the sequels of family strife throughout Genesis – Kings inscribe the event as a threat to every generation.
>
> *(Gunn and Fewell 1993: 157–8)*

It is evident from the examples that Gunn and Fewell adduce that exile is associated by the Hebrew Bible with punishment. On each occasion, the exiles are depicted as suffering the consequences of trespass, whether the failure to respect divine instruction, murder, hubris or religious defection. Looking back at the history of the nation in the wake of the Babylonian exile, the writers/compilers of Genesis understood the loss of homeland and related comforts as prefigured in the earliest dealings between people and the deity. Adam and Eve lose not only a home but a way of life, and their banishment from Eden foreshadows what follows throughout the Hebrew Bible. Genesis ends, as it begins, with representation of people cut off from their roots: the last of the patriarchs, Joseph, is buried, not in the land promised to Abraham and his descendants but in Egypt. It is a sad recalling of the original moment of cosmic estrangement. The myths with which the Hebrew Bible opens, then, form a prologue to the history which it traces, uncovering the roots of exilic experience in the soil of the primal garden.

Soil is a fitting metaphor since the name Adam is derived from the Hebrew word meaning earth or clay. In keeping with earlier ancient Near Eastern creation myths, God forms Adam from the ground, and his name/title reflects his origins. After the Fall, the first thing to suffer God's curse is the soil:

> Cursed is the ground for thy sake; in toil shalt thou eat of it all the days of thy life; thorns also and thistles shall it bring forth to thee; and thou shalt eat the herb of the field; in the sweat of thy face shalt thou eat bread, till thou return unto the ground; for out of it wast thou taken: for dust thou art, and unto dust shalt thou return.
>
> *(3.17-19, RV)*

The punishment is not simply exile from the garden but also from life itself. In the same movement, Adam and Eve are uprooted and buried, suffering the double blow of being cut off from the ground which bore them and being condemned to return to the soil. The ending of the book with the burial of Joseph in Egypt is a dramatic fulfilment of the curse: he is returned to dust, but in foreign ground.

The point is reiterated in the way Genesis describes Cain's murder of his brother Abel in ch. 4. The story is a version of a familiar motif in ancient Near Eastern mythology. In the Sumerian tale of the cattle and the grain, for example, divine brother and sister, Lahar and Ashnan, fall out over which of them achieves greater success – he in animal husbandry, or she in arable production (Kramer 1972: 53–4). What occasions the first murder in Genesis is precisely Cain's relationship with the soil and food production. While Abel is a herdsman, Cain is 'a tiller of the ground'. The two make offerings to Yahweh of their produce: Abel sacrifices young lambs, while Cain brings things he has grown. Yahweh is said to regard Abel's offering more highly than Cain's and the latter's jealousy turns into a murderous rage. As many have observed, the conflict between the brothers reflects an ancient rivalry between nomadic herdspeople and settled farmers, coming down firmly against the farmers.[11] Such rivalry between the nomadic and the settled probably underlies the text's animus against the city, marked most obviously in the story of Babel.

In ch. 4, Cain's bloody vengeance returns us to the identity of flesh and soil, not only in the nature of his offering to Yahweh but also in Yahweh's response to the murder: 'What hast thou done? the voice of thy brother's blood crieth unto me from the ground. And now cursed art thou from the ground, which hath opened her mouth to receive thy brother's blood from thy hand' (4.10-11, RV). This divine condemnation reverses the Mesopotamian myth recorded in the *Epic of Atrahasis* in which humans are created from a mixture of clay and the blood of a sacrificed god. In Genesis, humans are made from clay and fashioned in the image of God, but what animates the lifeless form is the breath of Yahweh rather than his blood. When blood and earth mingle here, it signifies murder rather than enlivening, and the earth which went to the making of the parents is now turned against their offspring. A tacit rejection of the older mythology, the murder of Abel and the cursing of his killer represent human life as cut off from its home ground, exiled and forced into nomadism. By divine fiat, Cain will be a wanderer, for whom neither a settled life nor farming are any longer possible: 'When thou tillest the ground, it shall not henceforth yield unto thee her strength; a fugitive and a wanderer shalt thou be in the earth' (4.12, RV).

Cain thus forms the nexus point of key narrative elements: the turning of agricultural settlement into a cursed mode of existence, estrangement from the ground as both source and sustainer of life, and the rejection of cities as places of corruption. The latter emerges at the end of Cain's story: 'And Cain went out from the presence of the LORD, and dwelt in the land of Nod, on the east of Eden. And Cain knew his wife; and she conceived and bare Enoch: and he builded a city, and called the name of the city, after the name of his son, Enoch' (4.16-17, RV). It is only when he has left the LORD behind, dismissed from his presence, that Cain turns into a city-builder. Robert Alter points out that the distrust of cities made plain in the destruction of Babel is implicit in the narrative at this point: 'The first recorded founder of a city is also the first murderer, a possible reflection of the antiurban bias in Genesis' (Alter 1996: 19).

When we learn (in ch. 11) that the condemned tower of Babel is made of clay bricks, we may well be reminded (by the construction materials) of the fallen nature of those first earthy beings and the blood of their murdered son. The tower thus takes on the character of a hubristic, but futile, attempt to reverse divine judgement. Cain, the progenitor and spiritual father of its architects, was condemned to wander, and so the city becomes a symbol of transgressive settlement and gathering, echoing the offence which issued in the Fall and expulsion from Eden. The people who build it carry the taint not only of disobedience but also of murder, and just as clay-born flesh has fallen into mortality, so the clay-built monument to their knowledge and technological prowess will, likewise, be condemned to fall. Cain's children will be returned to a nomadic lifestyle, partaking of his curse.

If there is a paradox in the representation of nomadism as both a curse and the way of life favoured by the text (over city life, at least), it should come as no surprise: Yahweh imposed fugitive status on humanity when he closed the gates of Eden behind it, and exilic experience became the hallmark of his chosen people. When they were exiled in Babylon, the city as a cultural phenomenon looked more than ever like a corrupt ideal and the product of fallen nature. In this light, the demise of that city depicted in the story of the tower of Babel takes on the character of an apocalyptic reversal of the empire's fortunes. But rather than suggesting Babel's abandonment is over and done with, a matter dealt with once and for all, setting the event in the distant past has the inverse effect. It suggests Yahweh's permanent opposition to, and power over, the chief city of the region and contributes to a universalizing movement:

> The story proposes to mention all the ancestors of mankind by this projection back into prehistory and thus to involve all its readers. . . . This retrospective move has released the universal. The same ascendant movement back in time to ancestors who exemplify all of us, the same inclusive way of thinking which pictures all of us as partners of God, can be found in the story of paradise.
>
> *(Fokkelman 1991: 41)*

Genesis, then, always has both the universal and the particular in view: it creates a towering mythical structure which relates a specific national identity to cosmic purposes. In the same movement it shows the cosmos contracted to the span of a single life in its depiction of Abram/Abraham, to whom Yahweh memorably says: 'in thee shall all families of the earth be blessed' (12.3). That very blend of universalism and particularity which embodies all humanity in Adam and Eve, in Noah, in the builders of Babel and in Abraham is also the tracing of a specific genealogical line. In tandem with this double vision, the evocations of Mesopotamia and Egypt look back to a past which has been transcended and, simultaneously, reveal the exilic nature of all such progress.

In its evocations of older formulations such as *Atrahasis*, *Enuma Elish* and *Gilgamesh*, Genesis conducts a kind of critique of mythology, supplanting their polytheistic depictions of primeval figures and events with the will and action of a transcendent deity of whom no story can be told and whose name cannot be pronounced. This too is exile and nomadism, since like Cain and his parents, we are all dismissed from Yahweh's presence: in the book of Exodus, he says to Moses: 'Thou canst not see my face: for there shall no man see me, and live' (Ex. 33.20, KJV).

Notes

1. For a brief history of scholarly approaches to Genesis, see Ska (2012).
2. See, for example, Yudkowsky (2007). The identifying of parallels and chiastic structures is not approved of by all Bible scholars.
3. J. P. Fokkelman's brilliant reading of the story reveals its complex patterns at every level from vocabulary to narrative structure. He concludes that 'this vision of the history and the nature of the dialogue between God and man required and was realized in a rigorously designed composition' (1991: 44).
4. Ronald Hendel notes that this story 'reflects broadly the historical context of the first half of the first millennium BCE when Babylon was a great cultural center' (2012: 60).
5. See, for example, Rohl (2002: 113).
6. Where the word 'LORD' appears in capital letters in English translations of the Hebrew Bible, it marks the presence of the name Yahweh in the Hebrew text. The name appears without the vowels in Hebrew tradition, since it is not to be spoken.
7. David Rohl identifies Nimrod with Enmerkar whose name appears in the Sumerian King List as king two generations after the flood. Nimrod is, correspondingly, a great grandson of Noah (2002: 58–9).

8. The Babylonian empire deported many of the people of Israel following its conquest of Jerusalem in 597 BCE. The exile lasted until the Persians overthrew Babylonia in 538 BCE. The Pentateuch is now thought by many scholars to have been composed in the post-exilic period.
9. 'The existence of primordial monotheism is an odd biblical notion that seeks to reinforce the universalism of the monotheistic idea' (Alter 1996: 21).
10. Alter points out that the distinction between clean and unclean animals refers to fitness for sacrifice rather than for food (1996: 30).
11. It should be noted that Nahum Sarna rejects this interpretation of the story of Cain and Abel, not least because significant aspects of the nomadic lifestyle such as cattle-rearing, music and metalwork are said to have been initiated by Cain's descendants (1966: 28).

Translations used in preparing this chapter

Alter, R. (1996), *Genesis: Translation and Commentary*, New York and London: W.W. Norton & Company.

The King James Bible (1611).

The Revised Version of the Bible (1885).

The Revised Standard Version of the Bible (1952), National Council of Churches of Christ in the United States of America.

CHAPTER 5
THE BOOK OF JOB

The story

The story told by the book of Job is a deceptively simple one. It opens with a brief character sketch of the protagonist as an extremely wealthy and pious man with ten children and an enviable reputation. The scene quickly shifts to a gathering in the heavenly court attended by Satan. In this context, *Satan* renders not a proper name, but a title: *hassatan*, meaning Prosecutor, or Adversary.[1] He appears to be a functionary of the court rather than an interloper. Yahweh draws his attention to Job as an exemplar of piety, only for the Prosecutor to point out that he has no reason *not* to be a good man: he has everything, and he has it in spectacular abundance. Take away his perfect family and vast wealth, the Prosecutor argues, and he will curse God to his face. Willing to gamble on the outcome, Yahweh permits the Prosecutor to take everything away from Job. Proving his religion more than a complacent acceptance of divine favour, Job refuses to curse God despite the death of his children and loss of his flocks. The Prosecutor returns to point out that Job still has his health; attack his flesh and he will soon vent his misery and anger in a blasphemous outburst. Again Yahweh agrees that Job should be afflicted, and so his entire body is covered with sores so painful and disfiguring that when three friends arrive to offer comfort, they fail to recognize him.

The friends – Eliphaz, Bildad and Zophar – sit with him in sympathetic silence for seven days before Job begins to pour out his misery. At this point, the prose tale gives way to poetic dialogue. In his speeches, Job defends his innocence against the assumption that he must have done something to deserve punishment. His friends make the case for his need to repent, since, in their view, his suffering is certain proof of his guilt. Putting things right with Yahweh, they believe, will see his fortunes restored. Job insists that if there is any justice in the cosmos, Yahweh will come and speak with him face to face to explain why a blameless man should be tortured in such an appalling way. Eventually the god appears, making a devastating contribution to the debate. The poetic dialogue ends with Job recanting, before the prose tale resumes to show him being restored to health, recompensed with twice the number of sheep, camels, oxen and donkeys that he had previously and blessed with ten children even more beautiful than their predecessors.

The apparent simplicity of the tale belies its literary, moral and religious complexity, as well as the many perplexing aspects of its composition, form and subject matter.

The puzzle

For many reasons, the book of Job is a puzzling text. No one has any idea who composed it or knows for sure where it was produced. There is no agreement about the date of composition either, though modern translators such as Raymond Scheindlin, Robert Alter and Edward Greenstein all place it between the fourth and sixth centuries BCE.

Then there is the issue of the language in which the work was originally written. Some scholars (such as N. H. Tur-Sinai) have asserted that the book was written in Aramaic (a language similar to classical Hebrew), while others (such as Frank Foster) argue that it was first produced in Arabic. But even those who are content that Job was always a Hebrew text find its language deeply problematical. Cristian Rata refers to the language of the book as 'arguably the most difficult in the Bible' (2008: 5–6). Edward Greenstein observes that linguistic difficulties posed by the Hebrew text make the work of translation especially tricky: 'the meanings of many words and expressions in Job are based on guesswork' (2019: xviii). The extremely challenging character of the text, both its strange language and its paradoxical content, has led to a variety of divergent interpretations, most of which reflect the religious or theological traditions of the interpreters (Greenstein 2019: xviii).

Something of the difficulty can be illustrated by means of a particularly telling example. The Revised Standard Version of the Bible (1952), renders Job 19.25-27 like this:

> For I know that my Redeemer lives,
> and at the last he will stand upon the earth;
> and after my skin has been destroyed,
> then without my flesh I shall see God,
> whom I shall see on my side,
> and my eyes shall behold, and not another.
> My heart faints within me!

This is the translation proffered (very tentatively) by Edwin Good (1990):

> As for me, I know that my avenger lives,
> and afterward he rises upon dust.
> And after they have flayed my skin, this –
> and from my flesh I perceive Eloah,
> whom I perceive to me,
> and my eyes saw, and not a foreigner.
> My kidneys are ended in my bosom.

Of other recent translations Raymond Scheindlin's (1998) and Edward Greenstein's (2019) bear some similarities with Good's, while Robert Alter's (2010) is not very different from that of the RSV. The latter's rendering smooths out some of the linguistic wrinkles, glossing over the uncertainties to present what appears to be a confident assertion of Job's trust in God to save his soul. It is a translation which unabashedly makes Job's speech sound like an expression of Christian commitment to the doctrines of redemption and resurrection. Despite the fact that the book of Job is in no sense a Christian text, dating from long before the time of Jesus, the presence of the Redeemer standing at last upon the earth has often brought to the minds of Christian readers the triumphant return of Christ at the end of days, while Job's certainty that he will see God without his flesh has tended to evoke the prospect of a spiritual entry into the divine presence after death. In fact, the word translated as 'Redeemer' is *go'el*. It has multiple meanings, two of which appear in other texts in the Hebrew Bible: a legally appointed avenger of bloodshed (Num. 35.19; Deut. 19.6), and, in the book of Ruth, a figure who buys back property lost to his tribe or clan. In Job, the term denotes not a divine saviour in the Christian mode, but a legal role in keeping with the suggestions of trial and justice found throughout the book (Alter 2010: 83).

Such a religiously slanted translation as we find in the RSV is perhaps unsurprising given that the copyright holder of that translation is the National Council of the Churches of Christ in the United States of America. Greenstein's version (like Alter's and Scheindlin's), clearly less influenced by religious commitment, allows the language to seem difficult and the imagery strange; he leaves the name Eloah (the singular form of Elohim) in place rather than opting for the less Hebrew more Christian-friendly form 'God'. Edwin Good's translation is even less willing to paper over the cracks, foregrounding the (possibly idiomatic) thorniness of Job's locution, and making plain the unyieldingness of the Hebrew text. While not every line is as resistant to interpretation as the verses just considered, the book has proved capable of provoking as much controversy as it has admiration, as much uncertainty as devotion.

Composition and genre

Another puzzling aspect of the book is the question of its generic identity. This is complicated because, like Genesis, it is considered by many to be a composite work, bringing together at least two originally separate sources – the prose tale and the poetic exchanges: 'Before there was a book of Job, there was very likely a story of Job, an exemplary tale designed to teach a simple idea about religion and man's duty to God' (Scheindlin 1998: 9). The text might be understood as an imaginative extension of such a traditional moral or didactic tale by the insertion of a poetic dialogue.

But, when it comes to the unity, or disunity, of the work, there are other considerations. For example, although just three friends turn up at the end of ch. 2 to offer their support to Job, a fourth figure – Elihu – takes part in the debate. His arrival has never been signalled, and he is not mentioned in the closing portion of the framing narrative when Yahweh addresses Eliphaz and his two companions (42.7-9). The scholarly consensus is that his speeches were not the work of the poet who composed the rest of the dialogue; they were a later addition (Alter 2010: 133). Carol Newsom describes Elihu's intervention as a problem which 'bedevils every interpretation of the book' because whoever added him to the original appears to many to be guilty of defacing 'a cultural monument with his graffiti' (2003: 200). But at least one commentator has argued that Elihu is an integral part of the work who should be understood as a bystander who intervenes after overhearing the debate (Habel 1975: 443). Angered by Job's presumption in proclaiming himself innocent, Elihu responds to his legal rhetoric by insisting that God 'does not pervert justice' (34.12). For Newsom, his contribution is significant as an act of principled interruption, but she nonetheless accepts that his speeches are a belated insertion (2003: 233).

Just what kind of text did the Elihu poet interrupt? Most obviously, Job belongs to a class of literary compositions known as 'wisdom literature': a form of writing practised widely in the ancient Near East, dealing with questions thought to be of universal significance, such as morality, social values and the meaning of human life.[2] The Hebrew Bible includes two other texts which have been placed alongside Job in this category: Proverbs and Ecclesiastes. Despite its presence in the Hebrew Bible, wisdom literature is not a distinctively Israelite form, and the biblical examples draw on materials from a range of intercultural sources (Alter 2010: xiv). Job and his friends are, in fact, not described as Israelites, but as coming from places probably located somewhere to the east of ancient Israel. In keeping with the conceit of a wisdom which transcends culture and location, each of Job's friends has a different geo-ethnic origin: Bildad is referred to as a Shuhite, Eliphaz a Temanite and Zophar a Naamathite. The whereabouts of their origins have been subject to scholarly debate, but placing them on a map of the region is less important than recognizing their geopolitical diversity as an index of the book's universal pretensions.

But if Job is an example of wisdom literature, it is related, too, to a different literary tradition. Archaeologists have uncovered quite a few stories from the ancient Near East about gods punishing a righteous man, some of them in dialogue form, and they may have provided models for the tale. Such stories dating from as early as 4,500 years ago have been found in ancient Egyptian, Akkadian and Sumerian, but despite certain common features, Job is not quite like any of them in every respect. A poem known as the 'Babylonian Theodicy', for example, stages a dialogue between a suffering man and his friend.[3] The sufferer, having lost his family and his health, questions the value of religious observance in the face of his miserable experience. His friend admits that the ways of the gods are not easy to understand, but advises him to 'seek the kindly wind of the god', and what he has lost will be regained. The similarities with Job are evident, but the Babylonian text is nowhere near as long, has no prose framing narrative, and shows nothing approaching the sheer religio-moral complexity of the Hebrew work.

Edward Greenstein points to an Egyptian story known as 'The Eloquent Peasant' (*c.*1850 BCE) as being structurally comparable with Job in that it frames poetic speeches with a prose narrative (2019: xxi–xxii). The peasant in question repeatedly defends his actions before a magistrate, his linguistic artistry eventually winning him justice. While the formal properties of the work are far closer to Job than is the content, the legal rhetoric of the latter may be an echo of the Egyptian dialogue as a trial-based composition.

Nor are these the only generic resonances in Job. Newsom has argued that a rich set of genre-based conventions are woven into the book forming a crucial aspect of its structure and enabling its production of meaning. She points to the writer's inclusion of a didactic tale, a wisdom dialogue, a distinct wisdom poem (forming ch. 28), and forensic discourse (concerned with legal proceedings), none of which enjoys a privileged status in the composition. The divergent perspectives represented by these discursive modes remain 'unmerged', creating the impression that no single consciousness or approach to the question can grasp a unitary or overarching truth about the relationship between piety and suffering (Newsom 2003: 3–31). I will return to Job's self-contradictory character a little later in this chapter, but here I want to note that, for Newsom at least, the unresolved tensions scholars have frequently perceived in the text are neither incidental nor unimportant; they are at the heart of the book's design and closely related to its generic hybridity. So, what for many readers – both scholarly and non-specialist – has appeared to be a confusing moral and religious inconsistency in Job, for Newsom, turns out to be the core of its highly distinctive offering.

The debate

The structure of the work gives central position and the majority of the text over to the dialogues, focussing attention on a debate which deals with the question of why Job is suffering. The symmetrical structure of the text – beginning and ending with the wealth and well-being of Job and his family – suggests an overarching order, but, in fact, Job is far from offering a clear or comforting picture. There is a tension between the order implied by the text's structure, and the sense of irresolution which emerges from the dialogues.

David Clines has explored the ways in which the text falls into apparent self-contradiction, seeming to undermine its own theology, philosophy or religious worldview. He describes the central point of contention as the conventional belief that suffering is the result of sin and that, conversely, prosperity is the reward of piety. The framing narrative describes Job as 'blameless and upright', and as fantastically prosperous, suggesting that there is a direct link between these two facts about him.[4] His extreme wealth is related to his extreme goodness, but the nature of the relationship is open to interpretation: 'According to the Satan, God must be thinking . . . that the piety of Job is the origin of his prosperity. The Satan's own suspicion is that it is Job's prosperity that is the origin of his piety, that it is only in order to become prosperous or remain prosperous that Job is so exceptionally pious' (Clines 1990: 68).

Since, according to the framing narrative, Job, though blameless, has everything taken away from him, the connection between goodness and prosperity is broken. Conversely, his innocence combined with his multiple bereavement and physical affliction shows that there is no necessary link between sin and suffering. The idea that people get what they deserve, for good or ill, is known as the doctrine of retribution, and, Clines argues, the book repeatedly proves that doctrine wrong. Job and his friends all set out with the conviction that the traditional dogma is trustworthy, but while the friends hold on to that position, concluding that Job must have committed some unacknowledged sin for which he is being punished, Job himself comes to feel that what has befallen him throws into question everything he once believed (Clines 1990: 69). So it seems that the book argues the doctrine of retribution to be wrong: prosperity is not linked to piety, nor suffering to sin. But the epilogue undermines this argument by depicting a penitent Job having his fortunes restored by Yahweh. At the close of the narrative, Job's wealth is not only returned, but is greater than ever before. 'What the book has been doing its best to demolish, the doctrine of retribution, is on its last page triumphantly affirmed' (Clines 1990: 71).

Showing Yahweh to be part of a moral experiment in this way would appear to make the doctrine of retribution something of a joke. If the supreme being is unclear about whether and how it works, then there is no guarantor of the system of judgement. In a monotheistic religion, there is no other god to appeal to, so if Yahweh is not in command of the processes of punishment and reward, then such processes can hardly be said to hold sway in the cosmos he created. Little wonder, then, that some scholars read Job as a satirical response to the matter of cosmic justice: 'By using the conventional tale as the frame for the poem, the poet satirizes its claim that we inhabit a world governed by justice and meaning. . . . Job has grasped and intrepidly maintained the most terrifying reality' (Scheindlin 1998: 17). Such perceptions of Job as a man rejecting deep-laid beliefs have led to his being celebrated by some as a man with the courage to confront head-on the fearful prospect of a world devoid of moral structure. For George Myerson, he is 'a heroic character' who conducts 'a fraught argument against terrifying odds', while David Lawton pays tribute to his 'extraordinary audacity' in challenging God's management of the universe and in forcing him to speak (Myerson 1992: 136; Lawton 1990: 113).

Job's audacity is made all the more pointed, and his anger the more sharply appropriate, by the fact that he knows nothing of what has taken place in the heavens; his suffering is a complete mystery to him and makes him question whether the cosmos is ordered or chaotic. If the god in charge is just, then he should come and explain himself; it cannot be just for him to punish someone without making clear what it is they have done to deserve their fate. Job's friends are committed to the idea that their god is just, while Job himself is clear that, although he once believed exactly what his friends do, his experience renders such a belief unsustainable unless and until Yahweh appears to answer for his actions. Effectively, Job wants to put his god on trial.

Trial and justice

There are many suggestions of trial in the book of Job. Since the book begins with a question of just how righteous Job really is, we might assume that he is the defendant. Much of the language used in the dialogues by Job's friends makes them sound like witnesses for the prosecution. But, in the wider scheme, Yahweh himself is also on trial, and Job's friends seem at times like witnesses in his defence.

Eliphaz is the first to address Job. He introduces the question of justice and the morality of the cosmic order, arguing that those who sow wrongdoing reap trouble, while the innocent come to no harm (4.7-8). Eliphaz is not expressing a personal opinion, so much as reiterating a widely held belief, as Michael Dick makes clear: 'Sickness implied guilt even as early as the Third Dynasty of Ur. . . . More pointedly there are even Mesopotamian texts which describe in the language of the court man's suffering as a legal judgment of guilt. . . . This causal relationship between sin and illness can be equally documented in the OT' (Dick 1979: 39–40).

Eliphaz thinks that all mortals are guilty: 'Can mortal man be righteous before God? Can a man be pure before his maker?' (4.17, RSV). The rhetorical question is its own answer, implying that Job's claim to be pure is misguided. But this does not really answer Job's more fundamental question: 'Why is light given to a man whose way is hid, whom God has hedged in?' (3.23, RSV). He is asking what use moral sensibility can possibly be to someone whose life is constrained by God. Trying to do good rather than evil is pointless if we cannot see what our choices may lead to. Eliphaz claims that even God's own messengers, the angels, can be 'charged with error' (4.18, RSV), so how much more are mere mortals subject to judgement? In that case, Job responds, why does humankind matter to the deity at all? 'What is a mortal that you treat him as important? / Why do you pay him any mind?' (7.17, Greenstein 2019). These questions show just how deep are Job's misgivings: he is asking why Yahweh cares what humans do. Since, as Eliphaz says, his judgements are not within our moral or intellectual grasp, how could what a mere mortal does affect or concern the deity?

Bildad's view is similar to that expressed by Eliphaz, but he is more pragmatic. He assumes that the deity is just and thinks that Job had therefore better accept his guilt and try to put things right: 'If you are pure and upright, surely then he will rouse himself for you and reward you with a rightful habitation' (8.6, RSV). Job's counterargument is that he can never know how to please God, since he has lived his life trying to do just that, but to no effect: 'I who, though innocent, couldn't answer / must beg my opponent for mercy? / If I summoned and he answered me, / I wouldn't believe he was hearing my voice' (9.15-16, Good 1990). As well as pointing out the impossibility of his position, Job identifies a problem which monotheism necessarily struggles to address. Just as in Genesis the same god both sent the flood and thwarted his own plan by saving the lives of Noah and his family, Job reveals the same god to be counsel for both prosecution and defence.

The third friend to speak, Zophar, has no time at all for Job's protestations of innocence. He claims that Job is simply ignorant of who/what the god is. The deity, in Zophar's opinion, is so far beyond Job's understanding, that to claim to be innocent in the face of extreme suffering is tantamount to blasphemy. He insists that far from being innocent, Job is getting off rather lightly: 'Know then that God exacts of you less than your guilt deserves' (11.6b, RSV). In response to this outrageous insult, Job loses patience and becomes sarcastic: 'No doubt you are the people, and wisdom will die with you' (12.2, RSV). He calls his 'friends' liars (13.4), and he accuses them of showing partiality for God against him – a sick, helpless mortal who needs all the friends he can get (13.7-8).

Job thinks his friends are missing the point: he already knows the religious conventions of which they are reminding him, but he cannot any longer accept those conventions in the same way; they are now questions for him rather than answers. Eliphaz, Bildad and Zophar, rather than making a case for those conventions which might answer Job's questions, do no more than repeat them.

In 32.2, Elihu enters the debate as if he has been there all along. His basic point is that pain and suffering are forms of divine communication, like dreams:

In a dream, in a vision of night,
when slumber drifts down upon men,
as they drowse upon their beds –
that is when He opens the ears of men,
and frightens them with due correction,
deterring a man from evil deeds.

(33.15-17, Scheindlin 1998)

Each of the four positions adopted by Job's human interlocutors, in its own way, adds to the basic assumption that the cosmos is ordered and just: Eliphaz adds that all mortals are guilty before the deity, and so protestations of innocence are misguided; Bildad adds that since God is just, Job had better attempt to appease him; Zophar adds that Yahweh is simply beyond human understanding, so Job's anger actually compounds his guilt; Elihu adds that suffering is a form of divine communication and that its message is the need for reform.

Logically, the friends all adopt an underlying circular argument: the deity is just and the cosmos is ordered, therefore only the guilty suffer; since Job is suffering, he must, by definition, be guilty; Job's suffering for his actions is proof that the deity is just. Job's counterargument is that he is innocent and yet he is suffering, therefore Yahweh if he is indeed just, will come and give him some answers in person.

Michael Dick sums up the situation as one in which 'Job's disturbing new relationship with his God is expressed in the legal metaphor'. The deity is absent and hopelessly misrepresented by the three friends (13.7-1 1). Job demands a direct confrontation (23.4-5), confident that 'if he could only face Eloah a reconciliation could be effected' (Dick 1979: 45).

In the absence of Yahweh, Job is led to wonder if his own suffering implies that creation has gone into reverse, or whether the whole thing might have been a mistake. His language at this point is reminiscent of the creation myth in Genesis 1: 'Let the day perish wherein I was born, / and the night which said, / 'A man-child is conceived.' / Let that day be darkness!' (3: 3-4, RSV). Job's words invert those of the Creator: 'And God said, "Let there be light," and there was light. And God saw that the light was good; and God separated the light from the darkness. God called the light "day," and the darkness he called "night"' (Gen 1: 3-5, RSV). Job thinks that the cosmic order is undone – the act of bringing order out of chaos reversed – by the fact that he suffers for no reason. If the doctrine of retribution is mistaken, then how can it be maintained that the cosmos is regulated by a just god? How can there be divine order if the innocent are punished?

In cursing the day of his birth, Job evokes the return of chaos and this chimes with his comparison between a notional trial in which he confronts Yahweh, and the primeval battle between chaos and order: 'God will not relent His fury. / Beneath Him Rahab's minions stoop' (9.13, Alter 2010). In some biblical texts Rahab is a mythical monster killed by God in order that the world could be created (Isa. 51.9). Psalm 89.9-10 associates Rahab with the sea, recalling the myth of Tiamat: 'Thou rulest the raging of the sea: when the waves thereof arise, thou stillest them. Thou hast broken Rahab in pieces, as one that is slain; thou hast scattered thine enemies with thy strong arm' (KJV).[5] As we will see, the language of primordial confrontation is picked up by Yahweh when he finally enters the debate in ch. 38.

The imagery of combat mythology forms a striking counterpoint to legal discourse: they are opposed modes of conflict resolution, one suggesting a life-or-death struggle with no rules, the other an established, civilized and highly developed system of arbitration. If Job is right, the fact that his life has been reduced to 'turmoil' (3.26) – the personal equivalent of chaos (Newsom 2003: 94) – indicates that chaos has never been finally defeated, and the cosmos remains darkly unpredictable. If his friends are right, order reigns. The question of which view is closer to the truth persists into Yahweh's concluding intervention.

By the time we arrive at ch. 13, all three of Job's friends have spoken for the first time, and Job is replying. He begins by observing that he knows very well all that they are saying to him: 'Lo, my eye has seen all this, my ear has heard and understood it' (13.1, RSV). Underlying his reply is a frustration that he cannot speak with his accuser in order to understand the charges against him. Speaking with his friends is no substitute since they do not know, any more than he does, the nature of the case he must answer. Michael Dick relates this to legal practices in the ancient Near East: 'In accordance with Ancient Near Eastern principles God appears to initiate the charges and Job seems to be the defendant. Job's request for a writ of particulars implies that he is the victim of a prior juridical action' (1979: 38).

Job, then, is making a legal point when he addresses God directly and demands disclosure of the charges he faces. He is confident that he has a watertight case and that no witness can be called who will be able to testify against him successfully. He is prepared to stake his life on his innocence: 'Here: I am laying out my lawsuit. / I know I am in the right. / Who would argue the case with me? / I would then keep silent – and expire' (13: 18-19, Greenstein 2019). It is clear, then, that Job believes, as do his friends, that disease and suffering are the effects of divine punishment, but he sees his own suffering as unjust. He does not doubt that his terrible experience owes its origins to divine action, but he is appalled at, and mystified by, that action, and feels that he has a right to a fair hearing.

Towards the end of ch. 13, Job compares himself with a dead plant: 'Wilt thou frighten a driven leaf and pursue dry chaff?' (v. 25, RSV). The images suggest the excessiveness of the deity's aggression towards him. 'Having destroyed the moral order, the arbiter of justice orchestrates uncontrolled violence against an innocent victim who must plead for mercy, an intolerable perversion of justice' (Crenshaw 2007: 94). What is the point of the continued punishment once everything has been taken from Job and he is as good as dead? It is like chasing a dead leaf or the chaff carried by the wind during winnowing (the process by which the wind is used to separate grain from straw and husks).

Chapter 14 picks up on the image of dead vegetation and uses it to meditate on human finitude: 'Man that is born of a woman / is of few days, and full of trouble. / He comes forth like a flower, and withers; / he flees like a shadow, and continues not' (14.1-2, RSV). Does it make sense, Job wants to know, to put fleeting and inconsequential lives on trial? Since there is nothing to be gained from plaguing mere mortals whose lives pass almost as quickly as flowers or shadows, Job appeals to the deity to just let humanity be: 'Look away from him, and desist, that he may enjoy, like a hireling, his day' (14.6, RSV). Then Job returns to the comparison with plants, but now with an even deeper sense of pessimism: 'But for a tree there is hope. / If it's cut, it will come new again, / and its shoots will not cease. /. . . / A hero dies, is prostrated, / humans expire – and where are they?' (14.7-10, Good 1990). If human life is plant-like in its brevity, well a tree has more hope than a human since it can spring new shoots despite being cut down. As Edwin Good notes, the 'earlier plant images (13:25; 14: 2) were similes or metaphors of the human. The analogy with the felled tree which renews itself and grows again is opposed to the human who, as verses 10-12 put it, "lies down and doesn't get up"' (Good 1990: 240).

But then Job wonders if the analogy of the tree might be more appropriate than that of the leaves and flowers. Perhaps he too could enter a kind of suspended animation like the cut-down tree, and, in time, be revived. Could God not put him into a kind of stasis until such time as his sins were either atoned or forgotten? 'Oh that thou wouldest hide me in Sheol, that thou wouldest conceal me until thy wrath be past' (14.13-14, RSV).[6] Although this verse might seem to allude to it, life beyond death was a part neither of ancient Israelite belief nor of other ancient Near Eastern religions, but, as Jack Sanders indicates, it is clearly an idea of which the writer of Job was aware. 'The book of Job', he says, 'raises the issue of existence after death but rejects the concept' (Sanders 2005: 268). A few verses later, Job lapses back into despair: 'But the mountain falls and crumbles away, / and the rock is removed from its place; / the waters wear away the stones; / the torrents wash away the soil of the earth' (14.18-19, RSV). Although mountains and rocks seem permanent, even they crumble away eventually, and so do human life and hope. Overseeing the human condition, the brevity and misery of existence, is the deity who appears to be immune from prosecution: 'so thou', Job says to Yahweh, 'destroyest the hope of man' (14.19, RSV).

The oath of innocence

According to Michael Dick, the petition for a trial in ancient Near Eastern legal practice required the accused to make a declaration of their innocence, often in the form of an oath. Chapter 31 appears to be an extended version of such an oath (Dick 1979: 47). And yet, as Edwin Good points out, it is not quite that straightforward (1990: 311). In the previous chapter, a trial has begun to look impossible: 'You have been changed to cruelty toward me, / With your powerful hand you attack me. / . . . / For I know you will return me to Death / And the house appointed for all who live' (Good 1990, 30: 21, 23). How could there possibly be any kind of trial, let alone a fair trial, with a god who appears to be Job's implacable enemy and who Job believes wants to kill him? It is as if the trial is already over, and God is carrying out the sentence. In this light, ch. 31 seems like Job contradicting himself and acting in utter desperation.

The chapter includes self-curses in which Job avows his innocence by calling down upon himself dreadful misfortune if he can be shown to have committed specific sins: 'If I raised my hand against an orphan, / When I saw my advantage in the gate, / let my shoulder fall out of its socket / and my arm break off from its shaft' (31.21-2, Alter 2010). As this example makes clear, the curses Job calls down fit the crimes they might avenge, and they cover all the major fields of moral and ethical behaviour, from telling lies to responsible use of land and resources. In ancient Israelite culture, curses were taken very seriously, and their use by Job is intended to force Yahweh to act.[7] So, ch. 31 is not merely a statement of Job's innocence which prepares for trial, though it certainly has that function; it is also a summoning of the deity by the strongest words possible.

After affirming his innocence and invoking the deity, Job makes his official plea for trial in v. 35: 'Oh, that I had one to hear me! Here is my signature! let the Almighty answer me! Oh, that I had the indictment written by my adversary!' (RSV). Michael Dick describes the plea as one for a properly constituted court with plaintiff, defendant and judge. Job knows, of course, that the plaintiff and the judge are one and the same, and yet he pursues the legal encounter because he has no other option.

Out of the whirlwind

At the beginning of ch. 38, Job's insistence pays off, and Yahweh appears in a whirlwind. This suggests a visible presence. Such occurrences are rare in the Hebrew Bible, but there are a few examples such as when Abram sees a flaming torch in Genesis 15, Moses encounters the burning bush in Exodus 3, and the prophet Elijah experiences earthquake, wind and fire on Mount Horeb in 1 Kings 19. These are highly significant moments, charged with great cultural and historical value, so the poet of Job effectively aligns this encounter with those of the greatest religious importance.

Despite the apparent privilege accorded to Job of being allowed this kind of one-to-one with Yahweh, inviting the reader to compare him with the great heroes of Israel's story, Yahweh's address to Job does not seem consonant with such a status. He does not appear concerned with Job's suffering nor take any account of the great virtue about which he boasted to the Prosecutor at the story's opening. He addresses Job with deep sarcasm, challenging him to display knowledge of things only the world's Creator could possibly understand:

Where were you when I founded earth?
Tell, if you know understanding.
Who fixed its measures, do you know,
or who stretched a line upon it?
In what were its sockets sunk,
or who laid its cornerstone,
when the morning stars sang together,
and all the sons of God shouted for joy?

(38.4-7, Alter 2010)

Yahweh details how he created the world, couching his description in the form of questions. He depicts a cosmology with which Job should be familiar, but which nonetheless presents a challenge to his comprehension. Although Job knows very well who did these things, he can neither fathom the processes nor measure the power of one able to perform such feats. Put in his place as a mere mortal, he recognizes himself incapable of understanding his own life and the suffering he has endured.

Yahweh describes his creative activities in a series of images dealing with natural phenomena such as the sea, the weather, day and night, stars and constellations, birds and animals, in poetry of enormous power and rich imagination steeped in a mythopoeic understanding of the world. Thus, the stars are depicted as singing alongside 'the sons of God', perhaps implying the presence of lesser gods looking on in admiration.

In vv. 8-11, some of the details echo other ancient Near Eastern mythologies which represent the control of the oceans as a battle to overcome chaos and establish order:

Or who shut in the sea with doors,
when it burst forth from the womb;
when I made clouds its garment,
and thick darkness its swaddling band,
and prescribed bounds for it,
and set bars and doors,
and said, 'Thus far shall you come, and no farther,
and here shall your proud waves be stayed'?

(38.8-11, RSV)

In 38.36 there is another mythological reference in the text which is obscured by the RSV's translation: 'Who has put wisdom in the clouds, or given understanding to the mists?' Scheindlin renders this verse very differently: 'Who gave wisdom to the ibis, gave the cock its knowledge?' The words translated as *clouds* and *mists* in the RSV and as *ibis* and *cock* by Scheindlin are obscure. Their mythological significance, however, is suggested by Edwin Good's translation of the verse: 'Who put wisdom into Thoth? Who gave understanding to Sekwi?' Thoth was the Egyptian god of wisdom and writing, who was depicted with the head of an ibis. Like Thoth, Sekwi is a proper name, but no one is sure who it refers to, nor what it represents in this context. Scheindlin's rendering of Thoth as *ibis* is understandable, and his rendering of Sekwi as *cock* follows Jewish tradition. The RSV's rendering of the verse seems designed to disguise the presence of pagan mythology in Yahweh's discourse.

Yahweh's intervention continues in ch. 39, which is rich in images of the animal kingdom, starkly contrasting his comparison between creation and the building of a city. The measuring, fixing and foundation-laying of the cosmos implicitly link it with the human imposition of order on the world and with civilization as the other of disordered nature. Yet within the cosmic order, animal life seems to be wild and uncontrolled.

> Who gave the wild ass his freedom,
> undid his bonds –
> the beast I made to live in wasteland,
> gave the salt flat as a home,
> so that he might laugh at crowded cities
> and never hear the driver's call?
>
> *(39.5-7, Scheindlin 1998)*

The image of the wild ass scorning human influence suggests that within Yahweh's world there are elements which do not conform to the picture of civic structure painted in his opening description of carefully crafted foundations and meticulous building work. He follows his depiction of the wild ass's rejection of the city, with the untameable nature of the wild ox: 'Is the wild ox willing to serve you? / Will he spend the night at your crib? / Can you bind him in the furrow with ropes, / or will he harrow the valleys after you?' (39.9-10, RSV). Just as the wild ass is seen to roam freely well beyond the confines of the city, the wild ox spurns the efforts of human agriculture to control the environment. This is a beast which cannot be domesticated or made to serve human ends. The animal referred to here is probably the aurochs: a now extinct ox which stood six feet high at the shoulder. Its presence again suggests the power of the forces lying outside human influence and control.

Yahweh's questions to Job at the beginning of ch. 40 carry the weight of the foregoing account of the world he has made: 'And the LORD said to Job: / "Shall a faultfinder contend with the Almighty? / He who argues with God, let him answer it"' (40.1-2, RSV). The RSV's translation of these questions does not clearly indicate their significance to the overall pattern of the book. Edwin Good translates them differently, and points out the importance of Yahweh's terminology: 'Will an accuser of Shaddai yield, Eloah's arbiter answer?' (40.2). He writes: 'Job wanted a trial, and now Yahweh uses legal language. The "accuser" and "arbiter" are both legal terms' (Good 1990: 348). This legal language is picked up in v. 8 when Yahweh asks if Job would treat him as guilty in order to make himself innocent. The implication is that Job really knows far too little to enter into legal confrontation with his god. His idea of a trial is ridiculous given that human law does not apply to either Yahweh or to most of his (largely untamed) creation. Job's unavoidable reliance on his accuser to be an impartial judge of his case combines with images of ungovernable nature to reveal that the cosmos cannot be ordered according to the dictates of any human understanding of law and justice. That there is no other legal system to which the suffering innocent can appeal is one of the terrors this extraordinary book confronts.

Job has picked an argument with the deity in ignorance of who he is up against. Now he has been apprised of Yahweh's power and the sheer unknowability of his world, does he still want to press his case? Job is forced to acknowledge that he is overwhelmed and reduced to silence by the questions with which Yahweh has confronted him:

> But Job answered Yahweh:
> 'I see how little I am.
> I will not answer You.
> I am putting my hand to my lips:
> One time I spoke;
> I will not speak again;
> two times I spoke,
> and I will not go on'.
>
> *(40.3-5, Scheindlin 1998)*

This response has been interpreted in many different ways by Bible scholars. Some see it as Job's acceptance of his personal guilt in questioning Yahweh, while others have argued that it is an acceptance that human finitude is itself a kind of guilt in the eyes of God. Is it that Job here regrets a failure to take the situation sufficiently seriously because he did not expect to be confronted so forcefully? Or is Job merely submitting to a bullying and tyrannical deity because he has no power to resist? Whatever we make of it, the text presents us with a powerful representation of divine–human relations in a world which exceeds human comprehension and domination.

In vv. 6-8, Yahweh poses a question which goes to the heart of the preceding dialogues between Job and his friends: 'Will you even put me in the wrong? / Will you condemn me that you may be justified?' (40.8, RSV). The question implies that if Job's argument is accepted, then Yahweh must be condemned: Job's case has put his god in the dock. The implication of Job's charges is that what Yahweh has said about the world, his creation, knowledge, organization and command, must all count for nothing so that Job might be proved innocent. As Edwin Good puts it: 'Job has wanted to have it only one way, supposing that unless his goodness is rewarded with prosperity, goodness is meaningless and the world unjust' (1990: 355). What Yahweh's reply makes clear is that the world is simply not like that. Job has wanted to believe that his own sense of morality and justice prevails throughout the created order; Yahweh's portrayal of the world shows that not to be the case.

As we have seen, the representation of the animal kingdom is at odds with the image of the cosmos as an architectural construct built to exacting standards and comparable with a human city. The presence of wildness and disarray in Yahweh's creation is made even more disturbing in ch. 40 with the introduction of Behemoth and Leviathan. These creatures have been interpreted in a variety of ways, some concluding that Behemoth is a hippopotamus, and leviathan a crocodile, while others have seen Behemoth as a crocodile and leviathan as whale, but it is clear that these are legendary or mythical beasts. The presence of such monsters in the world reveals that its order contains disorder; its structured character is in tension with the chaotic elements it houses. This means that Job's belief in the universality of moral law and his expectations of cosmic justice are hopelessly naïve. The world is not organized according to the principles of human justice; there is much that cannot be accounted for, explained or superintended by the conventions and protocols of civilized humanity.

After the whirlwind

Like so much about the book of Job, the resolution is not easy to understand. Silenced by Yahweh's assertions of incomprehensible power and his depiction of a world beyond the reach of mortal understanding, Job is left with no option but to back down.

> Job reacts to the speeches of his Divine Respondent by giving up his case against Him. In so doing, he implicitly acknowledges that what he had perceived as corrupt in the divine administration of cosmic order was an error generated by his human vantage point and a notion of justice that is not appropriate for the cosmos as a whole.
>
> *(Lasine 1990: 191)*

Understandable as it may be, Job's reaction to what Yahweh says, does not resolve the issues raised by his story or by the revelation of divine power and its effects in the world Yahweh has created. As Lasine points out, Job's 'vantage point' (by which he seems to mean the opposite of 'vantage point' – a viewpoint with severe restrictions) prevents him from seeing the whole cosmic picture. But those very limitations have been a significant part of Job's complaint. When Zophar tells him that God is beyond his understanding (11.7-9), Job's response is to say that he already knows this, but that is not enough to answer his case. It has often proved tempting to interpreters to reduce the book's moral message to an assertion of the need to trust that God knows more and better than any mortal. Alan Cooper remarks on the inadequacy of such a reading:

> I have often heard the 'teaching' of the book of Job characterized as the idea that 'God is just, but not in the sense that "we" use the term.' But what other sense is there? I doubt that the book of Job teaches us that God is, after all, what we want him to be (just and good), but only in a hazy sort of way.
>
> *(Cooper 1990: 72)*

To say that Yahweh and his world are ultimately incomprehensible does not mitigate the effect of suffering when Job has, to the best of his knowledge, done everything demanded of him by the moral law. If the moral law does not operate consistently, then it cannot be just, and to imagine a version of justice which is inaccessible to human understanding is to miss the fact that justice is a profoundly human concept. To project a notional, radically different idea of justice onto the deity is pure speculation based on its apparent absence from the world. If Job's perception of injustice stems from his failure to understand God and the world, then there would be little point in him trying to live a righteous life, since he can never know whether his actions are right or wrong. To demand that one lives by a law one cannot understand makes a mockery of the very idea that a human is a moral agent answerable for their actions.

Nevertheless, Job acknowledges he was wrong and repents. Exactly what he is repenting of is not entirely clear, although Michael V. Fox argues that it is of speaking in ignorance, especially when he claims that his suffering shows God to be hostile to him and indifferent to humanity (2005: 354–5). Such a response appears to be a matter of experiencing Yahweh's presence and being overawed. But, in a disconcerting twist, Yahweh says Job was right all along: 'After the Lord had spoken these words to Job, the Lord said to Eli'phaz the Te'manite: "My wrath is kindled against you and against your two friends; for you have not spoken of me what is right, as my servant Job has"' (42.7, RSV). Job's repentance is what the friends urged him to do from the start, and he does it in response to Yahweh's speeches. Yet Yahweh is angry with the friends for what they said to Job, even though, as Carol Newsom points out, the outcome is precisely what they predicted:

> When Job reorients himself towards God and puts the 'iniquity' of his arrogant words aside, God turns to him in kindness, removes his misery, and restores him to a life in which he 'rests secure' (so Zophar, 11:13-20). Indeed, God makes Job's 'latter days' more blessed than his 'former days' (cf. Bildad's words in 8:7 with 42:12). And as Eliphaz had predicted, God protects Job through his many trials, so that Job lives to experience prosperity, abundant offspring, and a peaceful death at an advanced age (5:19-27). (Newsom 2003: 20–1)

While the post-debate conclusion seems to offer narrative closure, restoring Job's fortunes, the divine judgement that Job was right and his friends wrong undermines that closure. Job, it appears, was right all along and yet, paradoxically, he is also right to repent. The friends were right – inasmuch as they foresaw the outcome of Job's penitence – and yet they are condemned by Yahweh. The idea of divine retribution has been shown to be wrong by the terrible suffering of an innocent man, and by the deity's depiction of a cosmos to which human morality is largely irrelevant. And yet, in the end, Job is rewarded for being right about Yahweh, suggesting that the doctrine of retribution is right. 'Job is inconsistent, but so is God', as Michael V. Fox puts it (2013: 22). Yahweh cannot be pinned down to the ideas of justice asserted by Job's friends, any more than he can be made to answer Job's questions. He is simply not to be constrained by human attitudes and beliefs – not even those of pious people. And, in a sense, this is a hard lesson for the reader: Job is a book which, like its god, refuses to conform to any of our readerly demands or expectations. It is no more consistent, moral or fair than the deity it puts in the dock.

As Nahum Sarna observes, most ancient peoples did not expect their gods to be principled or fair: 'The pagan worshipper had no reason to believe that the decrees of his god must necessarily be just, any more than he could be convinced that society rested upon a universal order of justice' (Sarna 1966: 17). That Job *does* expect both morality and justice from his god is a mark of the shift from polytheism to monotheism. But that shift brought its own problems when it came to issues of suffering with no court of appeal or alternate source of comfort in the face of Yahweh's displeasure. David Robertson understands Job's idea of the avenger (*go'el*) in ch. 19 in this light. Briefly, Job imagines the existence of a figure who might contend with Yahweh, but 'when we realize that Job never even so much as alludes to this figure again, it seems fair to conclude that he himself knows that such a figure is a pipe dream' (Robertson 1973: 460).

Job's challenge to the orthodoxies of his day is a powerful reminder of human resilience in the face of suffering, and of the will to call the powerful to account despite the overwhelming odds. Because the book ends with irresolvable strains and contradictions still in play, it remains an open-ended and infinitely re-interpretable book. It challenges beliefs and ideas about the relationship between human beings and the divine like nothing else from the ancient world. But it challenges the modern reader, too, however sceptical or irreligious, with its disconfirmation of narrative order. While Genesis makes of narrative a power akin to the world-making voice of Yahweh, Job reveals the profound difference between narrative closure and conceptual, or argumentative, resolution. All ends well for Job, but the book makes us doubt not only the likelihood of such an outcome but also the morality it represents. Ultimately, the story has a satisfying shape which belies the terror it evokes, and so calls into question the viability of the order which narrative seems to impose on experience.

Notes

1. Robert Alter comments that the Hebrew term '*hassatan*' 'invariably uses the definite article because the designation indicates a function, not a proper name. . . . Only toward the very end of the biblical period would the term begin to drop the definite article and refer to a demonic figure' (2010: 12).
2. Robert Gordis associates wisdom literature with the upper strata of society and points out its use in training young men for leadership and administrative roles (1943-4: 85–91).
3. 'Theodicy' denotes a defence of divine justice and providence in the face of suffering and evil.
4. Alan Cooper rejects the idea that the text makes Job's prosperity a consequence of his piety; such a conclusion, he argues, 'is a mere inference drawn by the reader of the text' (1990: 69).
5. According to W. R. F. Browning (2009), Rahab also came to be used as a symbolic name for Egypt (Ps. 87.4; Isa. 30.7).

6. 'Sheol is referred to as "the chambers of death" (Prov 7:27) and seems to connect the physical grave with an underground abode of the dead. . . . The term can also be used metaphorically to connote a place of shadowy afterlife existence or even an insatiable (Hab 2:5), harsh (Song 8:6) power that can destroy the living (Isa 5:14)' (Dolansky 2022: n.p.).
7. 'Curse can be defined as the use of powerful words to invoke supernatural harm. . . . Depending on their purpose and context, biblical curses can be approved (as in Deut 27-29) or condemned (as in Job 2:10), collective or individual, and they may combine political and theological aims' (Britt 2022: n.p.).

Translations used in preparing this chapter

Alter, R. (2010), *The Wisdom Books: Job, Proverbs, and Ecclesiastes: A Translation with Commentary*, New York, NY and London: W.W. Norton & Company.

Good, E. M. (1990), *In Turns of Tempest: A Reading of Job, with a Translation*, Stanford, CA: Stanford University Press.

Greenstein, E. L. (2019), *Introduction to Job: A New Translation*, Grand Rapids, MI: Yale University Press.

Scheindlin, R. P. (1998), *The Book of Job: Translation, Introduction and Notes*, New York, NY: W.W. Norton & Company.

The King James Bible (1611).

The Revised Version of the Bible (1885).

The Revised Standard Version of the Bible (1952), National Council of the Churches of Christ in the United States of America.

CHAPTER 6
THE *ODYSSEY*

Texts and historical setting

Few works from the ancient world have had the enduring impact on Western literatures and cultures of Homer's *Iliad* and *Odyssey*. Among the literary products of antiquity, perhaps only the Bible has been more influential over such a protracted historical span. Long viewed as the pinnacle of poetic achievement and as triumphs of narrative composition, the twin epics served for generations as touchstones of artistic excellence. Despite a wide range of challenges to traditional beliefs about their production, status and integrity, many still regard them as an unrivalled cultural highpoint.

Probably dating from the late eighth or early seventh century BCE, the true story of their creation remains unknown, but however they were originally composed, transmitted or preserved, they were passed down through the Greek-speaking world for centuries before translation broadened their sphere of dissemination and influence. There must have been texts in circulation as early as the sixth century BCE because there are reports of recitations of the work in Athens, and there are echoes of Homer in sixth-century Greek poetry. The *Odyssey* was known to fourth-century BCE scholars in ancient Alexandria – home of the most famous library of antiquity – probably on papyrus scrolls (Griffin 2004: 31–2). A poem as long as the *Odyssey* would have required multiple scrolls and this may be the origin of its division into twenty-four books. Some have speculated that the number of books echoes the twenty-four letters of the Greek alphabet, though why such correspondence would have seemed desirable, and to whom, is a matter of speculation (Powell 2007: 9). Copies of the poem were preserved, too, in Byzantium – capital of the eastern part of the Roman Empire from the time of Constantine (fourth century CE) – in bound manuscript books.

Following the collapse of the Roman Empire, widespread knowledge of the Greek language as well as first-hand familiarity with its literature were lost to Western Europe for the best part of a thousand years. In the fourteenth century CE, it was reintroduced to Italy from Byzantium where a Greek-speaking, Christian empire had persisted. The first printed edition of Homer's texts was produced in Florence in 1488, but the epics had circulated in handwritten copies for about a hundred years before that time (Knox 1996: 4). As more and more works from the classical age surfaced during the fifteenth and sixteenth centuries, they spread across Europe fuelling the growth of what became known as Renaissance humanism: the rediscovery and celebration of ancient Greek and Roman writing and the promotion of its perceived values. Homer was translated into

English by George Chapman (1559–1634), his version of the *Iliad* appearing in 1611, and his *Odyssey* in 1616.

In the wake of the rediscovery of his master works, Homer came to be seen by Western scholars, poets and artists as an ancient genius who composed the poems much as a modern poet would. That view prevailed until it was undermined by the work of American scholar Milman Parry (1902–35), who showed that the Homeric epics drew on the kind of formulaic expressions and phrases typical of oral composition rather than textual authorship. 'Parry argued, with a far more elaborate documentation than had ever been attempted before, that Homer was what is now called an "oral" poet – that is, a poet who composed his poems without the use of writing and who presented them orally and often more or less extemporaneously to his audience' (Combellack 1959: 193).

While there are undoubtedly abundant markers of orality in Homer, recent scholarship suggests that writing did play a part in the composition. The Greek alphabet is thought to have developed around 800 BCE: probably a comparatively short time before Homer's epics were composed. This fact is considered significant by some critics, their work envisaging 'a highly creative oral poet, master of the repertoire of inherited material and technique, who used the new instrument of writing to build . . . an epic poem on a scale beyond the imagination of his predecessors' (Knox 1996: 20).

Although the origin of Homer's works has been much disputed, scholars now mostly agree that his world is more or less that of the early Archaic Period (eighth century BCE). By then, Mycenaean civilization had been lost for about 300 years and succeeded by the 'Dark Age' (Powell 2007: 59).[1] While Homer's works were composed after the Dark Age had begun to recede, the world they depict is not the one in which they were composed. The *Iliad* and the *Odyssey* evoke 'a distant mythical past – even from the point of view of their earliest audiences' (Graziosi 2016: 35). Mycenaean culture flourished between 1600 and 1100 BCE, and some of the stories which found their way into Homer's epics were probably based on folk memories and oral narratives of the exploits of its heroes.

The society in which Odysseus is placed is, in a sense, a fantasy: it is neither an accurate portrayal of the way of life familiar to the composer(s) of the Homeric epics nor a realistic vision of a Mycenaean past (Graziosi 2016: 36–7). Heroic figures, stronger and more determined than ordinary mortals, peopled the land and enjoyed a closer relationship with the gods than had been possible since. It is a world dominated by nobles and kings who appear to be landowners, warriors and judges who retain power only as long as they are strong enough to do so. In certain respects, the power struggles and dynastic conflicts which emerge in the epics reflect cultural and political shifts during the Dark Age (roughly coterminous with the European Iron Age): 'In its general setting Homer describes the historical transition from rule by petty kings, the Big Men (*basileis*) in the Iron Age to rule by aristocratic oligarchies in the early historical period in the eighth century BCE. In Homer's story the older generation of Big Men is triumphant' (Powell 2007: 153). Odysseus, of course, is one of the 'Big Men', and his eventual overcoming of the suitors who plague his home during his absence reasserts the right to rule of such traditional overlords.

Mythical geography

If the historical setting of the *Odyssey* is a blend of reality and fiction, suspended between the time of composition and an imagined past, its geographical character is no more securely rooted in fact. The route of Odysseus' journey has been the subject of a great deal of enquiry and speculation, with commentators divided between those who wish to pinpoint the significant locations and those 'calling efforts to map the *Odyssey* a complete waste of time' (Zazzera 2019: n.p.). Divergences among the mappers have sometimes been wide, as Howard Clarke observes: 'There have been some seventy theories proposed since Homer wrote the *Odyssey*, with locations bounded only by the North and South Poles and ranging within the inhabited world from Norway to South Africa and from the Canary Islands to the Sea of Azov' (Clarke 1981: 251). At the other extreme from such cartographic enthusiasm, Bernard Knox sees Odysseus' wanderings as taking us 'off the map and into a world of wonders and terrors' (Knox 1996: 29).

Barbara Graziosi notes that from the point at which Odysseus and his men are blown off course while rounding Cape Malea (Book 9), until the end of the voyage, their travels cannot be traced with any certainty on modern maps (2016: 35). They seem to sail beyond the limits of the known world, crossing an imperceptible divide to enter strange, uncharted waters. The Phaeacians, who eventually take Odysseus home, ply the boundary dividing the phantasmagorical realm through which the hero passes from places familiar to the epic's original audience. Douglas Frame sees this peculiar people as inhabiting a contact zone between adjacent realities: 'a liminal place between the real and the unreal' (Frame 2020: 1, S3).

It is in this 'liminal place' among these marginal people that Odysseus unfolds the story of his adventures. At this point, he is on the cusp of restoration, transitioning from the fantastical back to the everyday. His arrival in the country of the Phaeacians – washed up on a beach, naked, battered and alone, followed by a death-like sleep in a pile of leaves – is suggestive of sloughing off the past in preparation for a renewal of life and purpose. The episode becomes, in the words of Charles Segal, 'the principal point of crisis and transition' (1962: 22). Unlike the other figures Odysseus has encountered in his off-the-map wanderings, the Phaeacians are welcoming and hospitable: they use neither violence nor enchantment against him, so that they 'appear as a neutralization of the dangers he has met' (Segal 1962: 22). His stay with them allows him to 'integrate the real with the unreal, the imaginary with the familiar' (Segal 1962: 23).

Odysseus' encounter with the Phaeacians, although forming the final stage of his homeward progress, occurs in books 6–8, so most of the story is yet to unfold. In books 9–12, he tells the tale of his tumultuous journey. From Book 13 on, the second-half of the epic is taken up with his return to Ithaca.

Plot and structure

As the placing of the Phaeacian episode midway through the poem suggests, the structure of the *Odyssey* is complex. It opens twenty years into the story with the hero's son Telemachus travelling in search of news of his father, and the first four books are taken up with these events. Books 5–8 deal with Odysseus and his current situation; books 9–13 bring us back to the beginning of the story when Odysseus recounts his adventures. The remaining books are the continuation of the story from the middle to the end. Bernard Knox explains why the story is organized in this non-sequential way: 'If the poet had begun at the beginning and observed a strict chronology, he would have been forced to interrupt the flow of his narrative as soon as he got his hero back to Ithaca in order to explain the extremely complicated situation he would have to deal with in his home' (Knox 1996: 10). Such an interruption would weaken the narrative tension forged by the threat facing Penelope, Telemachus and their home, and the continued delay in Odysseus' return.

The underlying timeline disguised by the complex narrative structure can, with a little effort, be recovered from the poem. Odysseus has been away from home for twenty years; the first ten were taken up with the Trojan War. During the first year after leaving Troy, he and his men encounter the Circonians, the Lotus Eaters, Polyphemus, Aeolus and the Laestrygonians. The following year is spent on Circe's island, and the year after that travelling to the underworld, encountering the Sirens, negotiating the terrors of Scylla and Charybdis and being stranded on the island of the sun god, Helios (or Hyperion). Odysseus then remains with Calypso for seven years; after leaving her, he meets the Phaeacians and is brought by them back to Ithaca. Telemachus' travels occur during the last month of Odysseus' absence (while he is with the Phaeacians).

The reason for the long delay in Odysseus' homecoming, his being blown off course, facing an array of natural and monstrous obstacles, confronting threats to life and limb, and being captivated by magical enchantments, lies with the gods, particularly the sea god, Poseidon. Odysseus earns his enmity by blinding his son, Polyphemus (the Cyclops), and so the offended deity does his utmost to prolong the hero's misery. Fortunately for Odysseus, the goddess Athena is sympathetic to him, pleads his case before Zeus, and wins for him a hard-earned return to Ithaca. The roles played by the gods, then, are crucial to the story.

The gods

The Olympian gods (taking their name from Mount Olympus, on which they were thought to live) who feature in the *Odyssey* were the third and fourth generations of deities. They descended from the Titans, who were themselves descended from the primordial parents Gaea (Earth) and Ouranos (Sky). There were six male Titans (Coeus, Cronos, Crius, Helios, Iapetus and Oceanus) and six female (Mnemosyne, Phoebe, Rhea, Theia, Themis and Tethys). They claimed power when Cronos, in a plot with his mother and his brothers, overthrew his father Ouranos. Cronos, in turn, was overthrown by his son, Zeus, who defeated chaos and became the founder of order in the world and chief of the gods. The first generation of Olympians were descendants of Cronos and Rhea: three sons (Poseidon, Hades and Zeus) and three daughters (Hera, Hestia and Demeter).

The second generation of Olympians were Athena, Ares, Hermes, Dionysus, Apollo, Artemis and Hephaestus. Aphrodite is also sometimes considered a second-generation Olympian, but was originally from the Titans' generation.

According to the Greek historian Herodotus (fifth century BCE), it was Homer who 'first fixed for the Greeks the genealogy of the gods, gave the gods their titles, divided among them their honours and functions, and defined their images' (Finley 1971: 26). A survival of Mycenaean culture, those gods had been known since at least the Bronze Age. The beliefs and rituals associated with their worship are often described in both the *Iliad* and the *Odyssey*, and these forms of religious practice, typical of archaic Greece, probably differed little from those of Mycenaean times.

B. C. Dietrich argues that the gods 'were real figures of faith, no less real in fact to Homer's audience than the epic heroes themselves, and no less "historical" than the account of the conflict about Troy' (1979: 136). But the *Odyssey* depicts the gods as quarrelsome and partisan and makes their disagreements integral to the narrative as a form of entertainment. If these gods were figures of religious belief and devotion such characterization would seem irreverent to say the least. As early as the fifth century BCE some commentators objected, the philosopher Xenophanes (*c.*570–478 BCE) being among those who condemned the shameful behaviour ascribed to the gods by Homer. Emily Kearns argues that Homer's epics are about human heroism, glory and suffering, and that these are pursued 'at the expense of a plausible and satisfying treatment of the divine'. While the gods are a necessary part of the Homeric world, they 'are there to illuminate, comment on and contrast with the depiction of human actions and the human condition' (Kearns 2004: 71). Their presence and character in the *Odyssey*, then, remain paradoxical: they seem to both demand and resist religious acknowledgement. Arranged in a human-like society, they fall into squabbles, rivalries, vendettas, favouritism, jealousy and resentment. Barry Powell characterizes them as 'ill-tempered, often ridiculous beings' whose immortality made them susceptible to triviality and pettiness 'unconstrained by the seriousness of human life. Our acts count because we are going to die, but the gods are free to be petty forever' (2007: 70).

Given the anthropomorphism of Greek theology, and its tendency to represent the gods as sometimes feckless and ill-disciplined, it is perhaps unsurprising that sexual desire and promiscuity play a significant part in the stories told of them. They often interbreed with humans, and many of the greatest heroes were of mixed human and divine parentage:

> I saw Antiope, daughter of Asopus; it was her pride to have slept in the arms of Zeus himself. She bore two sons, Amphion and Zethus, primal founders of Thebes of the seven gates. . . . After her I saw Alcmene, wife of Amphitryon, who lay in the arms of mighty Zeus and brought forth Heracles of the dauntless spirit and lion heart.
>
> *(Shewring 1980: Book 11, 134)*

Unlike Achilles, Heracles, Perseus and other heroic figures in Greek mythology, Odysseus, although he displays inordinate strength and cunning, is not a demigod; both of his parents were mortals. Nonetheless, his story has a divine dimension, being bound up with the ancient discord between Athena and Poseidon.[2] Athena acts as Odysseus' advocate and protector while Poseidon persecutes him.

The only other gods who have major parts to play are Zeus and the sun god, Helios. Zeus is in overall control of events, deciding Odysseus' fate, while Helios' involvement is to demand recompense after Odysseus' men slaughter and eat his cattle (Book 12); the guilty are condemned to pay with their lives. Bruce Louden notes that epic poetry typically relates divine character and action to the experience of the hero: 'how the gods are depicted is partly determined by their relationships to the hero. . . . In a given epic a small group of key deities are closely concerned with the hero, and either interact with him directly or influence his circumstances from a distance' (Louden 2009: 90). Although the role of the gods in the *Odyssey* is allied to Odysseus' experience, they are shown to exercise control over the wider world.

As the epic begins, once the muse has been invoked to assist with the telling of the tale, the gods appear as characters and the plot begins to unfold from their perspective. The combination of the invocation of the muse (implying some kind of divine inspiration) and the framing of Odysseus' tale as a matter of divine concern and action anchors the epic in a mythopoeic world in which human affairs are shaped by the will and intervention of the gods. Not only is the fate of Odysseus and his men shown to be determined by Zeus, Poseidon, Athena and the other Olympians, but the preservation and propagation of their story is also under divine control.

The first god mentioned is Poseidon, and this is a telling detail because his actions have the greatest consequences for the hero and his crew. Odysseus' blinding of his son, Polyphemus, earns the god's anger and enmity to such an extent that he does everything he can to destroy the hero, or, at least, prevent his homecoming. Since homecoming (*nostos* in Greek) is the central theme of the story, Poseidon's role is pivotal.

The next god to be mentioned is Zeus. As the most powerful of the Olympians and their leader, his will is decisive. When we first encounter him, he is pondering the idea of homecoming, particularly that of Agamemnon whose return from the Trojan War was also the moment of his murder at the hands of his wife's lover. The fact that homecoming and the danger facing a king who has been away for a very long time are on Zeus' mind indicates both Odysseus' stature as a hero with whom the gods are concerned, and the part Zeus will play as one of the 'key deities'. It has implications, too, for Penelope's character, as we shall see.

The other major divine player in the story is Athena. She appears on the scene shortly after Zeus, to express her concern for Odysseus:

> He has long been far from everything that he loves, desolate in a wave-washed island, a wooded island, the navel of all the seas. A goddess has made her dwelling there . . . who keeps poor Odysseus pining there, and who seeks continually with her soft and coaxing words to beguile him into forgetting Ithaca; but he – he would be well content to see even the smoke rising up from his own land, and he longs to die.
>
> *(Shewring 1980: Book 1, 2)*

In the goddess' words we learn of Odysseus' current whereabouts and of his quest to reach his home. They inform us, too, that Athena is a major player in the story, and that she sides with Odysseus against Poseidon.

We know from this opening on Mount Olympus that the story we are about to hear, or read, is one at the very heart of which is divine action and its relation to human affairs. From the mouth of Zeus himself we learn that their relations with the gods shape human lives:

> What a lamentable thing it is that men should blame the gods and regard *us* as the source of their troubles, when it is their own wickedness that brings them sufferings worse than any which Destiny allots them. Consider Aegisthus, who flouted Destiny by stealing Agamemnon's wife [Clytemnestra] and murdering her husband when he came home, though he knew the ruin this would entail, since we sent Hermes, the keen-eyed Giant slayer, to warn him neither to kill the man nor make love to his wife.
>
> *(Rieu 1946: Book 1, 26)*

Heeding the warnings of the gods and behaving in ways which respect their laws underlies human destiny, and this fact shapes what befalls Odysseus' men: despite being told not to, they killed and ate the cattle of the sun god Helios; so 'the god saw to it that they should never return' (Rieu 1946: Book 1, 25).

Zeus makes clear that the gods do not decide individual destinies on a whim. As we saw in the story of Job, there is an underlying belief in divine retribution: people are punished for their folly and rewarded for the right kind of behaviour. But the problem of retribution in the *Odyssey* is of a slightly different order from that faced by Job, since ancient Greek culture was polytheistic while Job has to deal with a single deity. When Athena complains to her father that Odysseus has not been treated appropriately, he responds by recognizing the hero's goodness and pointing out that human experience is shaped by more than one divine will:

> How could I forget Odysseus the godlike, he who
> is beyond all other men in mind, and who beyond others
> has given sacrifice to the gods, who hold wide heaven?
> It is the Earth Encircler Poseidon who, ever relentless,
> nurses a grudge because of the Cyclops, whose eye he blinded . . .
> For his sake Poseidon, shaker of the earth, although he does not
> kill Odysseus, yet drives him back from the land of his fathers.
>
> *(Lattimore 1967: Book 1, ll.65–75)*

Odysseus will not be killed because Zeus recognizes his righteousness, but the conflict over his case among the gods results in a tumultuous experience.

The *Odyssey* and folktale

If the opening of the epic locates the story in a mythopoeic setting, showing the inseparability of human and divine affairs, the role of Polyphemus indicates the subtle interweaving of myth with folktale.[3] The story is told in far more detail than any other episode Odysseus relates to the Phaeacians.[4]

The episode begins when Odysseus and his men put in on an island opposite the country of the Cyclopes. They have plenty to eat and drink, but curiosity drives Odysseus to explore the dangerous territory across the sound. On landing, the party sees a cave 'overhung with laurels', and, keen to find out whether Polyphemus will be welcoming, Odysseus enters the cave with twelve of his men. In the initial exchange with the monster, he specifically appeals to the laws of hospitality, invoking the protection of Zeus as guardian of travellers and divine patron of strangers. Polyphemus' answer expresses a chilling disregard for civilization and for the gods:

> We Cyclops never blink at Zeus and Zeus's shield
> of storm and thunder, or any other blessed god –
> we've got more force by far.
> I'd never spare you in fear of Zeus's hatred,
> you or your comrades here, unless I had the urge.
>
> *(Fagles 1996: Book 9, ll.309–13)*

When Polyphemus enters the cave, he blocks the entrance with a massive boulder, and rather than feeding Odysseus and his men, as the laws of hospitality would demand, he eats two of them, and then another two the following morning. Following his grim breakfast, he leaves the cave to tend his flock, imprisoning the remaining men in the cave. On his return, he eats two more of them. Odysseus gives him wine to drink, and he falls asleep. While he sleeps, Odysseus and his men sharpen a stake by putting the end in the fire until it forms a point, which they drive into Polyphemus' single eye, then, when he lets his sheep out in the morning, they escape by clinging to their bellies.

There are many ancient versions of this tale which come from a wide range of sources across a geographical region stretching from Britain to Russia, and reaching into Turkey, the Near East and North Africa (Edmunds 2009: 38), but the Homeric text makes it integral to Odysseus' story: 'The Homeric version of the folktale projects both a past (the prophecy concerning Odysseus that Polyphemos recalls) and a future (the anger of Poseidon), so that Odysseus' role as protagonist of this story becomes continuous with the narrative of the *Odyssey* as whole' (Edmunds 2009: 39). By giving the tale past and future, its character as a freestanding story is undercut, and it is effectively woven into the fabric of the epic. A number of other strategies contribute to this effect, including Polyphemus' expression of disregard for the gods. Since his unruly and inhospitable behaviour would not be acceptable within Homeric culture, it has to be adapted to the context by making lawlessness and irreligion the hallmarks of the Cyclopes' barbaric society.[5] Maureen Alden describes their way of life as 'the antithesis of agriculture and the Greek pattern of settlement in πόλεις (cities)' (2017: 224–5). All the more striking, then, that – as both she and Egbert J. Bakker observe – the episode parallels that in which Odysseus kills the suitors at the epic's close. Odysseus becomes 'a grim reflection of the Cyclops' as he avenges the invasion of his home and the uninvited eating of his food (Alden 2017: 233). Such parallels are, Alden notes, beloved of ancient literature (5).

The remaking of oral forms and traditions by means of the technology of writing allowed the emergence of a kind of storytelling which had not been possible before. As we have seen, Bernard Knox observes that the *Odyssey* is a blend of oral and written modes. As such, it represents a highly significant moment in the development of narrative: the creation of a story on a scale not previously attempted, and with a technical sophistication unmatched in earlier works.

The heightened complexity of the new mode – supremely evident in the transformation of an earlier independent tale into an integral episode – allowed myth and folktale to be yoked by a narration divided, principally, between the poet and the hero.[6] The use of Odysseus' voice to tell some of the story has attracted a lot of scholarly attention. Graham Wheeler calls him an '*anti*-Bard' who 'speaks on his own authority . . . and, obviously, lies' (Wheeler 2002: 35). Thus, the Homeric tradition developed many of the techniques and conventions of narration which we have come to associate with the novel, including reworking earlier stories, non-chronological ordering, unreliable voices and multiple narrators. And yet, it remains a text steeped in an ancient mythopoeic worldview, drawing into its world of gods, heroes, monsters and magic, material originating well beyond its confines.

But in its careful organization, studied technique and prefiguring of the novel, the *Odyssey* might be understood to question the very mythopoeic worldview which gave rise to it. Theodor Adorno and Max Horkheimer argued that the shape of the Homeric cosmos is the product of fiction rather than myth, its organization determined more by the demands of plot and narrative than by primordial relations between gods and humanity (1992: 109–11). This means that the emergence of Odysseus as an individual undermines, or calls into question, the cosmic order of myth, inasmuch as his goal of self-preservation leaves all other concerns in its wake. His quest and its telling in crafted, highly wrought form might be thought to fracture the picture of a world inhabited by divine, demonic and monstrous figures and controlled by superhuman and magical powers. Such presences and effects, the argument runs, are in tension with the reasoning processes behind the epic's sophisticated structure. And yet, the kind of parallels between episodes pointed out by Bakker and Alden might be interpreted as the inverse: as expressing a profoundly mythopoeic worldview, because narrative parallels can be taken to suggest transcendent order reflected in a range of different human experiences and actions.

Adorno and Horkheimer's argument anachronistically divides myth from reality:

> Our mentality as modern readers invites us to see Odysseus at home as 'reality' and Odysseus abroad as 'myth,' as if the myth of the hero contradicted the reality of the hero. Such a split vision is a false dichotomy. The reality of Odysseus is in

> fact the myth of Odysseus, since that myth derives from the historical reality of Homeric poetry as a medium of myth.
>
> *(Nagy 2020: n.p.)*

If the reality of Odysseus is indeed also the myth of Odysseus, then the *Odyssey* cannot depict a 'flight of the individual from the mythical powers', as Adorno and Horkheimer contend. Such a perception depends upon opposing myth to 'ordering reason', but as we saw in Chapter 2, this is not as clear cut a distinction as some interpreters would have us believe. If the arguments made in that chapter are accepted, then the thematic patterns in the epic and the order they create might be read less as the destruction of myth than its integration with narrative in a more complex form than had been seen before.

Women and *xenia*

One thematic pattern which reveals the intricacy of the epic's narrative is its representation of female figures, whether mortal women, goddesses or monsters. In the familiar and uncharted territory of his wanderings, most of the fearful and the desirable figures Odysseus encounters are female: Calypso, Circe, Scylla, Charybdis and the Sirens. Despite the monstrous nature of Scylla and Charybdis and the near humanity of Calypso, no distinction is made between their modes of existence: each is equally, physically real, and, as we shall see, they are united in a continuum of fear and desire.

When it comes to the place of women in ancient Greek society, a mixed picture emerges in the scholarly discourse. For example, H. D. F. Kitto argued that Athenian women were marginalized and severely constrained in various ways, while Simon Hornblower shows Spartan women to have enjoyed greater freedom and more legal rights (Hornblower 1991: 220). Collette Hemingway makes the important point that even though women in classical antiquity suffered under a range of restrictive impositions, they were, nonetheless, aware of potent female deities who presided over many aspects of their lives: 'Demeter was able to retrieve her daughter Persephone, Artemis could send a fatal arrow, and Athena had the ability to resist marriage and motherhood, and to provide advice to respected Greek heroes. Aphrodite, Hera, Hestia, and Hekate were also powerful goddesses, intensely honoured and greatly admired by women and men alike' (Hemingway 2004: n.p.).

Jonathan Hall observes that while much archaic Greek literature is deeply misogynistic, Homeric poetry, aimed at an aristocratic audience, 'testifies to an attitude of respect and affection for women' (2007: 199). Similarly, Kostas Myrsiades argues that in the *Odyssey* women 'enjoy a status and dignity equal to their husbands', and he points to examples such as Penelope, Arete and Anticlea, among others (2019: 279–80). On the other hand, he notes that 'feminine charm' can be 'a negative force for mortals. The Trojan War was due to the abduction of a woman, Helen, while the ongoing disorder in Ithaca is due to Penelope's refusal to select a husband' (Myrsiades 2019: 71).

There are other aspects of the narrative, too, which need to be considered as a counterbalance to the idea that women enjoyed anything approaching equality in Homeric culture. For example, suspicion of infidelity falls on Penelope, and she is judged by a different standard from her philandering husband; Odysseus hangs the housemaids without so much as a trial; throughout the epic the hero encounters predatory females. Embodying all manner of threats, from distraction to being eaten alive, women and female monsters are an ever-present danger. Barbara Graziosi notes that even Penelope is a potential killer: 'The story of Agamemnon's return from Troy is told prominently in the *Odyssey*, at the very beginning of the poem and at regular intervals throughout the epic' (Graziosi 2016: 114). As Odysseus moves ever closer to home, the shadow of that violent death grows darker. Penelope, surrounded by suitors, might always yield to temptation, join forces with one of them and re-enact Clytemnestra's plot against her husband.

Consciousness of such a possibility is sharpened by the representation of women as inscrutable, and therefore unpredictable, in the *Odyssey*. Jasper Griffin reveals the pattern: 'Odysseus never knows why Calypso suddenly let him go; the Suitors are completely baffled by Penelope; Circe, with her sinister magic passing directly into the offer of sexual union, terrifies the sailors and remains opaque to the hero' (Griffin 2004: 81). The 'inscrutability' of women to Homeric men perhaps helps to explain the extent to which the figures encountered by Odysseus in the unmapped regions are female. Such a perception would link the female sex with the strangeness, danger and attraction of the unknown.

That combination of danger and attraction is most readily apparent in the figure of Calypso – a minor goddess who keeps Odysseus on her island in Book 5. Her sexual allure is one threat among many to Odysseus' homecoming, testing his resolve to return: 'I know that my wise Penelope . . . is far beneath you in form and stature; she is a mortal, you are immortal and unageing. Yet, notwithstanding, my desire and longing day by day is still to reach my own home' (Shewring 1980: Book 5, 60).

In Book 10, Odysseus and his men land on the island of Aeaea, home to another minor goddess: Circe. She is slightly more threatening than Calypso. She keeps animals, weaves, sings and prepares food, but each of these domestic, and, in context, female, functions is given a perverse twist: her animals are actually men she has placed under a spell, her food is laced with poison, her singing enchants her victims and her weaving is (metaphorically) a spider's web. She seems to represent fear and desire in equal measure.

Again, in the case of the Sirens (Book 12), female attractiveness turns out to be potentially deadly: 'If a man in ignorance draws too close and catches their music, he will never return to find wife and little children near him and to see their joy at his homecoming' (Shewring 1980: Book 12, 144). The sea monsters Scylla and Charybdis are female figures from whose presence desire is completely absent: they embody unalloyed fear. So there is a kind of continuum in the representation of these female figures: Calypso – desire with an admixture of fear; Circe – a balance between desire and fear; the Sirens – fear with an admixture of desire; Scylla and Charybdis – undifferentiated fear.

There is a parallel progression of hospitality, or *xenia*, in the representation of societies Odysseus and his men encounter, from the most ordered and welcoming, to the utterly lawless. *Xenia* is the law/custom of offering protection and hospitality to strangers. It was felt to be so fundamental to civilized life that its patron was *Zeus Xenios*: 'Zeus the god who protects strangers.' The highly civilized Phaeacians offer Odysseus rich hospitality; the Lotus Eaters are likewise civilized and hospitable to a point, but they fail to ask the guests' names because they have no real interest in them. The Laestrygonians pretend to be hospitable but eat some of Odysseus' men (reversing the demand of *xenia* that guests should be fed), while the Cyclopes have no social order or law, and Polyphemus also eats some of Odysseus' men.

By creating a continuum of female figures which shades from desire into fear and a parallel continuum of *xenia* and its denial, the epic relates the theme of home (the locus of *xenia* as cultural practice) to marriage and sexual fidelity. The story begins with a reminder of the centrality of marriage to society, and its significance for homecoming, when Zeus speaks of the murder of Agamemnon. In the light of these interwoven thematic strands, Penelope's character is of great moment. While Odysseus is away, she is at home being badgered by suitors who want to marry her and accede to Odysseus' power. They are the antithesis of *xenia:* they abuse hospitality in the home of Penelope and treat strangers with contempt. In the middle of their depredations, Penelope is depicted as a devout practitioner of *xenia*, and as a faithful wife who resists all attempts to replace her husband. She thus embodies both *xenia* and marriage. But, as Laura Slatkin points out, despite the importance to the plot of her trustworthiness, the epic 'repeatedly raises the specter of wifely infidelity' (2009: 325).

> If some scholars have read the Odyssey as a triumphalist celebration of the married couple, others have drawn attention to the opaqueness of Penelope, as the poem represents her, and to the ambiguity of such elements as her dream of the geese [Book 19], where she seems to lament a proleptic image of the suitors' destruction. From the standpoint of the characters within the poem, of course, the duress of Penelope's situation makes her dangerously susceptible to the suitors' pressure.
>
> *(Slatkin 2009: 325)*

Penelope recounts her dream to Odysseus (who is at the time disguised as a beggar), explaining to him how painful she found it to see her geese lying dead. The 'beggar' interprets the eagle who kills the domestic birds as a portent of Odysseus' return and his slaughter of the suitors. Curiously, the interpretation does not seem to comfort Penelope, nor compensate for the loss of her geese.

Given these carefully woven doubts about Penelope, the return of the hero represents more than the destiny of an individual; it indicates that Ithaca is a community in need of restoration and renewal. Odysseus' absence leads to a dysfunctional society in which the fundamental bonds definitive of social order – marriage and *xenia* – are under the greatest stress. Penelope's feelings about the geese, and therefore about the suitors, suggest just how close to collapse that order has been driven, since the suitors embody a double threat: they treat the demands of *xenia* with contempt, and woo a married woman. The representation of Odysseus' homecoming as the descent of an eagle symbolizes the coalescence of human action and divine intervention to remedy the crisis: elsewhere in the epic, eagles are sent as omens from the gods. 'Return thus becomes more than a private objective in the *Odyssey*: it becomes an instrument of justice, sanctioned by the gods, through which the social order will be rescued' (Slatkin 2009: 318).

While Adorno and Horkheimer represent the mythological elements in such patterns as a kind of sediment – the remnants of a dead or dying worldview – it is hard to see how such designs can be separated from the underlying mythological formation. As Slatkin indicates, Odysseus' return makes sense only in the light of a divinely maintained social order and that order is made plain in the epic's thematic patterning and its complex narrative composition. Rather than the 'flight of the individual from the mythical powers', Odysseus' return might be seen as precisely the opposite: the narrative revelation of the individual's necessary (re)integration into a cosmic whole.

Food and social order

A key symbol of the disorder in Ithaca, which Odysseus' homecoming must rectify, is the incontinent eating of the suitors – a point I will return to shortly. The order of *xenia* is marked by the provision and consumption of food, as we see in Book 1 when Athena visits Ithaca, disguised as Mentes, 'chief of the Taphians'. Telemachus welcomes and feeds him before enquiring about the nature of his business, punctiliously observing the protocols of hospitality, unlike the boorish suitors who leave the stranger at the gate. Food thus focusses attention on the conflict between civilized order and its opposite. The polite and solicitous behaviour of Telemachus forms a significant contrast with the noise and insolence of the suitors. While they are seated on the hides of oxen they have killed and eaten, surrounded by servants cutting up great quantities of meat, Telemachus places his guest on a richly decorated seat with a footstool, furnishes him with a golden ewer and silver basin to wash himself and has a servant bring the choicest food.

If food marks the divide between civilized life and brutality, between *xenia* and its denial, it also serves to distinguish order from chaos. This is particularly marked in the *Odyssey* by the kind of eating Odysseus and his men encounter in their uncharted wanderings: 'The situations they encounter', Egbert J. Bakker notes, 'present meat and its consumption as the essential prerequisite of civilization' (2013: xi). The episode on the island of Helios in Book 12 – in which Odysseus' men eat the oxen belonging to the sun god, despite being told not to – is a central point which determines their fate. They will be denied their homecoming because of inappropriate eating, while Odysseus refuses to eat the meat and so is allowed to return home. It is significant, then, that immediately prior to this episode, the crew encounters the monstrous Scylla, and a different kind of inappropriate feeding. She is a figure of the ultimate fear because she eats men alive, which is among the most insistent motifs in the epic. In feeding on human flesh, Scylla, Polyphemus and the Laestrygonians echo one of the most important cycles in Greek mythology – the Oedipus story. That myth has at its heart the monstrous, flesh-eating Sphinx.

The predatory figures encountered by Odysseus beyond the borders of the homeland are echoed by the suitors inside his house: the latter threaten his home just as the maneaters threaten his homecoming. Given that the suitors echo the role of the predators encountered in the wild regions beyond the known world, it is not surprising that they are consistently depicted as eating. Telemachus complains that they 'eating [him] out of house and home': they are literally consuming Odysseus' wealth and metaphorically consuming the social order. This is depicted with graphic violence when Odysseus returns and the killing begins. The first blood is spilled over the suitors' food:

> Odysseus aimed at his throat, then shot.
> The point pierced all the way through his soft neck.
> He flopped down to the side and his cup slipped
> out of his hand. A double pipe of blood
> gushed from his nostrils. His foot twitched and knocked
> the table down; food scattered on the ground.
> The bread and roasted meat were soiled with blood.
>
> *(Wilson 2018: Book 22, ll.15–21)*

The mingling of food with human blood is a powerful image, revealing the suitors' equivalence with the predators who consume Odysseus' men.

The relationship with the gods, too, seems to be strongly associated with food. This is part of a description of a sacrifice to Athena: 'Then quickly they divided the flesh; at once they cut out the thigh-bones in ritual fashion, covered them with the fat twice folded, and laid the raw meat above. . . . Having roasted the outer flesh and drawn it from off the spits they sat down and began to feast' (Shewring 1980: Book 3, 34). Jan Bremmer argues that such passages reveal an unease among archaic Greeks about the idea of the gods eating in the same manner as mortals. So, we are shown the careful preparation of the sacrifice and human consumption of the meat, but the gods' part in the feast is unspoken (Bremmer 2007: 137). That devotional practices are related to food suggests not only the intimate involvement of the gods in everyday life but also that sacrifice was perceived to be integral to the social bond. This is made clear at the outset when Zeus connects Odysseus' homecoming with his faithfulness in making offerings to the gods: 'How could I forget Odysseus the godlike, he who / is beyond all other men in mind, and who beyond others / has given sacrifice to the gods, who hold wide heaven?'

Food and the social mores shaping its production and consumption form an important aspect of the epic's opening: one of the first things we learn about the predicament of Odysseus and his men is that it has been exacerbated by their eating the cattle of Helios. The episode is narrated in Book 12, at the centre of the epic, and is the only experience of the hero mentioned in the scene-setting lines with which the epic begins, investing it with particular significance. While the most obvious aspect of its importance lies in its sealing the fate of Odysseus' men, Michael Nagler points out that it aligns the condemned companions with the suitors whose deaths are made inevitable by the hero's pre-ordained *nostos*. The slaughter and consumption of the cattle of Helios, attended by inappropriate ritual, using water and oak leaves instead of wine and barley, 'is uncannily mirrored in Ithaca by the suitors who never sacrifice properly but feast on the socially forbidden cattle of the absent hero' (Nagler 1990: 340). When Zeus subsequently destroys the offenders for their behaviour, he does so on behalf of Helios and, as Egbert J. Bakker observes, this is paralleled by Odysseus' eventual killing of the suitors on behalf of an outraged Zeus (2013: 113).

When the sun god's cattle are being roasted, their flesh and hides move and bellow ominously, indicating divine disquiet. This is paralleled at the end of Book 20 when, in order to stoke Odysseus' fury, Athena provokes the suitors to ever more egregious behaviour as they dine:

> Athena turned the suitors' minds; they laughed
> unstoppably. They cackled, and they lost
> control of their own faces. Plates of meat
> began to drip with blood. Their eyes were full
> of tears, and they began to wail in grief.
>
> *(Wilson 2018: Book 20, ll.346–50)*

A few lines further on, the book ends with a foretelling of the unwelcome 'dinnertime' soon to come: the slaughter of the egregious eaters. The killing scene is described in Book 22, and it happens as the suitors, once again, feed themselves at their host's expense. Odysseus' homecoming, then, is a depicted as a matter of justice administered by the gods, described, significantly, as a kind of meal.

Homecoming

According to the Harvard glossary, the word '*nostos*' is derived from an Indo-European word indicating a return to light and life and occurs in myths having to do with the Morning Star/Evening Star. In Book 13, 'the star which often ushers in the tender light of Dawn' appears as the Phaeacians row Odysseus homeward, signalling his return from the dead as well as from his journey. As soon as the oars catch the water, he drifts into a sleep 'delicious and profound, the very counterfeit of death', which enables him to forget 'all he had once endured' (Rieu 1946: Book 13, 204). The depiction of Odysseus falling into a deep, peaceful slumber in which his sufferings slip away is suggestive of his death; his rebirth is indicated by rising daylight as the ship approaches the coast of Ithaca. In Book 12, as Odysseus and his men return from their voyage to Hades to speak with the dead, Circe tells them they have done a brave and rare thing in going down alive into the underworld: 'One death is enough for most men; but you will now have two' (Rieu 1946: Book 12, 189).

So, Odysseus' *nostos* is a return not just to his home but also to life and light. Life and light, of course, depend on the sun, on Helios. When he hears that his cattle have been killed, the sun god threatens to deprive the world of both: 'Unless / these are made to give me just recompense for my cattle, / I will go down to Hades and give my light to the dead men' (Lattimore 1967: Book 12, ll.381–3). Helios' outrage and his threat to undo life are echoed in Odysseus' angry return to Ithaca and his drive to kill the suitors. He is like the sun god in suffering the illicit slaughter of his livestock and in his desire for vengeance (as he is like Apollo in his use of a bow, and like Zeus in avenging the denial of *xenia*) but contrasted with him in his mortality. Helios' joining the dead would be the return of chaos, while Odysseus' acceptance of death is what enables his return and the concomitant restoration of order. For Odysseus has to choose between immortality and return to homelife. In the *Iliad*, Achilles explicitly chooses *kleos* over *nostos*: he elects the immortality of enduring renown in the memories and stories of those who survive, over living to return home. Odysseus is motivated by *nostos* rather than *kleos*, and that choice goes along with an acceptance of a kind of normality: 'Calypso offers Odysseus immortality and, then, in the following adventure, Alcinous offers him the hand of a princess. The adventures on Ogygia and Phaeacia that follow one after the other in the *Odyssey* present two classic and parallel goals for a Greek hero. Each offer, because it is typically desirable, highlights Odysseus' fixed resolve to return home' (Crane 1987: 21). The 'cattle of the sun' episode, then, interweaves the key themes of *nostos*, food and justice. What connects them is a decidedly mythopoeic worldview in which heroic adventures and divine interventions reveal how basic human needs shape the lives of individuals and societies: the need for food, a home and a divinely sanctioned social order which protects the individual.

Charles Segal has argued that in the *Odyssey* we can see evidence of the emergence of a *refined* mythopoeic order through shifts in the representation of the gods:

> Homer has brought together into an artistic conceptual whole both older and more evolved notions of divinity and in this way grounds his epic in a self-consciously moral theology . . . juxtaposing gods of different levels of moral sensitivity (like Zeus and Poseidon) and bracketing the more 'primitive' divine behavior in a well-demarcated section of the poem, the fabulous realm between Troy and Ithaca in books 5-13.
>
> *(Segal 1992: 489–90)*

So, the off-the-map territories where Odysseus encounters the lawless, predatory and hostile beings represent traces of an older world in which the rule of the gods was yet to be fully established. Polyphemus – son of Poseidon – declares clearly that he cares nothing for Zeus or his laws. In this sense, Odysseus' *nostos* might be understood as allegorical of the quest for a new social order (the end of the 'Dark Age'?) marked by the defeat of residual chaos and the establishment of the rule of moral law.

The contrast between the 'more evolved' and the 'more primitive' orders becomes even clearer as Book 19 develops the theme of *nostos* in a very striking way by drawing attention to the question of recognition. Odysseus has been away for twenty years: How will the people of his homeland recognize him? He conceals his identity, disguising himself as a beggar. This serves to highlight that in Odysseus' home *xenia* is still practised by Penelope and Telemachus, who welcome the stranger, despite its gross transgression by the suitors. When Penelope commands the aged Eurykleia to bathe Odysseus' feet, the maid – his childhood nurse – recognizes the scar on his leg. In one of the most celebrated scenes in the epic, the story of how he acquired the scar is related. Taken hunting by his grandfather Autolycus, the young Odysseus was gored by a wild boar which he then killed. Barbara Goff reads the incident as part of a rite of passage from youth to maturity:

> Odysseus makes the boar hunt the stage on which he performs successfully the act designed to establish his claim to adult manhood. The timing of the *Odyssey*'s recollection of this successful transition seems significant. Odysseus is, after all, in the bath, in the hands of Eurykleia, and it is well known that women and baths can be dangerous to returning heroes.
>
> *(Goff 1991: 263)*

In noting that 'it is well known that women and baths can be dangerous to returning heroes' Goff is alluding to the story of Agamemnon and Clytemnestra: when Agamemnon returns from Troy he is murdered in his bath. The contrast between Odysseus' homecoming and Agamemnon's is emphasized in Book 19 by the depiction of Penelope in her exchange with her disguised husband. Her grief and loss are evident, as is her fading hope. If the dream of the slaughtered geese hints at an unspoken pleasure she takes in being courted, her contrast with Clytemnestra is all the more pointed for her resistance to their blandishments however tempted she might have been to enjoy their attention.

Entering the house incognito gives Odysseus the opportunity to observe his wife, gather information about the suitors and servants and assess the situation. The disguise also foregrounds the related issues of identity and recognition. Goff points to the scar as proof of who Odysseus is, not only as a visual marker but also as a prompt to the recollection of the episode which produced it: one which helped forge Odysseus' adult identity.

She notes, too, that 'it brings into play the important figure of the hunt' (Goff 262). 'Hunting is fundamentally linked with the ἀγρός [*agros* – field] that is, the land lying beyond the cultivated fields, with the *eschatia* [limits] which form the borders of the Greek cities. . . . In one sense hunting is altogether on the side of what is wild, raw, night' (Vidal-Naquet 1968: 60). Vidal-Naquet and Goff both see a connection between the hunt and rites of passage into manhood, but in what Vidal-Naquet writes, it is evident, too, that the hunt served to mark the limits of civilization. When Odysseus returns from beyond the *eschatia*, having been on a kind of extended hunt, he is reborn a civilized man. He has survived his encounter with the 'more primitive' world, becoming an embodiment of its replacement. This formulation may well owe its shape to Gilgamesh who likewise travels into the unknown, before returning to the city and reaffirming the values of civilization. He too is reborn, at least inasmuch as he is shown shedding his wild garb, bathing and regaining his home a changed man. There is also, perhaps, a parallel between Odysseus' rejection of immortality and Gilgamesh's failure to achieve it.

If we recall that *nostos* is not just homecoming but also, in a sense, rebirth and the renewal of a social order, then the story of Odysseus' naming and his transition from youth to manhood makes perfect sense at this point in the narrative. Like the boar hunt which marked his passage to manhood, his travels mark his transition to full maturity. Returning to himself as well as to his home, he is reconnecting with his past and with what made him who and what he has become. In doing so, he is also redrawing the limits, re-securing home against the wild, the raw and the night.

Notes

1. The Greek Dark Age lasted for approximately 300 years (1100–800 BCE). During this period, the people of the region were mostly nomadic herders. They left no written records. The Archaic Period followed, its inception being marked by the development of the Greek alphabet.
2. The conflict between Athena and Poseidon went back to their rivalry over patronage of the city of Athens. In his bid to win the honour, Poseidon struck a rock and salt water flowed from it. Athena planted an olive tree on the acropolis, and this was judged to be the better gift. As a result, the city was named after her and placed in her care.
3. The epic's overarching story of Odysseus' return is itself a version of a widespread folktale. See Hansen (2002: 201–10).
4. 'The Cyclops episode occupies 81% of *Od.9*, whereas the Cicones and Lotus Eaters episodes in the same book occupy 8% and 4%, respectively' (Myrsiades 2019: xiii).
5. Egbert J. Bakker (2013) argues that the episode is tightly woven into the epic by the drawing of parallels between Polyphemus' behaviour and that of Odysseus, especially the latter's slaughter of the suitors in the violent conclusion to the story. He refers to the episode as 'the centrepiece of the Odyssey' (9) and notes that 'Both tales revolve around a home invasion, the encounter of the intruders with the returning master, and the uninvited guests being trapped in the house they entered' (9).
6. On the relationship between the poet and Odysseus as narrator, see Bakker (2013: 1–12).

Translations used in preparing this chapter

Fagles, R., trans. (1996), *The Odyssey*, London: Penguin.
Lattimore, R., trans. (1965, 1967), *The Odyssey of Homer: A Modern Translation*, New York, NY: Harper and Row.
Rieu, E. V., trans. (1946), *Homer: The Odyssey*, Harmondsworth: Penguin.
Shewring, W., trans. (1980), *Homer: The Odyssey*, Oxford: Oxford University Press.
Wilson, E., trans. (2018), *The Odyssey*, New York: W.W. Norton & Company.

PART III

MYTH REWRITTEN

CHAPTER 7
FROM MYTH TO ROMANCE
THE LIFE OF ST CADOC AND *SIR ORFEO*

After the Romans

A long history of immigrations, invasions, trade and cultural exchange has meant that Britain, more than any other European country, has been a site of contact and conflict between divergent mythologies. Christopher Fee and David Leeming describe the drawn-out process of confrontation as a 'Battle for Mythic Britain', noting that well beyond their initial impact the influence of classical, Celtic, Christian and Germanic mythologies survived in a 'rich, fertile and volatile medieval literary tradition . . . through which it is possible to gain genuine insight into the shadowy gods of ancient Britain' (Fee and Leeming 2001: 6).

It is easy to assume that the pagan world, with its gods, demigods, monsters and larger-than-life heroes held neither power over nor fascination for Christian Britain in the medieval period, yet writings from the time provide powerful evidence that this was not the case. Both hagiography and romance – the two dominant literary forms of the age – are rich in mythological resonances. This chapter explores an example of each of these modes in order to illustrate both the survival and the transformation of myth between the end of the Roman Empire and the rise of science in the early modern period.

When the Roman Empire's grip on Britain loosened early in the fifth century, and the country entered the so-called Dark Ages, an extraordinary movement grew up in the West, giving rise to 'erudition and literacy, travel and religion, but within a broader political context that is only slowly acquiring stability' (Pryor 2004: 190). Although many aspects of the period have been hotly debated for decades among historians and archaeologists, it is clear that the great upheaval occasioned by the demise of the Western Roman Empire did not lead to the collapse of British society into chaos nor to the decline of the belief system (Christianity) which had become the imperial religion. There may have been occasional resurgences of paganism in Britain and Ireland, but Christianity was firmly established, deep-rooted and capable of inspiring energetic propagation on the part of its adherents. Its most zealous devotees were eager to carry its message to the world and to make disciples wherever they went.

The emergence of the 'Celtic saints' – people of enormous enterprise, imagination and passion – spread culture, learning and faith throughout Britain, Ireland, Brittany and the Mediterranean. Undertaking perilous voyages to learn, to share ideas and to establish international bonds, these were people driven by profound convictions and boundless enthusiasm. Figures such as Teilo, Cadoc, Illtud, Dyfrig, David, Patrick, Ciaran, Kevin, Finnian, Columba and many others were tireless in their efforts and prepared to travel great distances to spread not only the 'word of God' but also the learning which underpinned its interpretation and dissemination. Their stories, mostly written many years after they were dead, preserved as well as helped to establish traditions which interweave Christian and pagan motifs, offering a glimpse of what became of myth in the post-classical world.

Hagiographies, or the stories of saints' lives, although little read today, were once popular and highly influential. Christopher Fee describes them as 'one of the staple literary traditions of the Middle Ages' (2011: xx). As Christianity spread through the Roman Empire, stories began to circulate about heroes of the faith: martyrs, teachers, leaders, miracle workers and those who were instrumental in converting pagans. And as these extraordinary biographical narratives took shape under the cultural and political aegis of Rome, they were inevitably influenced by, and blended with, stories of pagan gods and heroes. In the curious hybridity of some such saints and their exploits, it is possible to trace the rewriting and repurposing of mythology, not only classical but also the mythologies of cultures coming under imperial sway.

The Norman period in Britain (1066–1154) saw a renewal of interest in the saints, prompting the seeking out, retelling and committing to writing of lives from the early Christian era. Sometime around 1086 CE, Lifris, a monk at the religious settlement of Llancarfan in southeast Wales, wrote *The Life of St Cadoc*. Composed in Latin, it tells the story of a sixth-century church leader, the son of a local ruler. No one now knows what textual or oral sources he drew on in composing it, but he produced a remarkable and highly important, if neglected, work. It is set apart from other hagiographies of the period by its length, its depiction of Cadoc (Welsh Catwg) as a kind of magician akin to Merlin, the appearance of King Arthur in a number of episodes, and its echoes of Celtic mythology.[1] It is notable, too, as an influence on the Welsh cycle known as the Four Branches of the *Mabinogi* (discussed in the next chapter). As a text which looks back at the Dark Ages from the perspective of the early Norman period, Lifris' *Life* helps to uncover the transitional phase through which ancient mythology passed in the British Isles after the fall of the Roman Empire.

Early post-Roman Wales was divided into multiple kingdoms which in many respects derived from the tribal divisions familiar to the Romans. The geography of the country made it difficult to traverse and almost impossible to unify either politically or culturally. This meant that rulers were local and their territories relatively small. They were often on hostile terms with their neighbours, so that raiding, skirmishing and entering into disputes seem to have occupied most of the time and energy of the chieftains (Walker 1990: 1–2). Saint Cadoc is said to have been the son of one such chieftain known as Gwynlliw, Gundleus or Woolos. Eventually converted by his pious son, and canonized by later ages, Gwynlliw was initially as much a bandit as a king. His domain was the southeastern corner of Wales, taking in much of modern Gwent and Glamorgan. Cadoc's main area of influence seems to have been closely associated with this region, stretching (roughly) from the Gower peninsula to the Severn, and from the south coast as far north as the Brecon Beacons.

It has been said that place names tell us more about the existence of saints and the organization of the post-Roman church than any other source of information (Bowen 1954: 6). They have printed onto the landscape traces of travel, settlement and religious activity. E. G. Bowen argues that the names of churches, villages and monuments strongly suggest that Cadoc's influence followed Roman roads. Churches dedicated to him are clustered in the eastern part of the Vale of Glamorgan, and around Llangattock, near Crickhowell in Powys (Bowen 1977: 93). Roman influence was considerably less marked to the west of a notional line that might be drawn between these two areas. For Bowen, the fact that important Roman sites at Gelligaer (in Glamorgan) and Caerleon (in Gwent) both have churches dedicated to St Cadoc adds to the impression that his sphere of activity was shaped by the aftermath of the Roman presence in southeast Wales (1954: 39).

Intriguing as it is, such evidence must be treated with a degree of caution since dedications of places and churches to local saints, date, in many cases, from the Norman era when renewed interest in them became fashionable (Laing 2006: 268). It is the case, too, of course, that place names are subject to corruption, modification and change. Nevertheless, in the geographical clustering of names there may well be hints of traditional associations, for although no Welsh dedications predate the Norman era, that age might have revived rather than established specific connections.

Norman incursions into Wales changed its politics and social organization in profound and lasting ways. Anglo-Norman religious institutions took possession of land and altered the administrative structures of the church. The new regime had little understanding of the pre-existing patterns of ecclesiastical governance and was unfamiliar with the ways and means of Welsh religious practice (Walker 1990: 67). Welsh churches were often based on the system of *clasau:* Christian settlements each of which, rather than belonging to any larger organization such as a monastic order, enjoyed autonomy under the rule of a single leader, or *abod.*

Cadoc is said to have either established, or to have been an early *abod* of, the *clas* at Llancarfan (formerly Nantcarvan), a small village lying some eleven miles to the west of Cardiff.[2] Along with the *clas* of Illtud at Llanilltud Fawr (Llantwit Major), it was probably one of the first seats of learning in Britain, the influence of which spread into Ireland, Scotland, Cornwall and Brittany. The *clas*-based organization was quite different from Norman monastic foundations, and as the latter replaced the former, the cultural shift gave rise to prolonged conflict over the ownership of church buildings, lands and rights. This is evident from the appendices attached to Lifris' *Life*, as well as from the *Liber Landavensis* (*Book of Llandaff*).[3] While there are clear disparities between these ancient sources, both make clear that power struggles and land grabs were significant factors in the way saints and the age of their activity were represented (Charles-Edwards 2013: 256–67).

Some of the documents appended to Lifris' *Life* strongly suggest that stories told about Cadoc were part of the argument over who owned what. For example, one appendix tells us that 'Guorcinnim bought the village Reathr of Meurig, for his own inheritance, for a sword, the golden hilt of which was worth twenty-five cows. . . . Guorcinnim himself gave this village to the church of Saint Cadoc in perpetual possession until the Day of Judgement' (Rees 1843: 389–90). Such claims make sense precisely inasmuch as ownership of the territory they name was disputed, or likely to become so, at the time the text was written. This may help to explain why cults of saints enjoyed a resurgence in the Norman period: they both registered the competing interests of parties in the religious and political upheaval and served as reminders of pre-Norman practices and traditions.

St Cadoc and mythology

While there is compelling evidence for the existence of Cadoc, there is very little reliable information about him. Almost completely ignored today, even within southeast Wales, Lifris' *Life* is, nonetheless, a very significant document for the study of British mythology. Far longer and more detailed than other Welsh *Lives* of saints, it was rewritten by Caradog of Llancarfan in the early twelfth century, but these narratives cannot be read as accurate historical records. Trafficking in unlikely events, spurious claims and exaggerated achievements, they tell some fascinating stories but lack credibility as biographical sources.

Cadoc appears in a number of Irish hagiographies as a teacher of saints who travelled to Wales to join his community.

Despite this comparative wealth of material, details such as where and when he was born, where and when he died and where he is buried are subjects of speculation rather than knowledge. His birth is usually said to have taken place in either Newport or Gelligaer, his death at Llancarfan, or Benevento (Italy). His alleged presence at Benevento is probably a mistake: there was a *Bannaventa* near Daventry in Northamptonshire, which might have been his actual destination. Perhaps more significantly, Edmund McClure suggests that documentary evidence points to a Beneventum much closer to Llancarfan, and that *Venta Silurum* (the Roman name for Caerwent) fits the case (1910: 34). Cadoc might be buried at either site associated with his death or at Mamhilad (a few miles north of Pontypool in Gwent). Lifris tells of Cadoc's remains being carried from Llancarfan to Mamhilad in order to preserve them from the depredations of a marauding English viscount (Rees 1843: 372).

Quite apart from the difficulty of establishing the accuracy of information about the so-called Dark Ages, the details of Cadoc's life are problematical because the Welsh saint has been confused over generations with other figures of around the same period: Cadog, son of Brychan (died *c.*490) and the Breton St Cadou, among them. It seems likely that most accounts of St Cadoc interweave details of the lives of more than one individual quite indiscriminately, and there is now no historically robust way of unpicking the knot. The problem has been complicated further by the work of Iolo Morganwg (1747–1826), who almost certainly forged the 'Sayings of Cattwg the Wise' included in volume three of *The Myvyrian Archaiology*.[4]

With these provisos in mind, it might be reasonable to assume that a broad outline can be given of Cadoc's life which bears some relation to real events. Educated by St Tathan at Caerwent, he subsequently became an itinerant teacher until he found a home at, or established, the *clas* at Llancarfan. At some point, he travelled to Ireland to advance his studies, before returning to Wales bringing with him a few Irish followers. His education continued under Bachan, an Italian teacher of classical rhetoric (sometimes identified with St Fagan). The stories of Cadoc's travelling to Brittany and settling for a time on the Ile de St Cado in Morbihan may be the result of his misidentification with the Breton saint. He is said to have built a monastery in Scotland (close to Kilmarnock) and to have undertaken pilgrimages to Rome and Jerusalem. His death was the result of an attack on a church, probably by Saxon soldiers; tradition has him run through with a spear or lance at the altar, midway through the Mass.

If the biographical details are both sketchy and uncertain, the stories which grew up around Cadoc over some 500 years following his death are rich in striking events, powerful images and mythological resonances. The hagiographies depict him as a hard-bargaining, clever and tough-minded individual, with a sharp sense of his own power, and as committed to a sometimes rather vindictive theology which saw his enemies peremptorily destroyed by divine intervention. Lifris records some memorable tales, which, if they are often far-fetched, are also a fascinating blend of pagan and Christian traditions, juxtaposing with the insistent Christian rhetoric the performance of fire rituals, magical associations of water and the presence of animals with supernatural significance.

From early on in his story Cadoc is associated with water and with fire. As a babe in arms, he was baptized in a river which sprang up especially for the purpose (Rees 1843: 315). Anne Ross writes: 'Springs, wells and rivers are of first and enduring importance as a focal point of Celtic cult practice and ritual' (1974: 46). Still a child, the young prodigy performed a miracle with fire: 'Yet he, trusting in the Lord, received the coals of fire into his cloak; and brought them to his master, without the garment being burnt.' Preserved by Cadoc's teacher (Meuthi), the coals kindle a 'sacred fire' which confers healing on sick cattle brought near to it (Rees 1843: 318–20). The story clearly echoes practices associated with the Celtic Beltane festival at which cattle were driven between two fires to purify them. As Fee and Leeming note, 'the lighting of sacred fires was an important druidic rite' (2001: 65).

Later in his life, Cadoc encounters a range of animals whose presence takes on supernatural significance, including a wild boar, a swan, a mouse, stags, a salmon, bees and a hawk. According to Miranda Green, Celtic culture venerated animals as part of a sacred natural world:

> Accordingly, wild and domesticated species were the subject of elaborate rituals and the centre of profound belief-systems. The Celts depended on domestic beasts for their livelihood, on wild creatures for hunting and on horses for warfare. This intimate relationship between human and animal in so-called secular life stimulated the concept of beasts as sacred and numinous, whether in possession of divine status in their own right or simply acting as mediators between the gods and humankind.
>
> *(Green 1992: 3)*

It is clear from just these few examples that what Anne Ross says of British and Irish lives of saints in general is particularly pertinent to *The Life of St Cadoc*: they 'modified the old pagan legends . . . used the old traditional learning as the basis of the new, thus preserving into the Middle Ages traditions and modes of expression stemming direct from a barbarian milieu' (Ross 1974: 43).

Occasionally, the stories Lifris tells bear resemblances to those found in the *Mabinogi*. In one episode, for example, King Arthur demands a hundred distinctively coloured cows as compensation for the death of three of his men, insisting the cattle have 'the fore part red, and the hind part white' (Rees 1843: 341). The man guilty of the killing has taken refuge with Cadoc and his community, and when Arthur comes to claim his due, the saint intervenes, taking responsibility for ending the dispute.[5] Cadoc sends men to round up cattle of any colour they can find, and, by means of a miracle, the cows' markings change to meet the king's requirements. Eager to get their hands on the animals, Arthur's men take hold of their horns to lead them away, only for the miraculous beasts to be changed into bundles of ferns. In the first branch of the *Mabinogi*, Pwyll, Lord of Dyfed, while out hunting, encounters hounds with similar markings to those insisted upon by Arthur: gleaming white with red ears. Sioned Davies notes that 'red and white are colours traditionally associated with the supernatural in Welsh and Irish tradition' (Davies 2007: 228). The white boar encountered by Cadoc in another of the stories probably derives from the same pagan tradition. It appears as a sign from God which shows the holy man where to erect the buildings for his new religious settlement.[6] The detail of Arthur's cows turning into ferns is reminiscent of an episode from the fourth branch in which the magician Gwydion conjures twelve horses and twelve hounds from toadstools in order to trade them for a herd of otherworldly pigs. After a while, the magic wears off and the animals return to their toadstool form.

Yet another story in Lifris involves the murder of an architect whose severed head speaks to convict his killers, recalling the second branch of the *Mabinogi* in which the giant Brân's severed head continues to speak to his companions. In the Celtic belief system, the human head was symbolically imbued with divine or otherworldly powers, and the severed head is a motif which occurs throughout the Celtic world, from the earliest times, in stories and in visual representations. Anne Ross notes that this superstitious interest was shared by many other cultural formations, but none took their idolization as far as the Celts. Their art and religious practice appear to treat the head as an object of veneration to a degree which is striking and peculiar (Ross 1974: 94–5).

There are a few more such intriguing parallels between *The Life of St Cadoc* and the Four Branches, some of which will be discussed in the next chapter. Adding to the store of what we might call 'Celtic' tales, and contributing to the compendium of Arthurian literature, the stories of St Cadoc form an important part of the history and heritage not only of southeast Wales but of Britain as a whole. They are among the earliest known references to specifically British mythology, and may well have influenced composition of the Four Branches. Lifris' *Life* brought with it traces of mythology, transforming older stories into a newer mode of entertainment and instruction, recasting pagan motifs as Christian symbols. If it carried neither the obvious religious nor political freight of hagiography, the other great literary tradition of the medieval period – the romance – also worked to translate myth into diverting tales. Like hagiography, it bore its own spiritual and temporal messages, and it too exerted a powerful influence on the *Mabinogi* cycle.[7]

Middle English romance

Originating in twelfth-century France, the romance arrived in Britain in the aftermath of the Norman conquest. Typically, romances tell stories marked by a concern with chivalry, quest, love and magic. Many of the earliest examples were written in a dialect of French known as Anglo-Norman, and some of these were translated into Middle English from the thirteenth century on.[8] A great many romances in verse form, composed in the thirteenth and fourteenth centuries, have survived, and the form spawned subgenres, including the Breton lay (such as *Sir Orfeo*) and Arthurian romance (such as those included in the *Mabinogion*).

The Middle English romances are marked by conformity to 'a very rigid set of literary and social conventions', and examples display regularities of structure in relation to themes of separation – restoration, love – marriage (Wittig 1978: 5, 179). They depend, too, upon expressive conventions which, according to W. R. J. Barron, reflect a particular worldview and communicate a distinctive set of values. They are delicately poised between entertainment and moral instruction, combining symbolic representations with a kind of realism, blending fantasy with idealism. The tensions between these discursive modes reflect the 'dual nature of man as sensualist and idealist, escapist and moralist' (Barron 1987: 5). In other words, the paradoxes of the romance bear witness to the conflict set up by Christian morality between duty and desire: a way of understanding human experience as a perpetual spiritual tussle permeating every area of medieval life, from literature and history to social expectations and ceremonies.

The conventions of romance, then, were less the product of the genre itself than of the cultural milieu in which it emerged and thrived. It was a culture shaped by Christian beliefs in tension with the pagan heritage of the classical world which had moulded Roman attitudes, ideas and practices. Romances often drew on ancient, pre-Christian sources, but invested them with values deriving from theological doctrine. Helen Cooper points out that the coincidence of romance with 'the great age of faith' is no accident. Christian teaching regarding salvation, at the heart of which is the story of Christ's suffering, death and resurrection, envisaged the restoration of fallen humanity to innocence and bliss in a heavenly afterlife, and this doctrine was outlined more fully than ever before during the eleventh and twelfth centuries. Romance reflects this religious development by creating a pattern of disrupted order, 'followed by a period of trial and suffering, even an encounter with death, yet with a final symbolic resurrection and better restoration' (Cooper 2004: 5). So romances bore great religious significance, helping to elaborate and propagate Christian teaching. They served to make concrete, theological concepts such as faith, endurance and redemption, by embodying them in characters passing through adversity and being reborn through affliction.

A group of English romances were based on the Breton lays (*Sir Launfal, Sir Degare, La Freine, Sir Orfeo*). All found in fourteenth-century manuscripts, the Breton lays were originally oral and were sung by minstrels. They are marked by recurring themes and motifs: the union of mortal with otherworldly beings, tests, wilderness passages and the presence of the marvellous (figures and events lying beyond the reach of normal human experience). The ideals of 'courtly love' often drive the behaviour of the protagonists and colour the narratives.[9] According to this chivalric code, the knightly lover must demonstrate subjection to love as a transcendent force, adhere to the principles of humility and courtesy, and be prepared to prove his devotion by daring deeds or acts of courage or self-sacrifice. For Sarah Kay, the formulation of courtly love highlights a 'tension between inner intensity and outward decorum' as well as between 'desire and regulation' (Kay 2000: 85). As she observes, the very term 'courtly love' implies the co-implication of the personal (love) and the political (the court), or the emotional and the social. As we will see, in *Sir Orfeo* the protagonist's emotional state, precipitated by the loss of his wife, undermines his ability to function at court: he neglects his kingly duties in favour of doleful and lovelorn wandering. Orfeo's temporary loss of self and status illustrates that 'love' and 'court' can never be in complete harmony. Thus, the narratives in which courtly love is a significant presence are necessarily shot through with various kinds of irresolution and unease. As Kay suggests, such tensions imply that courtly love is itself a problematical and rather slippery term.

Despite the difficulty of pinning down its precise meaning, it is clear that narratives associated with the courtly love tradition propagated the values and ideals of the highest social echelons and were pertinent to an aristocratic context. While ancient tales provided the settings and furnished elements of plot, the behaviour and mores of the figures depicted were decidedly contemporaneous. Times and places specified in romances as the when and where of their action are of little historical moment. Serving chiefly as indicators of class rather than of period, they helped to form and buttress a social ideology based on stratification and hierarchy (Burlin 1995: 2).

Emerging from the most influential and sophisticated centres of medieval France's courtly culture, the ideological background of romance allied it with wealth, power and high status. However far removed from those origins were Middle English developments of the genre, they 'perpetuated many of its assumptions and often introduced new ones better suited to a "petty" noble class or even a bourgeois taste' (Burlin 1995: 3). That the mythical figure of Orpheus is transformed into Sir Orfeo – an English knight, and noble ruler – is indicative of precisely such a measured adaptation.

Sir Orfeo and the myth of Orpheus

It is not known who wrote *Sir Orfeo*, but on the basis of the poem's linguistic character, scholars suggest that it was composed in the late thirteenth or early fourteenth century, probably in the south-east of England. The poem refers to its own origin in a Breton lay, but no French text has been found. Most scholars assume that an Old French source existed at one time, since there are references to a musical lay of Orpheus in a number of Old French manuscripts. The earliest of three surviving versions of *Sir Orfeo* is recorded in the Auchinleck manuscript – an important anthology dating from around 1330–40.

Although written in medieval England, the poem's setting is not directly related to the place and time of its composition. Robert Burlin's reference to the use of spatial and temporal markers as indicative of class interests in romances is pertinent to *Sir Orfeo*. The story's location is mentioned precisely as a way of signalling the hero's status: 'In Traciens Orfeo held his court, / A city strong, a goodly fort' (Weston 1914: ll.47–8). Traciens (Thrace) was a region of ancient Greece associated with many mythological figures, including Orpheus, and, the poem claims, was an old name for Winchester. Winchester was a suitable setting for the story of a king since it had effectively been England's first capital under Egbert (770–839), as well as being associated with Alfred the Great (849–899). Peter Hofstee explains the poem's place-based allusion making:

> In the classical version as told by Ovid, Orpheus is a 'Thracian bard' but in *Sir Orfeo*, the protagonist is of a higher status: he is a king, more specifically the king of England. Moreover, we are told that Thrace is said to have been, without doubt, the former name of Winchester. . . . Clearly, this first deviation from the classical myth serves as a transposition in order to familiarise the medieval audience with the setting of the poem.
>
> *(Hofstee 2014: 1)*

The classical setting is thus craftily identified with England, connecting the English aristocracy with much admired ancient nobility.[10] The key figures – Orfeo and Heurodis – are obviously versions of Orpheus and Eurydice, and *Sir Orfeo* retells the myth of their tragic separation, making significant changes which translate the story from myth to romance.

In the Greek myth, Eurydice was running through a meadow with Orpheus when she was bitten by a serpent and descended to the realm of the dead. Desperate to recover her, Orpheus decided to petition Hades, the god of the underworld, in person. A son of Apollo (the god of music), Orpheus was blessed with exceptional musical talents. His harp-playing was so sweet and so moving that Hades – who habitually refused such petitions – gave permission for Eurydice to accompany him on his return journey. There was only one condition: Orpheus was not to look back as he ascended. He had almost completed the journey when he looked behind him to make sure Eurydice was still following. At that very moment, she disappeared forever into the gloom.

Sir Orfeo retells the story as one of fairy abduction rather than death, as encounter with the Otherworld rather than the underworld. Orfeo's wife, Heurodis, falls asleep under a tree in an orchard, only to wake screaming and clawing at her face. The source of her anxiety is an encounter with the king of the fairies, who has demanded that she live with him, threatening that if she does not go willingly, she will be taken by force. Orfeo gathers his knights to resist the otherworldly invaders, but Heurodis simply vanishes. Mortified by his loss, Orfeo is unable to continue in his kingly role; he takes his harp (like Orpheus he is a skilled musician) and begins to wander through the wilderness. During his ten years of solitude, he sometimes sees the Fairy King and his retinue out hunting. On one occasion he catches sight of Heurodis, but the fairies usher her away before he can reach her. He follows them through a cave and into a beautiful landscape dominated by a richly appointed castle. Claiming to be a visiting minstrel, he gains access, entering the hall and playing his harp for the fairy court. The king is so charmed by his music that he offers whatever Orfeo wants as a reward. Orfeo requests Heurodis' release and, though the king is reluctant, he is bound by his promise.

Returning to Winchester with Heurodis, Orfeo approaches his steward who welcomes him but does not recognize him. When Orfeo plays, the steward recognizes the harp, but Orfeo tells him that he found it beside a dead body. Demonstrating his loyalty, the steward weeps for the loss of his king, so Orfeo reveals his identity and makes his steward his heir. The court celebrates and Orfeo is restored as king.

There are a number of significant contrasts between the myth and the romance:

Orpheus	Orfeo
Wife dies	Wife abducted
Visits death/underworld	Visits the fairy/Otherworld
Quests for his wife	Wanders aimlessly
Finds his wife as result of quest	Finds his wife by accident
Does not ultimately regain his wife	Regains his wife

The tragic character of the myth, the outcome of which is permanent loss and unbearable grief, is overturned by the happy ending of the romance. The outcome is doubly happy for Orfeo since he regains both his wife and his kingdom. As Peter Hofstee suggests, the transformation is not only of the tragic elements but also of the myth itself, 'as indicated by Orfeo's status as ruler over England' (2014: 2). The king's restoration after a wilderness experience shifts the story away from its classical origins and their dark vision of human experience, towards what might be termed 'Celtic' interests. Not only is the happy ending far more reminiscent of Celtic stories than of classical, but the loss of the wife and the search for her binds *Sir Orfeo* as tightly to Celtic legend as to Greek myth. The movement of women back and forth between two males is a repeated pattern in the tales of the *Mabinogion*, as is rescue from some kind of Otherworld enchantment.

The romance explicitly proclaims its Celtic heritage by relating its composition to the Breton lay: 'In Britain first these lays were wrought / There were they made, and thence were brought. / They told of venturous deeds and days, / Whereof the Britons made their lays' (Weston 1914: ll.13–16). 'Lay' is a musical term referring to 'a short lyric or narrative poem intended to be sung' (OED), and this might be said to indicate another Celtic feature of *Sir Orfeo*: the emphasis on the transformative power of music. A recurrent motif in many ancient Irish and Welsh stories, music is a potent presence in the romance which concludes with a tribute to the lay as a restorative force: 'Good are the words, the music good – / Thus came Sir Orfeo out of his care' (Weston 1914: ll.600–1). Jane Minogue argues that the presence of the harp shapes the narrative's key moments, whether we think of the consolation Orfeo finds in playing it after he has lost his wife, his calming of wild beasts in the wilderness, his enchanting of the Fairy King to the extent that he is prepared to release Heurodis, or the moment at which the harp helps Orfeo test the faithfulness of his steward (Minogue n.d.: n.p.).

Middle English romances frequently draw attention to their musical affinities. Linda Zaerr observes that they tend to connect plucked and bowed stringed instruments (especially harp and fiddle) with narrative performance (2012: 78–104). Many old Celtic tales associate music with enchantment and the supernatural. For example, in Irish tradition the father god, Dagda, possesses a self-playing harp with which he is able to summon the seasons, while in two branches of the *Mabinogi* people are said to be charmed by the singing of the magical birds of Rhiannon which could wake the dead or lull the living to sleep. Thus, when Orfeo takes his harp to the Otherworld and creates music so aesthetically potent as to win over the supernatural court, the poem draws together two motifs with strong Celtic resonance.

Otherworld

Jordi Sánchez Martí argues that the otherworldly features of *Sir Orfeo* are 'mostly of Celtic derivation' (Martí 2017: 134). The poem's representation of the Otherworld is particularly reminiscent of the *Mabinogi*, especially in the depiction of its people as largely indistinguishable from humans in form and appearance (Fee and Leeming 2001: 204). Not only do they look like us but encounters with them are accepted by characters in *Sir Orfeo*, as in the *Mabinogi*, with remarkable equanimity. The Otherworld lies in close proximity to our own, and it hardly seems out of the ordinary that one should come face to face with its denizens by accident as one is going about one's daily business. While both Gilgamesh and Odysseus wander far from home and enter uncharted territory before they experience marvels, figures in Celtic tales stumble across them in their own backyard.

The Celtic Otherworld, sometimes associated with the fairy folk – the Irish *Sidhe*, and the Welsh *Tylwyth Teg* – probably derives from pre-Christian beliefs relating to a sacred parallel realm considered to be the home of the gods, or even the dwelling place of the dead. Stories of contact between the familiar, everyday world and its shadowy other have been interpreted by some scholars as remnants of an ancient mythology based on ancestor worship, and of long-forgotten burial practices (Selling 1998: 293). In *Sir Orfeo*, there are intimations that the fairy castle in which Heurodis is held captive is not entirely distinct from the realm of the departed: 'There as he gazed his glances fell / On many marvels all around; / Folk long thought dead were by a spell / Brought hither, and as living found' (Hunt 1910: 21). A catalogue of gruesome sights follows, illustrating various means of death, both violent and peaceful, each corpse seemingly suspended in the condition of its passing.

The doubleness of the Otherworld which Orfeo encounters – its combination of hellish and heavenly aspects – contributes to a pattern of antitheses in the poem, often noted by critics: loss and restoration, sorrow and joy, wealth and poverty, the court and the wilderness, nature and art, self and society. Seth Lerer sees another, more subtle contrast at work in the depiction of the Otherworld, relating it to the art of painting in thirteenth- and fourteenth-century Britain. In the visual arts the fairy realm is marked by a high degree of craft and artifice which the poem contrasts with Orfeo's skill as a musician. While the beautiful surface of the Otherworld dazzles and deceives the viewer/reader, Orfeo's artistry has a power to move and bring about real change, so 'the poem contrasts deceptive structures which offer but the semblance of security with an art which can harmonize man with nature and with man' (Lerer 1985: 93). Geraldine Barnes, too, observes that the fairy domain is characterized by a rich façade which belies its true nature: it is a world of 'deceptive order', the 'dazzling front' of which 'mask[s] the disorder and horror within' (1993: 120). So the contrast between the Otherworld's elegance, style and beauty and the heartfelt art of Orfeo as a consummate musician draws attention to the disorder which has led to the loss of the queen and of the kingdom, as well as to its eventual overcoming.

But, despite Lerer's emphasis on the restoration of harmony by means of Orfeo's skill, the tensions remain. The combination of horror and sumptuous beauty, of paradise and Hades in the Otherworld, is matched by the ambiguity of the Fairy King who abducts Heurodis. He is not overtly identified as evil in the poem; rather, he is made to operate outside human categories. As Laskaya and Salisbury observe, he can be read as a demonic figure if we invoke a medieval Christian worldview, but other interpretative frameworks will produce other readings: 'he can serve as an image of fate, a representative of death, an adversary who comes to life to punish sin, a pre-Christian divinity or spirit, a rupture in meaning, the representative of artifice, irrationality' (1995: n.p.).

The multiple possibilities embodied by the Fairy King play out through the whole story; if we cannot know for certain how to understand either him or his world, then we can never be sure how to read the poem. Perhaps *Sir Orfeo*'s resistance to any simple or unified meaning is the result of its blend of unassimilable cultural sources: classical (Greek) mythology, the Christian worldview and Celtic traditions. The Celtic Otherworld is a fantastical setting for the kind of supernatural adventures into which medieval heroes fall – enchanting and exciting, but potentially dangerous. It is a world largely indifferent to humanity: 'the denizens of the otherworld have little regard for men or for their values and codes, and therefore are usually to be avoided' (Fee and Leeming 2001: 64). On the other hand, the ancient Celts tended to see the Otherworld as 'a sacred spiritual realm to be feared, respected and revered as the dwelling place of the gods, the supernatural and a place where spirits went after death' (Selling 1998: 293). Such a place, whether sacred or fearful, could not easily be grafted onto the medieval Christian understanding of the world. Neither, of course, could the ancient story of Orpheus and Eurydice, without a blend of euhemerism (assuming that gods were really mortals subsequently deified for their extraordinary achievements) and allegorizing. Once we think in terms of allegory, the interpretative possibilities necessarily multiply.

If the Otherworld depicted in *Sir Orfeo* can be read as both a fairy domain and the land of the dead, as both beautiful and deceptive, as both outmoded history and instructive allegory, it is at the same time a depiction of both inner states and political realities. Heurodis' initial encounter with the Fairy King takes place in a dream, and her behaviour on waking is indicative of great torment: 'But when she woke, ah me, the change! / Strange were her words, her actions strange; / She wrung her hands, and tore her face / Till that the blood ran down apace; / Her goodly robes she soon had torn' (Weston 1914: ll.75–9). Jeff Rider observes that 'this appearance of the King of Faerie in a dream shows the border between the central and other worlds may be psychic as well as physical' (2000: 117).

On the other hand, the invasion of Orfeo's realm and the kidnapping of his wife are acts of political aggression as much as of psychic trauma. 'The loss of Heurodis very quickly turns into the loss of a kingdom', and what might be understood as violence against her person, turns out to be a threat to the integrity of the state' (Battles 2010: 179). The Fairy King initially takes Heurodis on a tour of his kingdom before returning her to the orchard and then takes her again – on a more permanent basis – the following day. Dominique Battles argues that 'the intervening time turns what would have been a private act (i.e. an abduction/rape) into a public and political act', because Heurodis is able to tell Orfeo of the threat, allowing him to muster troops to protect her. Orfeo's failure to prevent the abduction is thus a public humiliation: 'a military defeat of sorts, witnessed by hundreds of fighting men, to a foe whose land holdings, as far as we can tell, outclass Orfeo's own' (Battles 2010: 179). The disruption of the aristocratic order by the incursion of its dark other is a complex business in which social, religious, psychological and political meanings are entangled. Their intertwining suggests that the movement between worlds is less to do with the development of supernatural fantasy than with the translation of myth into a distinctly medieval mode of entertainment.

As Corinne Saunders makes clear, magic in medieval English romances 'is always grounded in cultural reality' (Saunders 2010: 2). Whether psychic or political, that reality is not far below the surface. This is evident in the depiction of the Otherworld as, in certain ways, comparable with Orfeo's own realm. When he eventually finds his way into the court of the Fairy King, it is not an outlandish, fantastical or even completely unfamiliar place. Orfeo, it seems, does not cross from the real world into an unreal one, so much as he moves into a dimension not altogether unlike the one he has left. He enters a medieval castle, perhaps not so different from his own except in its scale and the lavishness of its appointment. As Seth Lerer puts it: 'the two kingdoms seem strikingly similar in the ways they show an apparently decorous civilization at work' (Lerer 1985: 97). Not only is the fairy kingdom modelled on the medieval court, but its supernatural character proves irrelevant to Orfeo's quest. He finds the hidden domain and its ornate castle simply by following the fairy folk home, and he succeeds in his quest not by magic but by the practice of a highly developed human skill – his harp-playing (Finlayson 1999: 391–2). But when it comes to comparisons between the two worlds, the differences are no less important than the similarities. The violence with which Heurodis is abducted and the presence of the tortured dead contribute to a sense that what the fairy world reveals is the shadow side of the culture idealized in the court at Winchester.

While the poem makes no attempt to account for either the presence or the darkness of the supernatural world in terms of Christian doctrine, John Block Friedman argues that it has a demonic aspect:

> In time, all evil supernatural beings of the Middle Ages came to be thought of as descendants of the fallen angels; some were evil fairies who attacked women, especially those who were so unfortunate as to be caught near trees and bushes . . . the author of Sir Orfeo had good precedent for putting Heurodis into the hands of a fairy abductor. The king of the other-world both in his satanic and in his fairy aspect, was traditionally a creature with a penchant for fair women.
>
> *(Friedman 1996: 27)*

The religious undertones of romances, and the fact that their conjoining of worlds may be 'psychic as well as physical', political as well as personal, distinguish their discursive universe from that of ancient mythopoeic culture. In *Sir Orfeo* the underlying myth has evidently slipped its moorings in lived experience and been recast in the mode of entertainment as well as of ideological and religious propaganda. The poem's narrative of restoration and return has a kind of mythopoeic function in that it encourages participation in the rituals and values of courtly culture, but it also indulges in a fantasy in the sense that it self-consciously draws on a myth from an older time.

Expressing detachment from its own material in referring to its origins in the Breton lay, and in setting the action in an unspecified past, allows the story of traffic between worlds to serve as entertainment or distraction as much as discussion or instruction: 'Like the other worlds of modern cinema, television, and print, the other worlds of medieval romance were the laboratories of fears and longings whose monstrous, elegant and fantasized elaborations medieval audiences enjoyed in the same ways that we do those of our media' (Rider 2000: 129).[11] Generalizations about how medieval audiences received and understood romances are inherently problematical, and the comparison between them and modern media is necessarily imprecise, but the value of such works as entertainment is an important consideration, and 'laboratories' is a useful metaphor. To the extent that myths, in peering at the unknown and bringing to light the inexplicable, might be said to be the 'laboratories' in which the 'fears and longings' of our distant forebears were formed and investigated, romances took on something of the function of the ancient stories they plundered. While those stories were cut off from their roots by changes of place, time and narrative detail, and therefore, in a sense, demythologized, they were also translated into culturally meaningful forms and invested with renewed potency for medieval consumers.

From pagan to Christian

Given that medieval romances did so much to transform ancient myth into contemporaneous modes of storytelling, the reference to the classical gods Pluto and Juno as ancestors of Sir Orfeo (ll.29-30) is, in some respects, a puzzling one. That aspects of pagan mythology survived into the Christian era in Europe is well known: the literature of the Renaissance (or early modern period) is rich in references and allusions to classical figures and stories. But in the medieval period, ancient mythological material was still widely considered tainted by demonic presences. Renate Blumenfeld-Kosinski explains that the pagan elements in medieval literature had to be managed in such a way that they could be assimilated into Christian culture: 'The practice of Latin in the schools was always dependent on classical models. A survival of the gods was thus assured within the learned tradition, and ways had to be found to integrate them into a Christian framework' (Blumenfeld-Kosinski 1985: 1).

According to Jean Seznec, the ways found to manage such integration included historical, physical, moral and encyclopaedic modes of interpretation. Thus, gods could be euhemerized (made human by suggesting that some historical process had in ancient times made gods of mere mortals), or they could be associated with heavenly bodies and constellations, and so made part of the physical universe as celestial or angelic presences rather than divinities. Alternatively, pagan deities could be used as allegorical figures, moral or spiritual meanings being derived from the stories of their actions and interactions. Each of these interpretative strategies could be used independently, and, sometimes, all three could be interwoven:

> If in antiquity . . . the different philosophical schools proposed different interpretations 'of the nature of the gods,' these interpretations were not mutually exclusive; they were accessible simultaneously to cultivated minds, which did their best to reconcile them. Logic would doubtless have demanded the adoption of one to the exclusion of the rest, but men felt that three keys were better than one. Sometimes one key, sometimes another, seemed more appropriate to the character of a given myth.
>
> *(Seznec 1961: 122)*

Blumenfeld-Kosinski argues that the euhemeristic view best served the purposes of the earliest French romancers, 'since it would remove the threat of paganism and steep the text in historical "veracity," a very desirable quality for the first vernacular romances' (Blumenfeld-Kosinski 1985: 2). *Sir Orfeo* seems to take this approach, carefully distancing the ancient view of divinity from its own:

> This Orfeo, he was king with crown,
> A mighty lord of high renown,
> A stalwart man, and hardy too,
> Courteous and free of hand also.
> His parents might their lineage trace
> To Pluto, and to Juno's race,
> Who, for their marvels manifold,
> Were held as gods in days of old.
>
> *(Weston 1914: ll.25–32)*

Pluto and Juno were held to be gods in 'days of old', but this was based on their actions and the stories told about them – their 'marvels manifold'. The poem's nudging and winking alerts its audience/reader to the mistaken notions of the ancients. Thus, Orfeo can be depicted as descending from notable stock, but he is a *stalwart* and *hardy* man rather than a demigod. Whereas in the Greek myth Orpheus learned his musical skill from the god Apollo, Orfeo's ability is attributed to no divine origin: it seems to be based on constant practice: 'Himself upon the harp would play, / And set thereto his mind alway, / Till such his skill that, far or near, / No better harper might ye hear' (Weston 1914: ll.37–40). Orfeo, then, is more like the biblical King David than he is like the mythological Greek hero. Just as David's harp-playing calmed the demonic rage of King Saul (1 Sam. 16.23), Orfeo's music has the ability to soothe the distressed:

> None before him was, I trow,
> Or in after days will be
> Held the peer of Orfeo
> When he struck his harp. And he
> Who could hear that minstrelsy
> Would have deemed his spirit were
> Housed in Heaven, such melody
> Was it, and such joy to hear.
>
> *(Hunt 1910: 3)*

Euhemerization seems to be a key strategy employed by the poem to wrest the myth from its pagan sources and suit it to the worldview of medieval Christianity. But Christian interpretations of the Orpheus myth were just as likely to be allegorical, as Anne Laskaya and Eve Salisbury point out:

> Through medieval commentaries, Christian re-readings of the narrative became well-known: 1) Orpheus's backward glance and his consequent loss of Eurydice becomes emblematic for temptation and sin; or 2) Orpheus becomes a Christ figure and the tale foretells redemption. The lay of *Sir Orfeo* blends these received cultural materials with both Celtic and Germanic folk materials, especially the Celtic journey to the Otherworld.
>
> *(Laskaya and Salisbury 1995: n.p.)*

The parallel between Orfeo and Christ emerges most clearly in the poem when he leaves behind his kingdom and lives as a beggar:

> He that was wrapt in fur withal
> And slumbered soft 'neath purple and pall,
> On the heather he now must rest his head,
> With leaves and grass for a covering spread.

He that had castles, halls with towers,
Rivers, forests, fields with flowers,
Must make his bed 'neath the open sky
Though it snow and freeze right piercingly.

(Weston 1914: ll.239–46)

This might be read as an echo of Christ's incarnation which meant his leaving behind the splendours of heaven to be born into a lowly family, and to take on the hardships of homelessness and poverty. There is also a parallel of what, in Christian tradition, is known as the harrowing of hell: between his death on the Cross and his resurrection, Christ descended into hell, overthrew the devil, released the ancient righteous along with Adam and Eve, and led them to heaven. As we have seen, the Otherworld is depicted as a paradise, but is also the realm of the dead from which Heurodis is taken back to Winchester.

Sir Orfeo offers just one example of how pagan sources could be repurposed in Christian culture. As Blumenfeld-Kosinski points out, the possible variations were many, and the strategies of deployment depended on the kind of story one wanted to tell and how its cultural function was perceived. Christian culture could not allow the pagan gods to remain in their divine milieu, but once transplanted they could be given a variety of roles and functions according to the needs of the story in which they make an appearance. 'Indeed, their functional variability seems to be the only common denominator in the roles assigned to them in the medieval period' (Blumenfeld-Kosinski 1985: 10).

If the stories of St Cadoc and of many like him offered the possibility of remaking myth by recasting the magical as miraculous and the marvellous as proof of divine influence, the route taken by romances was almost the inverse. Rather than remodelling historical paragons as mythical heroes, as the hagiographies did, romances took mythical heroes and remodelled them as Christian knights. Either way, the result was the same: mythology was irremediably severed from its ancient roots. In whatever forms it survived into the modern, or even the postmodern age, an unbridgeable gulf had opened between myth and narrative. The gap is visible in similarities and differences between, say, Cadoc and Merlin, between Orfeo and Orpheus, but is ultimately beyond repair by gods, saints, knights or even kings.

Notes

1. Some scholars contest the existence of Celtic culture and mythology. The issue is discussed briefly in the next chapter. While I use the term for the sake of convenience throughout this chapter, I consider it a problematical issue.
2. Jeremy Knight (former inspector of Ancient Monuments at Cadw and English Heritage) notes that despite tantalizing clues having been unearthed on local construction sites, 'there has been no archaeological excavation in the centre of Llancarfan', which 'has been oddly neglected by archaeologists' (2013: 90).

3. '*The Book of Llandaff*, (*Liber Landavensis*), is one of Wales' earliest ecclesiastical manuscripts. It is a manuscript of considerable bulk comprising 128 vellum pages. Inside its covers the early history of the diocese of Llandaff is chronicled and the contents also throw light on the state and position of the church in one area of Wales soon after the Norman Conquest...It is believed that the Book of Llandaff was written between 1120 and 1140' (National Library of Wales website).
4. *The Myvyrian Archaiology of Wales* is an anthology of medieval Welsh literature, first published between 1801 and 1807.
5. According to T. M. Charles-Edwards, some of the stories in Lifris' *The Life of St Cadoc* are 'designed to show the saint's power over even the greatest of kings. In particular they demonstrated the authority of Cadog's sanctuary or "place of protection", *noddfa*, confirmed even by such warlords from Gwynedd and further afield, far from Llancarfan' (Charles-Edwards 2013: 295).
6. On the hagiographical significance of wild and domesticated swine, see Jankulak (2003).
7. As the work of Jocelyn Wogan-Browne shows, there was a close relationship between hagiography and romance in medieval England. This is especially true of the lives of female saints in the twelfth and thirteenth centuries, which saw a shift in the depiction of saints 'from admirable to imitable' (Wogan-Browne 2001: 92).
8. '"Middle English" – a period of roughly 300 years from around 1150 CE to around 1450 – is difficult to identify because it is a time of transition between two eras that each have stronger definition: Old English and Modern English' (Crystal 2018: n.p.).
9. Geraldine Barnes considers Middle English romances to be characterized by opposition to some of the values of courtly love, especially its individualistic, 'anti-social' emphasis. For her, the 'socialization' of the hero – his interaction with court and counsellors rather than his inner life – is what matters most in these poems (Barnes 1993: 16).
10. Connecting English aristocracy to ancient nobility, especially Roman and/or divine forebears was a highly popular gesture in this period. 'The enumeration of a king's illustrious ancestry, especially a line of descent which includes a deity, serves to legitimize the claim to sovereignty' (Leckie 1981: 11).
11. As Nancy Partner (among others) has argued, instruction and entertainment have always been considered to be complementary aims of literature (Partner 1977).

Translations used in preparing this chapter

The Life of St Cadoc.

Rees, W. J. (1843), *Lives of the Cambro British Saints*, Llandovery: William Rees; London: Longman and Co; Abergavenny: J.H. Morgan.

Sir Orfeo

Hunt, E. E. (1910), *Sir Orfeo Adapted from the Middle English*, Cambridge, MA: Harvard Cooperative Society.

Weston, J. L. (1914), *The Chief Middle English Poets*, Boston, MA and New York, NY: Houghton Mifflin Co.

CHAPTER 8
THE FOUR BRANCHES OF THE *MABINOGI*

Charlotte Guest's *Mabinogion*

The stories collected in the *Mabinogion* were given their current form long after Roman rule and the medieval church had subordinated, if not submerged, Celtic culture and religion. They contain myth, folklore, history and invention, often overlaid with Christian mores and values. Despite their relatively late date, they are the earliest examples of tales which might be said to preserve elements of a specifically British mythology.

The title was given by Lady Charlotte Guest (1812–95) to her English translation (1847–49) of eleven stories, just four of which belong to the *Mabinogi* proper: 'Pwyll', 'Branwen', 'Manawydan' and 'Math'. Known as the Four Branches (*Pedair Cainc*), each ends with the formula, 'So ends this branch of the *Mabinogi*': a formula not found in any of the other tales. Taking her cue from that phrase, Guest mistakenly thought *mabinogion* to be the plural of *mabinogi*.[1] The word possibly means something like 'tales of the children', or 'stories of youth'.[2] So, the *Mabinogion* as it appears today – an edited collection of tales and romances – was created in the nineteenth century, but, as Will Parker points out, 'its constituent texts are authentic medieval productions, deriving from originals composed between the eleventh and the fourteenth centuries' (Parker 2010: n.p.). The stories which Guest drew together and translated are preserved chiefly in two medieval manuscripts: the *White Book of Rhydderch* (*c.*1350) which is held in the National Library of Wales, Aberystwyth, and the *Red Book of Hergest* (between 1382 and 1410), kept in the Bodleian Library, Oxford.

The stories in the *Mabinogion* are marked by a tension between orality and literacy, with some tales, especially the Four Branches, being more redolent than others of pre-literary form (Rider-Bezerra 2011: n.p.). At the opposite end of the spectrum from the Four Branches, 'The Dream of Rhonabwy' ends with a claim to being impossible to recite: no one can know it 'without a book' because of the richness of its descriptive detail. Such a claim suggests that it was from the first a literary rather than an oral composition.

As the contrasting styles of the Four Branches and 'The Dream of Rhonabwy' indicate, Guest included in her collection a diverse bundle of compositions. There are no obvious connections between them, and nothing to suggest that they belong together thematically, stylistically or historically. Tradition has labelled the Arthurian tales 'Peredur son of Efrog', 'Geraint son of Erbin' and 'The Lady of the Well' the 'three romances' since they are generically related to French and English works in that tradition (Davies 2007: x–xi). Each may retell a story found in Chrétien de Troyes (1130–1191) whose work formed the basis of the Arthurian legends. Despite his crucial contribution to the formation and dissemination of the familiar tradition, Chrétien did not invent King Arthur. The legendary ruler first appears in the work of the ninth-century Welsh historian Nennius, who lists twelve battles he fought against Saxon invaders. Welsh Chronicles from the tenth century also refer to battles fought by Arthur (Brown 2016: n.p.).

Subsequent shaping of the legend owes a great deal to Chrétien, but just how much is a controversial issue. The relationships between the Welsh romances and Chrétien have been debated since the nineteenth century, and there is still no consensus. Despite divergent interpretations, no one doubts that the similarities are more than coincidence: they are striking enough to imply shared origins. It may have been that Chrétien drew on Welsh sources, or, conversely, that the composers of the Welsh romances borrowed from Chrétien. It is possible, too, that both Chrétien and the Welsh writers were familiar with (now lost) sources or traditions, the similarities springing from common roots. Another interpretation of the exchange developed in the twentieth century, to the effect that the Welsh stories derived from Chrétien, but supplemented his work with material drawn from home-grown narrative styles and plots.

Arthur appears, too, in 'How Culhwch won Olwen', which is probably the oldest tale in the *Mabinogion*, though some elements of the Four Branches almost certainly predate it. This story has Arthur and his men hunt the giant boar Twrch Trwyth as part of a marriage quest. The latest of the stories, probably dating from between the twelfth and fourteenth centuries, 'The Dream of Rhonabwy', is an elaborate fantasia on Arthurian themes, 'satirizing . . . the structure of medieval romance itself' (Davies 2007: xii). In 'Lludd and Llefelys', Lludd – traditionally a British King in the period leading up to the Roman invasion – has to overcome three plagues with the help of his brother, the king of France. 'The Dream of the Emperor Maxen' is based on the historical figure of Magnus Maximus, the Roman British leader who became emperor in the West, but it refashions the details to suggest that the Welsh are the rightful inheritors of Roman rule in Britain.

The Four Branches

Since they contain ancient material which may well be mythological in origin, the focus of this chapter is on the Four Branches rather than the whole of Guest's *Mabinogion*. A masterpiece of medieval composition with roots in an undocumented pre-Christian past, the Welsh cycle weaves tales of magic, parallel worlds, social and sexual bonds, war, betrayal, transformation and redemption.

The first branch tells the story of Pwyll, Prince of Dyfed, beginning with his encountering Arawn, king of the Otherworld. The two exchange places and Pwyll defeats Arawn's rival Hafgan in single combat. The second part tells of Pwyll's meeting Rhiannon, with whom no one can catch up even though her horse never changes its steady pace. Pwyll, in his desire to meet her, simply asks her to stop. Rhiannon tells him that she is unhappily betrothed to Gwawl; Pwyll himself is the real subject of her affections. She tells him how he can contrive to capture Gwawl in a magic sack, putting him at Pwyll's mercy. Thus freed from her bond, Rhiannon marries Pwyll. In the third episode, the baby son of Rhiannon and Pwyll disappears. Fearing they will be blamed for failing to protect him, Rhiannon's maids smear her face and hands with the blood of puppies while she sleeps so that she is accused of killing the child. The same night, Teirnon Twrf Liant, Lord of Gwent Is Coed, finds the baby outside his door after chasing away a monster. He raises the boy as his own until his resemblance to Pwyll becomes apparent. Returned to his parents, the boy is re-named Pryderi (worry) because of the anguish suffered by his mother.

The second branch concerns Bendigeidfran (Brân the Blessed), the giant king of Britain, his sister Branwen and their trouble-making half-brother Efnisien. Married to Matholwch, king of Ireland, Branwen is subjected to violence and made to work in the castle kitchen. In desperation, she trains a starling to take a letter to her brother to let him know of her mistreatment. On receiving the message, Bendigeidfran leads his army in an invasion of Ireland to rescue her. Peace talks, complicated by the machinations of Efnisien and the treachery of Matholwch, end in a war which devastates both sides. Just seven soldiers return to Wales, carrying the still-speaking head of the slain Bendigeidfran. They stay in Harlech for seven years feasting, soothed by the singing birds of Rhiannon. From there they travel to the island of Gwales (Grassholm). A state of blissful forgetfulness prevails until one of them opens a door looking towards Cornwall and their pain and loss come flooding back. The men then set out for London to bury Bendigeidfran's head.

One of the survivors of the Irish war, Manawydan, is at the centre of the third branch. He marries Rhiannon, widow of Pwyll and Pryderi's mother. Manawydan and Rhiannon together with Pryderi and his wife Cigfa face the mysterious cursing of Dyfed from where everyone disappears. A two-year search finds the land to be completely deserted. After working unhappily in England, they return to Dyfed where Pryderi and Rhiannon become trapped in an otherworldly fortress. Manawydan and Cigfa try to survive by growing crops, but the fields are stripped clean overnight by a horde of mice. These are discovered to be the soldiers and servants of a magician who has transformed them as part of a campaign of vengeance for the treatment of Gwawl (described in the first branch). Manawydan catches and prepares to hang a pregnant mouse. She is the transmogrified wife of the magician, who comes to beg for her release, and so Manawydan is able to negotiate with him the lifting of the curse and the restoration of the kingdom.

In the fourth branch, Gilfaethwy, nephew of Math (a magician), rapes his uncle's foot-maiden Goewin and contrives, with his brother Gwydion, to start a war. Using a magical deception, Gwydion steals some otherworldly pigs from Pryderi thus sparking the conflict between the kingdoms of Gwynedd and Dyfed. After a bloody but indecisive battle, Pryderi and Gwydion meet in single combat and Pryderi is killed. Math returns to his court and punishes his nephews by turning Gilfaethwy into a hind and Gwydion into a stag. For each of the three following years, Math turns them into different animals forcing them to mate and to give him their offspring. Math then returns his nephews to human form. When he asks them to recommend another virgin who can serve as his foot-maiden in Goewin's stead, Gwydion suggests his sister Arianrhod.

Math uses magic to test Arianrhod's virginity and she gives birth to Dylan, who flees to the sea. As she runs away in disgrace, Arianrhod drops something small. Gwydion picks it up, carries it home and hides it in a chest at the foot of his bed. One morning he wakes to hear a child crying and finds in the chest a baby boy. Confronted with her son, Arianrhod refuses to acknowledge or name him until Gwydion tricks her into doing so. A further curse prevents the boy, Lleu Llaw Gyffes, from marrying a human woman, and so Gwydion creates a woman out of woodland flowers, naming her Blodeuwedd. Lleu and Blodeuwedd marry, but Blodeuwedd falls in love with a neighbouring lord, Gronw Pebr, and they plot to kill Lleu. Hit with a spear, Lleu turns into an eagle and flies off. Gwydion searches all over Wales until he finds Lleu perched in an oak tree near Yr Wyddfa (Snowdon). He returns Lleu to human form and carries him back to Math's court. When fully recovered, Lleu plans revenge on Blodeuwedd and Gronw Pebr. Gwydion turns Blodeuwedd into an owl, while Lleu kills Gronw with a spear.

Finely interwoven and highly wrought, the connections between these tales develop a set of elaborate patterns which are crucial to the expression of social and moral themes. But these characteristics also make plain their literariness, and their medieval production. Even if, as Geoffrey Ashe claims, they are rooted 'in Celtic antiquity, and pictured as taking place in a pre-Roman milieu' (1990: 99), the ancient society they evoke and the mythological material they encode are viewed through a Norman-era literary and cultural lens.

Composition and date

> The living oral tradition of Welsh story-telling died before more than a few examples could be noted and it can never be re-created. What we have are versions of prose tales written in the medieval period by particular authors. These are in each case literary versions rather than verbatim copies of the oral tales on which they are based.
>
> *(Roberts 1992: 205)*

As literary compositions, the Four Branches were necessarily shaped by the techniques and conventions of their day and yet they carry traces of orality. Chronological order, repetition of phrases, episodic structure and clear marking of the speaker in dialogue, are features of oral composition which appear in the medieval Welsh narratives. Sioned Davies argues that the narrators were 'drawing on a stock of traditional verbal patterns or formulas that were familiar to them, and that these formulas also derive from an oral style' (Davies 1992: 252). She goes on to point out that whether or not the stories were originally passed on by word of mouth their written versions were influenced by the characteristics of oral storytelling. There is no certainty as to when those written versions were composed, as Davies acknowledges, but the scholarly consensus is that they probably date from sometime between 1060 and 1120 (Davies 2007: xxvi–xxvii).

Arguing for a slightly later date than most scholars, Andrew Breeze notes that in the second branch Efnisien mutilates the horses of Matholwch (king of Ireland) in a way which echoes an episode in Lifris' *The Life of St Cadoc* (*c.*1086). Lifris depicts the saint ordering the cutting of lips and ears of horses belonging to men who raid his monastery. Breeze suggests that the episode in the second branch must be based on Lifris' text: 'Being effectively unknown elsewhere, the episode therefore surely reached the Four Branches from the saint's life (. . .) The alternative, that Lifris learnt it from the Four Branches, is improbable. Nor, given the motif's rareness, would it come to each from an independent source' (Breeze 2018: 49). If influenced by Lifris, the Four Branches must, of course, be later than his composition. Breeze concludes that they were written in the 1120s or 1130s.

His argument is interesting, not only for its contribution to the question of dating but also because it helps his case for specific attribution of the tales to a named author. In *The Origins of the Four Branches of the Mabinogi* (2009), he argues that the cycle was written by Princess Gwenllian (*c.*1096–1136) of Gwynedd. Evidence he adduces for female authorship includes the concern the texts show for the character and experience of women, the frequent weakness and passivity of male characters and the lack of interest shown in bloodshed and warfare (by contrast with other ancient texts, such as Homer). Evidence that Gwenllian was behind the composition includes its careful representation of the regions with which she was familiar (particularly Gwynedd and Dyfed), its demonstration of courtly, legal and governmental knowledge and its commitment to the viewpoint of the Welsh ruling class. Even though Breeze's theory is not widely accepted, it illustrates, as it adds to, the sense of uncertainty surrounding the origins and character of an enigmatic work.

Whoever composed the Four Branches, they were not products of free invention in the manner of a modern novel: traditional materials were recast in the fashion of the times, and the resultant narratives bear the clear imprint of medieval romance. The precise nature of those underlying sources reshaped by the conventions of a contemporaneous literary genre is now beyond recovery, but that has not prevented a good deal of speculation and sharp disagreement about them.

A significant question for scholars has been whether the extant branches represent the residue of a now unknown corpus. Some scholars have suggested that underlying what remains is a lost epic of which Pryderi was the hero. Patrick Ford, for example, writes of the first branch:

> What the tale is about, I would venture, is the issue of the parentage of Pryderi and the joint issues of fertility in the land and among men.
>
> Pryderi is a character of considerable importance in medieval Welsh tradition, though he does not figure largely in the four branches as a whole. He is certainly important enough to have a tale about his birth, and that is to be found in the first branch.
>
> *(Ford 1981–2: 113–14)*

Ford goes on to argue that although he was once a divine figure, whose father (Pwyll) is known as Lord of the Otherworld, over time Pryderi became a mortal hero. The story of his father's exchange of place with the Fairy King, Arawn, helps to explain Pryderi's dual nature since Pwyll is a mortal ruler who becomes an otherworldly lord. Pryderi's birth and childhood are similarly dual, as he is effectively fathered by both Pwyll and Teirnon Twrf Liant ('Lord of the Tempestuous Sea'); Ford claims the latter was originally a sea god. Pryderi's mother is Rhiannon, herself sometimes understood to be a euhemerized goddess (Ford 1981–2: 125). As a child, he develops far more quickly than any ordinary mortal, having at the age of three the strength and stature of a six-year-old. Like his mother, he is closely associated with horses, and his birth is attended by supernatural events. Traditionally, a special bond with a particular animal and accelerated development are characteristic of a superhuman hero (Davies 2007: 231–2). If his parentage and the peculiarities of his early life suggest a kind of divine–human hybridity, his death is no less indicative: Gwydion defeats him in single combat with a combination of 'strength and valour, and magic and enchantment' (Davies 2007: 51).

In a more recent development of the Pryderi case, Matthieu Boyd has suggested that the designation of the tales as 'branches' might imply the erstwhile existence of a 'trunk'. That is, the story of Pryderi may originally have been the central narrative from which the remaining stories are outgrowths. In the Four Branches, he can be seen to play a part in the stories of Pwyll, Rhiannon, Branwen, Bendigeidfran, Manawydan, Cigfa, Gwydion and Lleu Llaw Gyffes, but he is mentioned only as his impact or presence demand rather than being the focus of attention. 'This makes the Four Branches of the Mabinogi', Boyd asserts, 'a cycle, by the usual scholarly definition: a narrative circle around a center point. . . . The center point, the heroic biography of Pryderi, is decayed or suppressed' (Boyd 2010: 36).

Unless and until a Pryderi narrative is discovered, the relationship between the Four Branches and such a putative epic remains speculative. But along with various patterns and motifs, which I will discuss in due course, Pryderi's presence helps to establish the unity and narrative sophistication of the Four Branches even though he is at the centre of none of them. Carrying as he does certain mythological resonances, his insistent presence is indicative of the antiquity of the stories, suggesting that they belong to a tradition of which we know comparatively little. But whether or not there really is an underlying mythology is no less contentious an issue than Pryderi's place in the cycle.

Celtic mythology?

That there are magical and otherworldly figures in the Four Branches is beyond doubt, and that events sometimes take a supernatural turn is no less certain. However, not all scholars in the field accept that these features are traces of ancient mythology, nor that they belong to a tradition which can reasonably be called 'Celtic'. In 1986, anthropologist Maryon McDonald observed that what she called 'the Celtic idea' had permeated popular culture among the Bretons, Welsh and Irish. She saw it as having so potent an influence in politics, race, economics, culture and morality that no amount of contrary evidence could serve to falsify its claims, however unconvincing they may be. Based on 'muddling and uncritical employment of archaeology and philology', she argued, the 'Celtic' label was applied to all manner of cultural productions and political interests (McDonald 1986: 339).

A critical perspective known as 'Celto-scepticism' developed in the wake of McDonald's work. In *The Celts: The Construction of a Myth* (1992), Malcolm Chapman argued that Celts never actually existed as an identifiable group. The denomination was created and defined first by Greek and Roman writers, and subsequently developed by the marginalized peoples of Western Europe. Those who identify themselves as Celts today are connected by their resistance to dominant nations and ideologies rather than by any material geo-cultural or genetic heritage. Then, in 1999, Simon James claimed that there is no archaeological evidence connecting the people of Iron Age Britain and Ireland with the 'Celtic' populations of continental Europe. Cultural developments in Britain and Ireland were indigenous and diverse. Those modern people who identify themselves as 'Celts' must do so based not on their ethnicity but on political factors dating back to the early modern, rather than to the ancient, past.

In 2006, archaeologist Michael Dietler observed that the Celtic label persists in our culture, but with a wide range of meanings and applications which cannot readily be reconciled either with each other or with the available archaeological information. He called it 'an amazingly versatile concept in the politics of identity and collective memory', arguing that it is often used in contradictory ways in the service of ethnic and/or regional claims to community or kinship (Dietler 2006: 239). More recently, John Collis, Francis Pryor and Simon Rodway have added their voices to the chorus of scepticism aimed at the 'Celtic idea', especially as applied to the British context.

On the other side of the debate have been those such as Barry Cunliffe and John T. Koch, whose work reasserts the coherence of the archaeological, classical and linguistic evidence, to argue that there was a recognizable group of ancient peoples who can be identified as Celts. The work of Miranda Green, too, has been significant in relating the archaeological record, if not to a specific people or ethnic group, to a cultural phenomenon that has come to be known as 'Celticity'.

If the very idea of a Celtic people and culture is suspect, then what of Celtic mythology in the *Mabinogi*? This is how Simon Rodway diagnoses the problem:

> Using extant stories about euhemerized gods to reconstruct a myth, even if we accept that the attempt is a valid one, is going to involve a lot of arbitrary decisions. We cannot triangulate with ancient Celtic myths from the continent because none have survived. Trying to reconstruct them from the exiguous evidence for pagan religion in Celtic-speaking areas (divine names, iconography, propagandist Classical descriptions of druidical rituals, and so on) is every bit as speculative as trying to do so from medieval Celtic literature.
>
> *(Rodway 2018: 76)*

It is within the range of neither my scholarly expertise nor my current concerns to argue for or against the existence of Celts or Celtic culture. An emotive, sometimes bad tempered, and not always enlightening debate looks set fair to rumble on. In what remains of this chapter, I will use the term 'Celtic' to speak of mythological aspects of the Four Branches, but wish to alert my reader to the problematical character of such a policy. My interest is in the peculiar mutation of mythology in the texts rather than in archaeological or historical questions of ethnicity or cultural identity. Whatever its origins, there does appear to be a pre-Christian undercurrent to the Four Branches, call it 'Celtic' or something else. That is to say, the stories as we have them now include material which clearly predates their medieval composition, some of it supernatural and (possibly) mythological in character.

In the Four Branches we are probably dealing with material far removed from its original forms with no way of overcoming the distance which even archaeology, for all its fascinating discoveries, leaves unbridged. We can, perhaps, detect traces of mythological figures and happenings in certain aspects of the stories, but they are neither clear nor certainly related to any known belief system or pre-Christian worldview. But whatever their ultimate source or line of descent, these stories have given rise to a very rich cultural heritage. We have inherited from them stories of giants, fairies, witches, the wildwood, enchantment, rebirth, magical animals and parallel worlds. Whether or not they derive from an ancient mythology, they have passed into modern culture with an aura of myth clinging to them.

Magic and the Otherworld

Perhaps the most obvious and persistent supernatural features in the Four Branches are the practice of magic and the (often troublesome) proximity of the Otherworld. These are evident from the outset, the first branch opening with an episode in which both are prominent. Pwyll, Lord of Dyfed, while out hunting, encounters a pack of hounds which turn out to belong to Arawn, Lord of the Otherworld (*Annwfn*). A spell worked by Arawn transforms each ruler into the likeness of the other. From then on, magic is a material force in the events which unfold throughout the cycle. In the second branch a magic cauldron revives the dead during a battle in Ireland; in the third branch Dyfed is left desolate by a curse, and people are turned into mice as part of the same story; Gwydion and Gilfaethwy are likewise changed into animals and their children subsequently made human in the fourth branch; the fourth branch also sees Arianrhod's pregnancy revealed by magic, Blodeuwedd created out of flowers, and the magic-assisted defeat of Pryderi in combat. Will Parker writes: 'At regular intervals throughout the Mabinogi, the rational sequence of events is interrupted by a supernatural event, which often occurs immediately before, after or in conjunction with the outlandish and inexplicable behaviour of one of the protagonists' (Parker 2010: n.p.).

Whether it is Pwyll's failure to observe the etiquette of the hunt (in letting his hounds feed on a stag brought down by another man's pack), the trouble-making of Efnisien which provokes conflict with Matholwch (the Irish king), the mistreatment of Gwawl by Pwyll and his men, Gwydion and Gilfaethwy's rape of Goewin, or Arianrhod's cursing of her son (Lleu Llaw Gyffes), Parker's observation seems to hold true: recourse to magic is prompted by 'inexplicable' behaviour, often socially unacceptable or damaging in character. In each case, the situations arising from wicked or unwise choices have to be addressed by supernatural means, so that, typically, magic is used to remedy the ills brought on by poor decisions or disruptive actions. But it is used, too, for purposes of deception and predation, especially in the fourth branch. This is part of a complex and delicate balancing of light with shade, good with evil, transgression with justice. Sioned Davies observes that although it perhaps belongs to a more ancient tradition, the magical dimension of the Four Branches serves a distinctly medieval purpose in emphasizing 'a moral code of conduct' (Davies 1995: 790).

In the ancient world of the *Mabinogi*, then, magic is commonplace, and magicians play significant roles in the tales. But the relationship between magic and the Otherworld is not altogether clear. In the first branch, for example, Arawn (an Otherworld ruler) clearly has magical powers, but since this is true, too, of Math and Gwydion, it cannot be said that magic belongs exclusively in or to the Otherworld. Some figures such as Rhiannon, Teirnon and Llwyd son of Cil Coed (who curses Dyfed in the third branch) have associations with both magic and the Otherworld, but to which world they truly belong is never made explicit. All of which suggests that the boundary between worlds is porous, and everyday reality is rendered unstable by the proximity of its cosmic shadow. John Carey describes the contact zone as a paradoxical blend of the familiar and the strange: 'The Otherworld is nearby, perhaps indeed immediately present, but hidden and alien as well. It may be reached by way of the holy places. . . . The whole of the Otherworld may lie beneath a single well or hill; or a single Otherworld palace may be linked to points far distant from each other in the geography of mortals' (Carey 1987: 7).

The reference to access via a well attests to an oft-encountered motif. In the second branch, for example, while out hunting Matholwch sees 'huge, monstrous' Llasar Llaes Gyfnewid and his even larger wife emerging from a lake carrying a cauldron, as if the water formed or concealed a portal between worlds. Anne Ross writes of the votive offerings deposited in pools, lakes, wells and springs, asserting that 'Celtic peoples regarded all such places as entrances to the otherworld, and the literatures of the Celtic world support this supposition' (Ross 1974: 50–1). One of the three romances in Guest's collection, 'The Lady of the Well', draws on the same tradition, telling of otherworldly encounters following a ritual involving the drawing of water and the pouring of it over a marble slab.

Carey notes, too, that time operates differently in the Otherworld. In the second branch

> the survivors of Bran's disastrous expedition to Ireland spend seven years feasting in Harddlech and eighty feasting in Gwales, supernaturally entertained and forgetful of every 'affliction in the world'; when they return to the normal conditions of existence, no time seems to have passed in Britain. Otherworld time, as the Rees brothers observe, 'is both longer and shorter than the time of our world'.
>
> *(Carey 1987: 8)*[3]

The temporal discontinuity, familiar to anyone who has read C. S. Lewis' Narnia books, is a feature of many fairy tales in the Celtic mould. A number of traditional stories from Wales, probably medieval in origin, feature characters who experience lost time as a result of encounters with otherworldly beings.

While time holds the worlds apart, space brings them close. Pwyll's journey to, and sojourn in, the Otherworld illustrates their proximity. As far as he knows, he is on familiar territory when he encounters Arawn and his hounds, but otherworldly authority takes precedence. He arrives at Arawn's court without passing through any obvious portal, or entering a parallel reality, and yet he needs to be escorted to the realm by its king. Although he enters a court which appears to be not unfamiliar in its lineaments, it is made up of the most beautifully adorned buildings and peopled with the best equipped men and most beautiful women anyone has ever seen. The feasts have more food and drink than at any other court on earth, and they are served in golden vessels.

The blend of homelike and alien alongside the use of superlatives in depictions of the Otherworld may represent traces of a pre-Christian belief system, but they may, simultaneously, reflect the medieval context. Helen Fulton argues that 'the Otherworld in the Four Branches functions as a paradigm of the Norman settlements in Wales, in that it can be either friendly or hostile but in any case has an inevitable and unsurpassable power compared to the mortal world' (2000: 447). Such political aspects of the stories have tended to attract less attention than the mythological, but they are necessarily significant for our understanding of texts focussed on relations between rulers of neighbouring territories.[4] Joseph Shack makes the case for an Otherworld which serves as a figure for the power struggles of the time:

> Pwyll's initial meeting with Arawn . . . occurs at an ambiguous, liminal location on a Welsh territorial border, suggesting the encroachment of the Otherworld into Dyfed and perhaps indicating anxieties regarding the fluidity of borders. Dovetailing with this indistinct but earthly location of the Otherworld is the notably prosaic representation of the court of Annwfn, which is easily reached and lacks overtly supernatural elements, suggesting an Otherworld that seems decidedly familiar – perhaps denoting a foreign earthly court evocative of Norman settlements rather than a supernatural realm. Finally, during his stay in Annwfn, Arawn charges Pwyll with dealing with a territorial dispute: a politically charged task, betraying concerns regarding borders, identity, and the nature of alliance.
>
> *(Shack 2015: 175)*

While Shack's description tends to supplant rather than complement the mythological, there is no reason why a political reading should necessarily do so. The Four Branches is certainly a medieval text which bears the imprint of its time, and, inevitably, registers the power dynamics shaping the context of its production. But it is, nonetheless, a cycle of stories which draws on an older tradition. However faint they may be, the traces of contemporaneous political realities relating to Norman incursions might be said to show through here and there in the representation of a mythological Otherworld.

The hybridic character of the Otherworld – its politico-mythological constitution – is evident in the opening episode:

> Once upon a time he [Pwyll] was at Arberth, a chief court of his, and he was seized by the thought and the desire to go hunting. . . . He set out that evening from Arberth, coming as far Pen Llwyn Diarwya, and there he spent the night.
>
> The next morning, in the young of the day, he arose and came to Glyn Cuch to let loose his dogs beneath the wood.
>
> *(Parker 2005: 178)*

Sioned Davies writes: 'Hunting was a common pastime for the noblemen of medieval Wales, with its own terminology and legalities. The hunt is often used in medieval French and English tales and romances, as well as in the *Mabinogion* as a precursor to an encounter with the supernatural' (Davies 2007: 228).

Davies' point is a telling one since it makes the hunt evocative of both the medieval and the mythological. When Pwyll encounters a pack of white dogs with red ears, the significance is clear: white animals are associated with the Otherworld and the supernatural in Welsh and Irish traditions. In the third branch, Manawydan and Pryderi, while out hunting, are led to a magical fortress by a white boar, and the incident is very similar to the moment in Lifris' *The Life of St Cadoc* when a white boar miraculously indicates to the saint the divinely appointed location for his new religious settlement. More generally, animals are, at every turn, a part of the human story, deeply embedded in both everyday and otherworldly experience. As Sarah Larratt Keefer contends, some of the most powerful appearances of the Otherworld take the form of animal–human exchange, whether the transmogrifications of Gwydion and Gilfaethwy, Lleu and the wife of Llwyd Cil Coed, or the roles played by horse, colt, boar, pigs, eagle and owl (Keefer 1996: 7). Characters such as Rhiannon, Pryderi, Lleu and Blodeuwedd are intimately associated with animals; their hybridity representing traffic between adjacent worlds.

Gods in the *Mabinogi*?

Such hybridity may well be a trace of the pagan past, but is also integral to the medieval interweaving of Christian and pre-Christian motifs: an oft-recognized feature of the Four Branches. For some critics, the residue of ancient worldviews is associated with the divine origins of a few figures: 'Many of the characters derive ultimately from much earlier Celtic gods and goddesses, and many of the events and episodes draw on mythologies all but forgotten' (Bollard 2006: 9).

Rhiannon is one of the most important figures for such claims because her name and aspects of her character suggest that she might have begun life as a goddess. The name Rhiannon derives from the Celtic form *Rigantona* ('divine queen'). The male form is Teirnon, derived from *Tigernonos* ('divine king'): the name of the man who raises Rhiannon's son during his early years. First appearing on a magical mount, then condemned to carry passengers on her back, and, in the third branch, to wear an ass's collar, Rhiannon is insistently connected with horses, leading some interpreters to associate her with the Gallo-Roman horse goddess Epona.[5]

If her name is suggestive of supernatural origins, her character deepens the impression of a more-than-human individual. Rhiannon's wisdom and ability to turn events to her own advantage are often contrasted with Pwyll's tendency to act without thinking. It is she who brings the two of them together for the first time, actively seeking out Pwyll and ensuring that their meeting takes place on her terms:

> 'Lady,' he said, 'will you tell me anything about your business?'
> 'I will, between me and God', she said. 'My main purpose was to try and see you.'
> 'That, to me, is the best business you could have,' said Pwyll. 'Will you tell me who you are?'
> 'I will, lord,' she said 'I am Rhiannon, daughter of Hyfaidd Hen, and I am to be given to a husband against my will.[6] But I have never wanted any man, because of my love for you. And I still do not want him, unless you reject me. And it is to find out your answer on the matter that I have come'.
>
> *(Davies 2007: 11)*

This makes clear that the meeting is no accident; it has been contrived by Rhiannon whose mission is to free herself from an unwanted betrothal. She emerges as both driving force and presiding intelligence in the relationship. Catherine Byfield observes that Rhiannon and Pwyll serve as foils to each other: 'Pwyll's heedless actions are contrasted with Rhiannon's mental acuity, strengthening our perceptions of her incisiveness and wit, while Rhiannon's sharp tongue and "no-nonsense" attitude throw Pwyll's impulsive generosity and recklessness into relief' (Byfield 1993: 3).

Pwyll shows his rashness, and Rhiannon her cleverness, again in the episode of their wedding feast at her father's court. The man to whom Rhiannon was previously promised (Gwawl) turns up to claim her, and, without thinking, or even asking who the man is, Pwyll promises to give him anything in his power to offer. Rhiannon points out his foolishness in no uncertain terms:

> 'Never was a man more feeble in his own wits than you have been.'
> 'Lady,' he replied, 'I did not know who he was.'
> 'That is the man to whom it was intended I should be given against my will,' she said, 'Gwawl son of Clud, a wealthy man with many followers. But since it has happened that you said what you have said, give me to him, lest there be disgrace to you'.
>
> *(Bollard 2006: 29)*

Rhiannon has then to come up with a plan to rescue herself, making use of a magic bag in which Gwawl is trapped and from which he has to bargain his way out. The incident comes back to haunt Pwyll and Rhiannon's son Pryderi in the third branch, when, in revenge for the treatment of Gwawl, Llwyd son of Cil Coed puts a spell on Dyfed and changes his people into mice to eat its corn crops.

So, Rhiannon has characteristics which might suggest divine origins and the survival of an ancient mythology, but she is no less a figure of folklore.[7] Falsely accused of killing her child, she belongs to a European storytelling tradition: 'The Calumniated Wife has been part of European folk tradition since at least the twelfth century and forms an important episode in several folktales. . . . The motif occurs in some half dozen tale types and within these one finds variants which echo features in the Four Branches' (Wood 1996: 64–6). Facing a manifestly unjust charge of child-murder, Rhiannon derives as much from a class of folktales dealing with falsely accused wives as she does from mythology. She is, arguably, the figure in whom these different modes are most evidently, and most inextricably, entangled. She seems to have elements of myth, romance and folktale in her make-up. So, as Erica Sessle contends, she must be regarded 'as a literary character and not simply the remnant of a degenerated goddess' (1994: 11). Woven from a range of earlier figures and types, as well as from contemporaneous conventions and motifs, she serves to typify the representational character of the Four Branches as a whole, in the complexity of its form and multiplicity of its derivation.

While she is the most obviously hybridic figure in the Four Branches, Rhiannon is far from the only one. In the second branch we meet Brân (or Bendigeidfran). Brân is Welsh for crow or raven – a bird associated with a number of Celtic deities. He is a giant who possesses a magic cauldron, and whose severed head continues to speak and maintain companionship with his comrades. Anne Ross' work helps to explain the significance of the latter detail: 'The human head was regarded by the Celts as being symbolic of divinity and otherworld powers. The motif of the severed head figures throughout the entire field of Celtic cult practice, temporally and geographically' (Ross 1974: 94). Brân, then, may have his origins in some divine figure. The same is true of his sister Branwen, whom Patrick Ford refers to as 'the war goddess', noting her key role in the bloody conflict between Britain and Ireland. On this account, Brân is the male form of an originally female divinity (Ford 1996: 113–14).

Manawydan, son of Llŷr, who features in the third branch, is sometimes equated with Manannan mac Lir, the Irish god of the sea. Unlike Manannan, there is no evidence that Manawydan was ever thought of as a sea divinity in the Welsh tradition. Both names might derive from Manaw (the early Welsh name for the Isle of Man). But *manawyd is* the Welsh word for 'awl', so his name may be associated with his skill as a craftsman (demonstrated repeatedly in the story). In the fourth branch Lleu Llaw Gyffes, too, is associated with preternatural ability in making. He is probably to be identified with the Irish god Lugh Samildanach: *Llaw Gyffes* means 'Skilful Hand', while *Samildanach* means 'Skilled-in-many-arts'. Both Lleu and Lugh are connected with the Gaulish god Lugus. In the same branch, we meet Gwydion and Arianrhod who are called the children of Dôn. Dôn is etymologically related to the name Danu, mother of the Irish gods (the Tuatha Dé Danann).[8]

If there are indeed euhemerized gods in the Four Branches, they are made to serve a broadly Christian purpose: the communication of a set of courtly values. Ancient material is reworked to illustrate those values and the consequences of their transgression, rather than to update its settings or sanitize the behaviour of its characters for a Christian audience.

Structures and themes

While the presence in the stories of mythological figures and motifs has long been of interest to readers, critical appreciation of the underlying political and moral concerns and how they relate to the structure of the work is a more recent development. In an essay published in 1978, Jeffrey Gantz noted that up until that time Celtic scholars had tended to consider the Four Branches to be 'devoid of both theme and structure' (1978: 247). By means of a percipient structural analysis, revealing a skilfully wrought and highly complex narrative patterning, he showed such judgements to be a long way wide of the mark. The two major episodes of the first branch, for example, are designed to echo each other in the character and order of their incidents: in the first episode Pwyll meets Arawn and in the second he meets Rhiannon; in the first, he takes Arawn's stag, while in the second he gives Rhiannon to Gwawl; he journeys to Arawn's court in the first, and to Rhiannon's court in the second; he shows mercy to Hafgan in the first, and to Gwawl in the second; he bonds with Arawn in the first and marries Rhiannon in the second.[9]

Similar parallels occur between the episodes in the other three branches, but the patterning is not contained within individual branches; rather, it spreads across and throughout all four. Gantz shows, for example, that the first and fourth branches interlock in no less elaborate a fashion than the episodes within each branch, striking a series of direct and significant contrasts between the sophistication and gentility of the stories set in south Wales (branches one and three) with the comparative disorder and brutality of those set in the north (two and four). The alternation between north and south is neither simply ornamental nor geographical, Gantz concludes; it is thematic: 'In a sense, the structure is the theme; for, as alternating tales balance and sequences parallel each other, so the world of the Four Branches is an ideally just one in which good begets good, evil evil' (1978: 254). The 'interlacing' technique, which patterns both events and themes by means of repetition and variation, prompts readers to bear in mind various moral and political concerns as they return in different settings. Or, as J. K. Bollard puts it: 'The Four Tales are juxtaposed in order that the reader might compare the events of one with those of another . . . There is no incident or detail which remains isolated or superfluous in the Four Branches' (1996: 168).

Since Gantz's intervention, many scholars have written about these issues, seeing in the Four Branches the kind of densely woven structures typical of medieval romance and identifying a wide range of interconnecting themes. For Catherine McKenna (1980–2), literary modes designed for 'the education of a prince' might be seen to underlie the stories of Pwyll with their 'atmosphere of courtliness' and emphasis on 'the traditional virtues of Celtic sovereignty'. Brynley Roberts draws attention to a focus on insult, friendship and shame, referring to these as 'keywords' used to 'unify the material at a deeper level than the plot' (1984: 226). Roberta Valente (1988) has read the fourth branch as concerned with the cultural codes which constitute a social order, focussing on the consequences of transgressing prescribed gender roles. Andrew Welsh, discussing doubling and incest, suggests that the text is 'radically ambivalent about its values', and its characters are 'haunted by duality' (1990: 346–7). On Catherine Byfield's (1993) reading, the origins of conflict and strategies for its resolution take centre stage, each tale modulating the causes, settlements and consequences of disquiet. Patrick Ford (1996) shows how the second branch skilfully braids images of bags, cauldrons and births, not only in events but also in linguistic patterns and the use of names.

Underlying all these interpretations is a sense that fundamental moral values are at stake in the stories. Whether the focus is on the character needed to rule well, relationships between men and women, the mutability of cultural codes or the just handling of disputes, scholarly interpreters find a moral sensibility at work in both the architecture and the narrative detail of the Four Branches. Sioned Davies sees this emphasis emerging from the medieval recasting of ancient traditions:

> It is apparent . . . that the author of the Four Branches is drawing on traditional stories ultimately derived from earlier primary Celtic mythology. However, the author is using these tales and traditions from the past as a vehicle for his own ideas – underneath the magic and enchantment we are aware of his emphasis on a moral code of conduct which he tries to communicate to his medieval audience.
>
> *(Davies 1995: 790)*

The moral order comes under the most intense pressure in the complex final branch. It takes place in and around the Llŷn peninsula in north Wales and its episodes unleash a range of disruptive energies. Corruption appears in many guises: sexual, economic, political and familial. Gilfaethwy's lust for Goewin combines with his brother Gwydion's ruthless cunning in a horrifying sequence of crimes: rape, theft and warmongering. But the misdemeanours do not end there. Arianrhod, sister of Gilfaethwy and Gwydion, curses her own son (Lleu Llaw Gyffes), Gronw Pebr steals Lleu's land and his wife (Blodeuwedd), and conspires with her to murder her husband. Here the moral themes are writ large, and consequences of corruption are wide-ranging. Among the devastating effects of defection from the social code are personal tragedy for Goewin, Pryderi, Lleu, Blodeuwedd and Gronw Pebr, humiliation for Gilfaethwy and Gwydion, and the terrible massacre of the people of Gwynedd and Dyfed. The magical interventions of Math and Gwydion go some way to repairing the damage, but they cannot undo the violence done to an innocent young woman, the death of a hero, nor the loss of many lives in a pointless war.[10]

At the heart of this widespread and damaging disorder is sexual incontinence. Andrew Welsh observes that Goewin, Arianrhod and Blodeuwedd are each 'involved in some kind of sexual violation' (1990: 355). Such a focus is evident from the beginning of the story: 'At that time Math son of Mathonwy could not live unless his feet were in the folds of a virgin's lap, except when the tumult of war prevented this. The virgin who was with him was Goewin from Dôl Bebin in Arvon, for she was the most beautiful girl known in those parts' (Gantz 1976: 98–9). Goewin is described in sexual terms as 'virgin' and as the most beautiful girl in the region. Just a few sentences further on, we are told of the effect she has on Gilfaethwy: 'Now Goewin was always with Math, and Gilfaethwy son of Dôn set his heart on her and loved her so that he did not know what to do; his colour and looks and shape were all wasting away, and it was not easy to recognize him' (Gantz 1976: 99). Gilfaethwy's powerful desire becomes the driving force of the first part of the story. Since the only thing which can part Goewin from Math is war, Gwydion deliberately foments conflict between Gwynedd and Dyfed in order to provide his brother with the opportunity to rape her. The effects of this dark plot spread virally through the two kingdoms, leading to a disastrous war, the shaming of Arianrhod, the betrayal of Lleu by both his mother and his wife, the theft of his territory and usurping of his power, the eventual deaths of Pryderi and Gronw Pebr, and the permanent exile of Blodeuwedd from human society. Although the story of Blodeuwedd, Lleu and Gronw Pebr forms a separate episode from the rape of Goewin, the chain of events leading to the conflict can be traced back to that act of violation.

Math's punishment of Gwydion and Gilfaethwy is peculiarly appropriate to their crime: their animal-like sexual behaviour is exposed by their being turned into animals, who are forced to mate and bear young. Both men are thus made to experience sexual violation. Their punitive mating introduces another strand to the theme of disorderly desire: incestuous coupling. While this clearly happens between Gwydion and Gilfaethwy, that may not be the only example in the fourth branch, as Andrew Welsh indicates: 'There is also a strong suggestion in the Fourth Branch that the twins, Dylan and Lleu, are the result of the brother-sister incest of Gwydion and Aranrhod. This is not explicitly spelled out in the text, however' (Welsh 1990: 356). Whatever else indicates an incestuous relationship between the pair, the fact that Gwydion raises Lleu as his son suggests that he feels some responsibility. The image of the baby being gestated in a chest at the foot of his bed (as if it were a prosthetic womb) adds to the sense of his intimate connection with Lleu; it is almost as if he becomes a surrogate mother to him.

Lleu's estrangement from his actual mother, Arianrhod, connects sexual disorder with the cultural significance of motherhood, and motherhood comes under scrutiny in the fourth branch as in the first (in the calumny against Rhiannon). Arianrhod's disgrace as an unwed mother (and possibly the mother of a child born of incest), the unnatural mothering of the offspring of the transmogrified Gwydion and Gilfaethwy, the male mothering of Lleu by Gwydion, parallel the various forms of sexual misdemeanour: rape, incest and adultery.

The re-conception of motherhood as both male and female is part of a wider concern with gender and power in the fourth branch, the relation of women to political agency being significant in each episode. The women in this branch, as in the other three, are active and authoritative as well as threatened and abused: just as Rhiannon overcomes her unjust ignominy, Branwen her imprisonment and maltreatment, both Arianrhod and Blodeuwedd seek to shape their own ends despite strong social pressures. Women are depicted neither as merely victims of male aggression nor as the chattels of powerful men. Violence is done to them, but they too can be the aggressors, and they can wield power, hold court and command respect. As recompense for her rape by his nephews, Math marries Goewin and gives her real autonomy as ruler over Gwynedd: '"I will arrange recompense for you first, and then I will seek recompense for myself. And I will take you as my wife," he said, "and give you authority over my kingdom"' (Davies 2007: 52). Arianrhod appears to hold sway in Caer Arianrhod and to have control over what happens to Lleu. Blodeuwedd assumes a kind of rule in the absence of Lleu and is then involved in a plot to kill him and steal his territory.

Shamhat, Ninsun, Ishtar and Siduri play bit parts in *Gilgamesh*; Eve, Sarai, Rebecca, and Rachel yield centre stage to the patriarchs in Genesis; Job's wife is little more than a cypher; Homer's Penelope features in a story which is manifestly her husband's. By contrast, four powerful and memorable female figures – Rhiannon, Branwen, Arianrhod and Blodeuwedd – are at the heart of the Four Branches of the *Mabinogi*, not as adjuncts to male ambition, nor as trophies for triumphant warlords; they have unbridled agency in their own and other stories. It may be, then, that these tales bear traces of a matriarchal, or at least matrilineal, culture which had long since been replaced by patriarchy. Will Parker sees in the fourth branch echoes of the ancient process which brought about the change: 'A representation of the process by which the goddess was usurped . . . constitutes the narrative deep structure of the Fourth Branch' (Parker 2010: n.p.). This, of course, is a speculative reading, but one which perhaps helps to make sense of the various distortions of motherhood which characterize the stories.

Steeped in magic and myth, the fourth branch nonetheless deals with darkly realistic relationships between sex and power, and the dire implications of moral failings in these matters. The three main female figures – Goewin, Arianrhod and Blodeuwedd – are each implicated in some form of deviance from the sexual norm, and find themselves caught up in bloody power struggles between the dominant males. But even if Will Parker is right to see the stories as bearing traces of the overthrow of the goddess, they are far from celebrating or propagating patriarchal violence. Rather, they show it to be harmful and destructive: tragic for individuals and politically disastrous. The turning of the rapacious warmongers Gwydion and Gilfaethwy into animals is perhaps the boldest and most telling metaphor in the Four Branches. In that image of a magical act of judgement, which might be thought to echo the bestial torment of King Nebuchadnezzar in the biblical book of Daniel, it is possible to trace the refraction of contemporaneous social codes through more ancient mythological formations, establishing both their antiquity and their putative universality.[11] This is an important moment in the cultural life of mythology: rather than shaping societal values by means of belief and participation – as in the ancient world – myths come to serve as endlessly re-interpretable stories onto which contemporary values can be projected and by means of which the pertinence of those values might be immeasurably broadened.

Notes

1. Rachel Bromwich points out that Guest adopted the title from W. O. Pughe's *Cambrian Register* (1795) (1996: 11).
2. Eric Hamp has suggested that the term '*mabinogi*' derives from the name Maponos – a Gallic god known as Mabon in Medieval Welsh literature. Pryderi – also known as Gwri – is the father of Maponos (1999: 106–8).
3. The quotation from the Rees brothers is from Rees (1961: 344).
4. Byron Huws argues that the enchantment of Dyfed in the third branch is evidence of 'the Normans hiding in plain sight', inasmuch as the episode can be read as the trace of Henry I's (reigned 1100–35) policy of resettling England's Flemish immigrants in west Wales, causing a mass displacement of the local population (2009: 7–23).
5. On Rhiannon as horse goddess, see Dexter (1990a).
6. *Hen* means 'old'.
7. Building on the work of Kenneth Jackson, Andrew Welsh notes that many narrative incidents in the *Four Branches* are motifs or 'basic story elements' of folktales from many international traditions (1996: 124–5).
8. On the goddess Danu and the people named after her, see Dexter (1990b).
9. At around the same time as Gantz produced his essay, Seán Ó Coileáin, drawing on the work of W. J. Gruffydd, pointed out the correspondences 'which appear with remarkable regularity' between the two main parts of the first branch (1977–8: 79–80).
10. Damian Walford Davies suggests that insistent themes of violence and proscription found throughout the Four Branches might be read as 'an articulation of an inherited and contemporary (medieval) socio-political trauma', associated with Norman incursions (personal correspondence).
11. In Dan. 4.33 the Babylonian king Nebuchadnezzar is transformed into a beast as a divine judgement on his wickedness.

Translations used in preparing this chapter

Bollard, J. K., trans. and Anthony Griffiths, photographs (2006), *The Mabinogi: Legend and Landscape of Wales*, Llandysul: Gomer.
Davies, S., trans. (2007), *The Mabinogion: A New Translation*, Oxford: Oxford University Press.
Gantz, J., trans. (1976), *The Mabinogion*, Harmondsworth: Penguin.
Guest, C., trans. and Alan Lee, illus. (2000), *The Mabinogion*, London: HarperCollins.
Parker, W. (2005), *The Four Branches of the Mabinogi*, Oregon House, CA: Bardic Press.

CHAPTER 9
MYTH TODAY

Roland Barthes

I have borrowed the title of this chapter from the work of Roland Barthes (1915–80). An essay called 'Myth Today' appeared in his 1957 work *Mythologies* (English translation 1972). Barthes makes myth synonymous with bourgeois ideology: a means of imposing middle-class, capitalist values, beliefs and dispositions upon all who come within its sphere of influence. On this account, myth is a form of meaning creation (verbal or visual) which distorts our perception of the world in the interests of the powerful, the privileged and the status quo in Western states.

For Barthes, as Elizabeth Baeten notes: 'myth in the contemporary world is absolutely conservative in its function' (1996: 104). Myths, the argument goes, 'immobilize the world'; they 'suggest and mimic a universal order' (Barthes 2000: 145). In other words, they work against any kind of social and/or political change by making cultural and historical developments appear natural. For example, there was a time when the biblical myths of Creation and Fall were read to imply that women were naturally subordinate to men because God had made sexual difference hierarchical. The myths served patriarchal interests by disguising political oppression as an aspect of the created order and as a matter of God's will. For Barthes, such uses are definitive of myth, and modern mythologies – which he identified in examples of popular culture such as wrestling, movies and food – were no less oppressive than their ancient precursors.

Barthes, then, is among those modern thinkers discussed in Chapter 1 for whom myth is to be regarded with an all-pervading suspicion precisely because it blinds us to the capitalist system's strategies of domination and control. Following Paul Ricoeur, I suggested in that chapter that this is an inadequate response to myth, not because myth is innocent of the kind of charges Barthes lays at its door but because its potential to be re-read, reinterpreted and made productive is not necessarily negated by its regressive aspects. What Brian Attebery says of fantasy fiction is true of other contemporary uses of myth too: they 'provide new contexts, and thus inevitably new meanings, for myth' (2014: 3).

Barthes' analysis is of particular interest in this regard because the flaws in his argument make plain the problems with accounts of myth which fail to look beyond their preformed suspicion. Understanding the persistence of myth in contemporary culture depends upon an ability and willingness to tackle head-on these misperceptions. Barthes appears to me to make three grave errors in his attempt to expose the political work of myth in modernity. First, each of the illustrations he uses to make his argument clear is drawn from contemporaneous culture. This both neglects the ancient roots of myth and disguises the fact that its earliest forms and functions cannot be presumed to match up with modern practices. Second, he characterizes myth as the denial of history (in the sense that it naturalizes cultural values and makes them appear eternal rather than mutable and time-bound). But history itself is a set of traditions and conventions *with a history*: it too formed at a particular moment and has changed over time, so cannot be the source of stable or undistorted meanings any more than can myth. Not only so, but its roots lie *in* myth: before we recounted our ideas about the past in historiographical records, we did so in myths. History, like science, could not have emerged from nothing, nor formed in a cultural vacuum; it grew up as a mode of post-mythological thinking about the past, necessarily shaped, at least in part, by what it sought to escape, replace or supplant. Third, Barthes seems to me to have made a poor choice in using the term 'myth' to label cultural productions which propagate bourgeois ideology. Bourgeois culture is a relatively recent phenomenon which came into existence with the rise of larger towns and cities in early modern Europe, and the emergence of a mercantile middle class. By referring to ideological distortions as *myths*, Barthes makes them seem eternal (or at least persisting from very ancient times into the present) and universal, which is precisely what he says myth does to historical developments. Identifying bourgeois ideology with myth creates the illusion that modern beliefs and values are unproblematically comparable with those of prehistoric cultures in terms of their social forms and functions. Ultimately, Barthes presumes that myth and bourgeois ideology are identical because, for him, both mean 'falsehood', 'deception' or 'delusion' and, rather than interrogating that supposition, he makes it the basis of his entire argument, paying scant attention to myth's diversity, longevity or global reach.

As misleading as Barthes' analysis is in some ways, it alerts us to the potential dangers associated with modern uses of myth. It is not difficult to see that cultural productions which draw on mythological sources today include examples which serve to 'immobilize the world'. On the other hand, the limits of Barthesian suspicion are exposed by the fact that there are modern uses of myth which do pretty much the opposite: they mobilize resistance to established beliefs and practices.

Before considering some examples of 'immobilizing' and 'progressive' uses of myth in contemporary culture, I want to look at the broader picture, taking in literary and cinematic examples, and to think about how and why myth continues to enjoy popular appeal. This is necessarily an incomplete picture, but it is, I hope, broadly indicative of the current scene.

Literary and cinematic currents

As Barthes recognized, Hollywood, in its most glamorous aspects, offers modern Western cultures its own kind of post-religious mythology. Exceptionally beautiful, wealthy and famous individuals, who inhabit a world far removed from that in which most of us live, are adored (worshipped even) by people of whom they have no knowledge. We hear of their exploits, watch their performances, treasure their images and tell stories – true and untrue – about them as if they were a species apart. On screen they appear larger than life, and the magic of cinema can show them wielding powers beyond the reach of ordinary mortals. Even if we have little interest in the stars, the fictional figures they portray sometimes take on a cultural resonance not unlike that of their ancient divine forebears. We may not believe that Luke Skywalker, Batman or Spiderman really exist, but their presence has profoundly affected our imaginative lives.

While we nurture peculiarly modern dreams, fantasies and illusions in concert with the technicians and performers of the modern film industry, ancient myth remains as popular as ever, its best-known examples, especially those of ancient Greece, continuing to colour our fictional productions, whether in print or on screen. Perhaps the most insistent recycling of mythological sources is in fantasy fiction: a subject treated in depth by Brian Attebery, in his excellent book *Stories about Stories* (2014). He notes that authors working in that genre use myths 'to construct new ways of looking at traditional stories and beliefs', their main claim to cultural significance lying in 'redefining the relationship between contemporary readers and mythic texts' (Attebery 2014: 3–4). Since Attebery covers the field of fantasy, there is little need to re-examine it here. But the use of myth in contemporary narrative productions is not confined to one genre.

In recent years, the Edinburgh-based publisher Canongate and the Bridgend-based publisher Seren have both issued book series designed to retell mythological tales. Canongate's 'The Myths' includes contributions from Margaret Atwood (*The Penelopiad*, 2005), Jeanette Winterson (*Weight: The Myth of Atlas and Herakles*, 2005), Philip Pullman (*The Good Man Jesus and the Scoundrel Christ*, 2010) and A. S. Byatt (*Ragnorok*, 2018). For 'New Stories from the Mabinogion' Seren commissioned work by Gwyneth Lewis (*The Meat Tree*, 2010), Owen Sheers (*White Ravens*, 2010) and Cynan Jones (*Bird, Blood, Snow*, 2012), among others. We might add to these numerous examples of independently generated fictions such as Rick Riordan's Percy Jackson books, Suzanne Collins *Hunger Games* series, Neil Gaiman's *American Gods*, novels by Madeline Miller, Colm Tóibín, Pat Barker, Natalie Haynes, Kamila Shamsie, Daisy Johnson, Zoe Gilbert, Jennifer Saint and Claire North, to name but a few.

A significant majority of these works is based on Greek mythology, which has enjoyed something of a literary heyday since the turn of the millennium. Canongate's series was designed to represent a wide cultural range but classical mythology accounts for about one-third of the titles published so far. There are, of course, many contemporary writers who look to other ancient traditions: Joan London's *Gilgamesh* (2001), for example, uses the epic as a counterpoint to her modern-day story of escape, wanderlust and the quest for a home; Betsy Tobin's *Ice Land* (2008) recasts the Norse myth of the goddess Freya's necklace, Brisingamen, to tell a story of women finding love against the odds in a violent world on the brink of disaster; bestselling author Joanne Harris has produced three novels based on Norse mythology: *Runemarks* (2007), *Runelight* (2011) and *The Gospel of Loki* (2014).

Film production is no less fascinated by mythology. Since 2000 there have been many cinematic representations of, and variations on, the ancient stories, such as

Troy (2004), *Clash of the Titans* (2010), *Thor* (2011), *Immortals* (2011), *Noah* (2014), *Hercules* (2014) and *Gods of Egypt* (2016). As well as imaginative recreations of the ancient world, there are films which draw on mythological patterns, themes and/or narrative structures but are set in other historical contexts: *O Brother, Where Art Thou?* (2001), *Pan's Labyrinth* (2006), *The Secret of Kells* (2009), *Django Unchained* (2012), *Oldboy* (2013). In 2021, *Eternals*, based on figures from Marvel Comics, plundered a range of mythologies to offer cinema goers a fictional version of ancient astronaut theory, which interprets gods as misunderstood visitors from other planets. The same year saw the release of *Dune* – a remake of the 1984 adaptation of Frank Herbert's celebrated sci-fi novel. The story features a family called the Atreides – the name given in Greek mythology to the descendants of Atreus: Agamemnon and Menelaus – key figures in Homer's *Iliad*.

Offering exotic settings, dramatic conflicts, ready-made plots, heroic action and archetypal roles needing little by way of explanation or contextualization, the appeal of myth for filmmakers is not difficult to understand. Since, as Sylvie Magerstädt observes, the advent of digital technologies means that the film industry is better equipped than ever to produce convincing renditions of imaginary, magical and mythical worlds, the attraction of the ancient stories (especially the Greek ones) with their fantastical trappings has come to seem irresistible (2015: xiii). Perhaps, then, myth does no more nor less than provide a set of ready-made and highly versatile resources which lend themselves to remoulding, while, at times, creating the impression of layered, allusive or deep-rooted work.

Hollywood story consultant Christopher Vogler, drawing on Carl Jung and Joseph Campbell, makes the case for widespread dependence of films on narrative structures derived from mythology, especially the hero's journey motif. He writes: 'Stories built on the model of the Hero's Journey have an appeal that can be felt by everyone, because they well up from a universal source in the shared unconscious and reflect universal concerns' (Vogler 2007: 5). While such claims of universality seem to me highly problematical, Vogler's analysis of selected movies certainly shows the persistence and effectiveness of Campbell's pattern. But that may be no more than necessity: it has been argued that there are not many narrative possibilities with which to work. Myth's seemingly inexhaustible character as a source, and its undiminishing presence in our fictions, suggests that writers such as Christopher Booker may be right to claim that the number of possible stories is actually very limited; by virtue of their sheer age myths necessarily got there first, and so, perhaps, all writers can ever do is retell and remake them.[1]

Margaret Atwood has described myth as being something like a subterranean watercourse which springs up willy-nilly in creative productions:

> Myths are stories that are central to their cultures and that are taken seriously enough that people organize their ritual and emotional lives around them, and can even start wars over them. Such stories go underground, as it were, when the core statements about truth and reality repeated in the stories cease to be entirely,

> factually believed. But they then emerge in other guises, such as Art, or political ideologies.
>
> *(Atwood 2011: 41)*

Myth seems here to be a deep aquifer of narrative and ideological possibilities, leeching into the arteries of culture, for good or ill. But it re-emerges into a changed world from which its founding beliefs and values have been rinsed, potentially rendering its stories obsolete, atavistic or misleading.

Such a perception underlies the suspicion, hostility even, with which modern writers have occasionally regarded the use of myth in contemporary art. The poet Philip Larkin, for example, referred disparagingly to 'a common myth kitty' from which writers often withdraw images, motifs or patterns (Larkin 1983: 79). Poems, he insisted, should not recycle the cultural detritus of prevenient texts or discursive formations; they should shape their own universe afresh. Yet, despite this disavowal of the value of myth as a cache of versatile images, narratives, relationships or symbols, Larkin was, as Laurence Coupe has shown, actually rather fond of smuggling into his poems what might be called mythic resonances – whether the rites of fertility in 'The Whitsun Weddings', or the transcendence of cyclical re-creation in 'High Windows' (2009: 11–12). It is more difficult to dispense with myth than Larkin seems to have realized, not only because it formed the foundations of Western culture but also because its narrative archetypes, symbols, patterns and themes are those which necessarily shape all our stories.

So myth appears in many guises in today's cultural artefacts, leading some literary critics to devise categories by means of which to make sense of the diversity. Most famously, Northrop Frye claimed that in literature there are three organizations of myths and archetypal symbols: 'undisplaced myth' in which the divine, the magical or the supernatural is present; 'romantic' sources which employ mythical patterns in a world more closely associated with human than with divine experience; 'realism' which works with the same archetypical forms and patterns as myth but recasts them in line with everyday experience (1957: 139–40). Frye's analysis is historical, relating each mode of myth-appropriation to a specific period, from ancient to modern. Highly impressive as it is, in both its critical incisiveness and its command of literary history, his analysis is of limited use in describing contemporary practice. On his account, all uses of mythology in literature of the present day should be considered ironic since its prescientific terms are strictly meaninglessness for modern people. This is manifestly not the case, and so Frye's historical approach misfires when confronted with the sheer diversity of uses to which myth continues to be put.

With this failure in view, Mark Workman (1981) has redescribed Frye's categories as technical rather than temporal, replacing period-based categories with rhetorical labels: metonymic, metaphorical and metamorphic. In metonymic uses, the world of myth exists in parallel with that of everyday experience, much as, for example, C. S. Lewis' Narnia can be entered and left behind by normal humans without any change to their form or appearance. Metaphorical uses of myth forge comparisons between events and situations experienced by ordinary people, and those undergone by figures in mythology.

Such a pattern can be observed in Joan London's *Gilgamesh*: its key characters repeat in a twentieth-century setting the ancient hero's quest, undertaking a long and perilous journey in search of love and redemption. But modern literature is as likely to change, challenge or distort its mythological forebears as it is to echo or repeat them; this way of relating to myth, Workman dubs 'metamorphic'. Phillip Pullman's recasting of Eve and Adam as Lyra and Will in *His Dark Materials* might be understood along these lines: it is designed to challenge Christian beliefs regarding loss of innocence and the church's model of divine authority.

Why does myth persist?

Workman's taxonomy is useful inasmuch as it helps us to understand that the presence of myth in modern and contemporary culture takes more than one form and serves more than one purpose. It might offer us imaginative insights into the distant past, serve to refract our own experience through that of our ancient forebears, or reveal present-day practices, attitudes or values to be dangerously atavistic. Evidently, these divergent uses are not necessarily complementary: they are, potentially, at odds with each other, rendering ancient stories either instructive or regressive. This suggests that there is no single reason why myths continue to attract creative minds and entertainment seekers alike.

For some, myths appeal to our sense of shared humanity, revealing what connects us with each other, not only in the present but across time. Jean Shinoda Bolen writes of what she considers the 'ring of truth' in myths, and draws attention to their 'vaguely familiar' symbolism. She compares them with dreams which help us to process and so to understand our experience (Bolen 1985: 6). Kath Filmer-Davies takes a similar stance, suggesting that the 'cultural effects of the widespread physical displacement of populations across the world' produces a sense of exile which can be ameliorated, to some extent, by fictions rooted in mythology. They allow the consumer to tap into traditions generative of shared identity and belonging (Filmer-Davies 1996: xiii). Sylvie Magerstädt argues that myth, especially as recreated in films, has a kind of redemptive power: it offers 'unifying illusions' which help to overcome the fragmentation and alienation of postmodern societies, connecting us with each other by means of 'universal stories' (2015: xii, 28, 116–17).

But there may be considerable dangers in arguing for the unifying or connective power of myth: what provides a means of establishing community for some might well impose exile, dispossession, displacement or worse on others. It should not be ignored that community is always necessarily predicated as much on exclusion as it is on inclusion. Born of suspicion and a perceived need to repulse the invader, it is a concept whose origins lie in defence rather than welcome.[2] Myths have often been used to draw definitive boundaries between 'us' and 'them', between 'insiders' and 'outsiders', whether in terms of race, gender, language or religion, instituting privilege and creating disadvantage. If there are reasons to value myth and to invoke its power to aid identity formation, reasons to regard it with suspicion are no less pressing.

Similarly, while myth might be attractive as a means of connecting with a kind of pre-industrial, prescientific world, whose inhabitants were, notionally at least, less alienated from nature and from each other than we are today, it is also a world where violence can be unbridled and the weak have no power to resist the strong. Roger D. Abrahams wrote of the appeal for creative artists of 'the life of the folk, the peasant, an image of life which is familiar and comfortable, static and uncomplicated, and which therefore represents an attractive alternative to modernity and its attendant complexity' (1972: 85). Mark Workman's response is to reveal the flip side of such an apparently naïve view: 'It is fair to say that the literary attractiveness of mythology is due to its enduring depiction of significant and sometimes very uncomfortable relationships, some admittedly between man and his environment, but others of at least equal importance between man and his fellow men, and between man and his deities' (Workman 1981: 36). Myth may well take us to times, places and circumstances which hold a certain appeal for people confronting modern versions of timeless horror such as war, natural disaster, persecution, oppression or exile. It is surely no less attractive to those living comparatively settled and peaceful lives, but who are plagued with the uncertainties visited on us by imminent environmental collapse, economic crisis and global pandemics. It is not hard to understand why some, confronted by terrors which have no evident or recognizable horizon, might want to escape to a world in which divine presences and magical or miraculous interventions ensure the right outcomes for deserving heroes. Nor is it surprising that others might yearn for an age of omen, prophecy, oracle or even apocalyptic closure.

The kind of certainties available to Gilgamesh, Abraham, Job and Odysseus and the magical possibilities open to Math and Gwydion can offer imaginative solace, and may even prompt us to quest for just resolutions of our own, but we can neither take the meanings of such stories for granted nor presume that we fully understand their origins, their character or their consequences. In any act of appropriation, it would be unjust to overlook the outsiders, victims and silenced voices on the margins of many myths: ordinary people, forests, servants, slaves, sacrificed lambs, slaughtered children, drowned worlds, sacked cities, doomed companions, hanged women, and so on. When we recreate, reimagine, echo or modernize these stories, it is important to ask what new margins we draw, and who we leave on the altar, in the wilderness, under the rubble, below the flood or in the grave. That is not to say we should abandon myths; it is merely to argue that we should use them cautiously and with due regard to the risks.

Novels

It is precisely because myth, inherited from pre-democratic times, always brings with it a degree of moral and political jeopardy that we need to pay heed to some aspects of Barthes' treatment of the subject. I want to do so by distinguishing between broadly progressive and 'immobilizing' uses of myth. By 'progressive', I mean reinterpretations of ancient stories which refuse to leave their prejudicial aspects intact, or which are not content to allow the presumptive heroism of figures who act unjustly to go unchallenged.

Madeline Miller's *Circe* (2018) for example, gives a distinctive and memorable voice to the minor goddess branded a witch by patriarchal tradition, revealing not only the endemic maltreatment of women in classical culture but also their ongoing struggle to find autonomy and enduring peace in a male-dominated world. Her heroine makes a virtue of necessity, turning the island of her exile into a magical homeland over which she enjoys a kind of supernatural control, and which she protects from the malign power of the gods.

But it is legitimate to ask why contemporary writers like Miller, whose fiction works to expose misogyny and to create powerful, self-fashioning female characters, turns to myth as a source. Might she not have told a wholly contemporary tale to the same effect? And would it not have been politically more astute to do so? After all, as well as conducting a critique of the values encoded in the Greek myths, the novel reminds us of those very values, returns them to our notice, brings them into today's world rather than consigning them to the reject pile of history. Once again: myth carries risks. Conceivably, Miller might have set her fiction in present-day Boston and eschewed the presence of gods and monsters, but, even had the characterization and narrative arc been similar, its effect could not have been identical since it would lack both the temporal depth and social implications of a work steeped in an ancient and profoundly influential cultural formation. By reimagining and defamiliarizing a set of well-known figures and episodes, the novel simultaneously exposes the gender ideology of the originals and suggests their continuity with modern-day forms of marginalization and victimization. Myth is made, in this case, to mobilize rather than to constrain critical responses. In this, it is similar to Margaret Atwood's *Penelopiad* which gives a modern, independent voice to a Homeric woman denied autonomy in the myth.

In another feminist re-reading of Greek myth, Pat Barker's *The Silence of the Girls* (2019) explores the dark side of male heroism through the figure of Briseis. Once a queen, Briseis is given to Achilles as a sex slave following the sacking of her city, Lyrnessus. The novel retells Homer's *Iliad* confronting its glorification of male violence with the consequences of war for women, most of whom are deprived of voice and agency by the epic and by the storytelling tradition growing from it. The lights of imagination and critical thinking are thus shed on a world left dark by the Homeric text. Barker shows us the Trojan War from the point of view of its most abject victims: raped, enslaved and brutalized women whose menfolk and children have been murdered in front of their eyes. Traumatized and objectified, Briseis gives us a glimpse of the true cost of war, not only in blood but also in prolonged and irremediable suffering. The acclaimed heroes of the Western canon are here shown to be uninhibited killers, rapists, slave-owners and gangsters. Barker's choice of the *Iliad* as source text is neither random nor whimsical: it re-examines a work which stands at the fountainhead of Western literary and storytelling traditions, influencing much of its content and shaping many of its conventions. Her novel, which exemplifies Workman's metamorphic mode, does a very important job in exposing the poisonous roots of much of our fiction, poetry and drama.

Circe and *The Silence of the Girls* share a broad methodology with a number of recent novels: retelling ancient stories from unfamiliar perspectives in order to mount a critique of their ideological heritage. In line with Northrop Frye's analysis, we might call such an approach to myth *ironic*, inasmuch as it sets out to disrupt and destabilize the originary texts. In many cases, it is the ironic treatment of myth which makes it progressive rather than immobilizing. And yet, novels such as Barker's and Miller's are neither careless with nor dismissive of their source texts. Both authors preserve elements of the magical and miraculous, and each allows a role for the gods. They take into themselves other important aspects of those sources, too, such as setting, character and numerous plot points, finding in them something to be rescued, to be informed by, if in need of correction or updating. While Barker takes a hatchet to the heroic tradition, exposing the corruption of the Homeric ideal, Miller mounts an iconoclastic assault on the gods, depicting them as cruel, spiteful, vain and often stupid. And yet, despite the charges against them, the underlying stories remain of sufficient interest to be made contemporary in however highly emended a form. This, of course, is the approach advocated by Paul Ricoeur: that we be attentive as well as critical in our reading of myth.

Another variant of the creative criticism of ancient stories and the worldviews they encode can be found in Colm Tóibín's *House of Names* (2018). Tóibín treats myth in a way which echoes (albeit faintly) the demythologizing drive of nineteenth-century biblical criticism.[3] That is to say: the story includes very little which does not have a natural cause, or an explanation rooted in human psychology. The gods appear on the periphery of events as the remnants of a belief system on the verge of collapse: more than one character observes that divinity has had its day. Much praised for a pared-down style (which approximates oral storytelling), psychological depth and page-turning energy, the novel retells the story of Orestes, mentioned in the *Odyssey* and explored in plays by classical tragedians Aeschylus, Euripides and Sophocles. The perspectives of Clytemnestra and Electra are rendered in the first person, while Orestes' experience, which takes up most of the novel, is recounted in the third person. The effect of this strategy is to rebalance the gender bias of ancient attitudes, at least to some extent, so that once-demonized female figures are allowed to shape their own versions of the familiar tale. Orestes still dominates and emerges as a slightly more sympathetic figure than either his mother or his sister, both of whom appear ruthless and controlling. But they are depicted as women profoundly damaged by a brutal, male-dominated culture of self-preservation and vengeance, and each is caught up, against their will, in a cycle of bloody retaliation.

The novel's under-stated, but insistent, homoeroticism contributes to the depiction of Orestes as a character with more sensitivity and less bloodlust than those around him. His subtly depicted relationship with Leander (a character created by Tóibín, but probably based on Pylades) becomes the focus of Orestes' story, so that most of his actions are driven by his need for love and belonging more than they are by the desire for revenge which motivates the mythical figure.[4] He becomes, in Tóibín's hands, a victim of circumstance, traumatized, manipulated and teetering on the edge of an emotional abyss.

Such a focus on the inner life – the psychology, emotions and motivations of characters – relates many modern uses of mythology to Freudian interpretation: conflicts between key figures reflect confrontations between conscious and unconscious regions of the psyche. But instead of reducing myths to allegories of the divided self, the ancient figures are recast as rounded characters for whom the pitiless violence of the world has the kind of consequences we now associate with dehumanizing treatment and traumatic experience.

While most of the myth-based novels appearing in recent years have, like Freudian theory, been based on Greek sources, I want to draw attention to two notable exceptions, each of which combines modern scepticism with careful attention to what the ancient stories have to offer modern readers. Both grant us access to the interior worlds of their key characters, but expose those hidden dynamics in relation to alternative (non-classical) stories.

Joan London's *Gilgamesh* takes the reader on a journey across the globe, from Australia to Armenia and back, on the eve of the Second World War, the narrative echoing aspects of the ancient epic after which it is named. Following the death of their father, Edith and her sister Frances are raised in abject poverty by a mother whose mind is destroyed by grief and despair. They endure a semi-civilized, hand-to-mouth existence knowing little of the modern world. Edith's job at a local hotel, itself something of an unlikely outpost in the bush of Western Australia, offers her glimpses of a more sophisticated life, encouraging her to feel that mere subsistence cannot, ultimately, be her lot. Leopold (a cousin) and his friend Aram come to visit, bringing with them a taste of freedom, romance and exotic places, their tales shaping Edith's dreams of escape. Fresh from an archaeological expedition in the Near East, they tell her, too, of *Gilgamesh*: the story of a man who set out to find everlasting life.

Aram – an Armenian – unknowingly leaves Edith pregnant and, at the age of just seventeen or eighteen, she sets off in search of him. Fleeing her home with her young son (Jim) in her arms, it seems obvious that her quest for love, adventure and happiness aligns her with the ancient hero, but her origins in the semi-wild of a run-down patch of farmland, and her journey to London (initially), are more redolent of Enkidu's progress from animal to human. Much as the wild man's transformation begins with a sexual encounter, Edith's too is sparked by her time with Aram. The parallel becomes even more marked when, on finding herself in her mother's former home in London, she spends long periods bathing, and, in a bid to shed her past, cuts off her long hair, echoing the final stages of Enkidu's civilizing process. But the novel never allows the reader to settle for any neat parallels between the lives of its central characters and the myth. Each of them bears their own resemblance to either Gilgamesh or Enkidu, or even both at once, but none is like either of them in every respect. Furthermore, while the story is one of restlessness and searching, it rejects the idea of heroic quest and of homecoming as a permanent resolution. When he reaches adolescence, Jim sneers at what he considers myths for old men. He knows that his world is not that of the ancient heroes, not only because he comes of age in the aftermath of the Second World War, but also because he is brought up by a single woman and in poverty. He inherits his mother's sense of alienation and her wanderlust, but is unburdened by any sense of purpose or direction which might align him with Gilgamesh or any heroic tradition.

Edith's story exposes both the class-bias and gendering of myth. Penury and motherhood shape her decisions and drive her actions; necessity rather than a desire for power or glory underlie her bravery. She notes that myths are not about women: women are left to look after the children while the men undertake their self-validating quests. She might, in fact, be as close to the temple prostitute (Shamhat) who seduces Enkidu, or to Gilgamesh's mother (Ninsun) as she is to either of the male heroes, only that she refuses the prescribed subordinate roles. She embodies resistance to the fates outlined in the myth, courageously taking her small child with her on her epic journey. What she shares with Gilgamesh is the ultimate failure to realize her ambitions, and, like him, she eventually returns to her first home, seeing it anew. But while Gilgamesh comes to view his city and its people as his only hope of leaving a lasting legacy, for Edith it is her son, Jim, who inherits her restless spirit and carries her memory into the future. In taking inspiration from and simultaneously critiquing *Gilgamesh*, Joan London offers the reader a modern revision of myth with motherhood at its heart.

Perhaps the most unusual fictional treatment of myth to appear in recent years is another which focusses on a non-classical tradition. Lloyd Jones' *Mr Cassini* (2006) is a colourful collage of images and themes from stories in the *Mabinogion*. At its simplest, the strange, dream-infused plot can be read as a psychologically freighted retelling of the tale of Culhwch and Olwen: a quest narrative in which a giant boar is pursued across Wales as part of the hero's fulfilment of terms set by the father of his would-be bride. Jones' hero is not in pursuit of a bride; rather, he is seeking to recover a traumatic childhood which has left him with partial amnesia, a physical deformity and a debilitating form of depression. The quest is played out as a week-long recollection of dreams and fantasies in which a van driver called Duxie gathers a band of comrades, much as Culhwch does in the ancient tale, for a showdown with the villain on a mountaintop at the centre of Wales. Jones' Olwen is a beautiful young woman whom Duxie meets in a local café; she becomes both a sympathetic listener and the subject of his private desires.

Drawing on key images and motifs from Celtic mythology, such as wells, quests, magic, colour symbolism, the Otherworld, physical transmogrification and the land under a curse, the novel interweaves the inner life of its protagonist with aspects of Welsh history in a hallucinatory montage of the individual and the cultural. The convolutions of the novel are too many and too complicated to rehearse here: its blend of genres (gothic, crime, comic, magic realist), its rich weave of allusions, embedded stories and folklore and its eventual shift from oneiric to realistic make it all but impossible to summarize. I will, however, attempt to outline briefly what it does with its mythological sources.

The story of Culhwch and Olwen is mentioned specifically in the text, furnishing the name of its central female character (Jones 2006: 97). The name Olwen means 'white trail'. It is no less important that the name Culhwch means 'pig-run'. In *Mr Cassini*, the image of the white trail emerges mainly in the form of the protagonist's obsession with snow obliterating the features of a landscape and freezing the earth, while creating something visually beautiful. Duxie's childhood has disappeared under a combination of fear and emotional coldness, while Olwen's presence suggests the possibility of aesthetic and sensual pleasure, close at hand yet always unreachable. She thus comes both to represent an unattainable beauty and to embody Duxie's quest to remember and overcome his past. At one point she disappears, and pursuit of what is buried within himself becomes indistinguishable from his search for her. In both roles, she echoes the Olwen of the ancient tale. But at the heart of that old story is the pursuit of a giant boar, from which the hero's name (Culhwch) derives. Picking up on that pursuit, and on elements of the Four Branches, Jones uses pig imagery (among other things) to suggest that Duxie is as much a symbol of his country as he is a damaged individual.

The most obvious sense in which Duxie represents Wales is that he (misleadingly) characterizes himself as a former captain of the national football team: he thinks he has 'represented his country' on the pitch. On one occasion, he refers to his body as 'a small country' (Jones 2006: 61), and the identification is enhanced by the description of his journeys across the land and of specific locations within it, the assembling of a group of figures from Welsh history and legend to hunt Mr Cassini and multiple allusions to the nation's cultural ur-text, the *Mabinogion*.

The insistent pig imagery, bizarrely, helps to focus that identification, not least because, in the fourth branch of the *Mabinogi*, pigs are the cause of a devastating war between Gwynedd and Dyfed, the national epic ending with the bleak aftermath of that conflict. The vampiric Mr Cassini who plagues Duxie's dreams – an avatar of his abusive father – is associated with pigs in more than one way. He owns a pig called 'Golly', the name suggesting surprise, subsuming the name 'Olly' (which is how Duxie refers to Olwen), and punning on the Welsh *gollu* ('to lose'). The loss of Olly thus merges in the protagonist's troubled mind with the presence of the figure who has taken everything from him. Informed that the front door of Mr Cassini's house bears a knocker in the shape of a pig's head, the reader may well recall that Wales is often thought of as forming precisely that shape on the map (Jones 2006: 61). In this sense, Mr Cassini, like his son Duxie, represents both Wales – 'land of my fathers' as the national anthem calls it – and the forces which have combined to leave it stunted, deprived and with no obvious path to redemption.

The only indication that Duxie can imagine surviving and moving beyond his intermittent psychosis comes with suggestions of his finding the Celtic Otherworld (*Annwfn*). At times this takes the form of seeking out wells and bodies of water – characterized as portals in the ancient stories – and at times an obsession with islands, all of which evoke King Arthur's final resting place on Avalon. As discussed in Chapter 7, red and white are traditionally indicative of the presence of the supernatural in Celtic stories, and so the insistent association of Mr Cassini with the colour red, and the constant reminders of snowy whiteness combine to make the Otherworld an ever-present background to the narrative. But, of course, these phenomena are effects of Duxie's retreat from reality, his inability to adjust to the world outside his head, and so the mythological elements are, ultimately, the products of a disturbed imagination: the Otherworld is all in the (broken) mind.

By refracting a story of contemporary Wales through its most ancient myths and legends, Jones creates an image of his country as damaged and deformed; its real past all but forgotten while its present remains in the icy grip of a delusory sense of national identity. Taking the pattern of an ancient quest narrative, and applying it to modern lives, the novel's use of myth is akin to London's *Gilgamesh*, but is also strikingly different in its layered, allusive and linguistically playful evocation and disruption of its sources. Its closest English-language comparator, to my mind, is James Joyce's *Ulysses*.

Films

Cinema is typically less discriminating in the way it treats myth, partly because novels can deal with their subjects in greater detail and more depth. Quentin Tarantino's *Django Unchained* (2012), for example, explicitly derives its narrative structure from the Nordic/Germanic myth of Siegfried and Brunhilde. There are variant forms of the story, Tarantino taking his version from the final act of Richard Wagner's opera *Siegfried* (1857), in which the hero rides through a wall of flame to rescue the heroine. *Django Unchained* sets the action in the American south, recasting the tale as a version of the Western. Its hero is a freed slave looking for his stolen wife and for vengeance on those who have mistreated her.

The film is controversial for its continual use of racially provocative and demeaning language, its unrealistic depiction of slavery in the United States and its extreme and gratuitous violence. Replacing the white heroes of the Western genre with Black central figures, it is damning of the institutions and practices of slavery, graphically depicting the injustice and cruelty of the trade. While it uses its story for broadly progressive ends, it accepts and promotes (or, at least, does nothing to question or challenge) the bloodlust of Norse mythology, drawing the viewer into a desire for vengeance, as if the abusive and murderous actions of the hero were justified by the vicious behaviour of the film's villains. There is little subtlety or ambiguity about the world the film creates, and the only solution it offers to social ills is eye-for-eye repayment of wrongs. It is not unusual among Hollywood films in treating vengeance as a social good, or, at least, as a necessary corrective to failed institutions of state, but it combines that dangerous and destructive value with indefensible gender politics.[5] There is no woman in a significant role: the main female character ('Broomhilda') has few lines, is depicted as devoid of agency and is utterly dependent upon her male rescuer.

Although it belongs to a very different cinematic genre, the gender politics of *Thor* (2011) are not dissimilar. The product of an all-male writing team, its female characters are made to rely on the strength and courage of the male hero. Even the female lead, who is a scientist, has a senior male academic overseeing her research.

Using myth in a more light-hearted, escapist vein than Tarantino's film, *Thor* freely reworks Norse mythology in a tale of familial conflict and redemption. Following the banishment of Thor from Asgard, the (mostly male) gods play out a power struggle in a small, contemporary, American town, wreaking havoc and, in the case of the hero, falling in love with a mortal woman. Staple Hollywood values of physical beauty, male strength, explosive spectacle and the division of the cast into good guys and villains dictate the shape of the narrative. Its moral focus is on the hero's achievement of a degree of self-knowledge and humility following his rash and ill-judged invasion of Jotunheim (the world of giants).

Despite its depiction of the attack on neighbouring territory as an act of irresponsible warmongering, the inhabitants of the violated world are never anything but villainous monsters. Even though the film's arch villain, Loki, is an inhabitant of Asgard and at home among the gods, his treachery is closely associated with the fact of his being fathered by a Jotun. Red-eyed, blue-skinned, scarred and highly aggressive, Jotuns are the antithesis of the movie-star inhabitants of Asgard. The latter, of course, come to be identified with Americans in the earthbound finale, as they fight to protect the mortal realm on US territory. The conflict is, as ever, resolved by extreme violence and destruction, at the heart of which is the self-sacrificial action of Thor himself.

This is straightforward comic-book storytelling of the kind one might expect from Marvel Studios, and, as such, it turns the ancient tales into an evanescent fantasy. Its use of mythology asks the audience to suspend disbelief, encouraging us to imagine gods not only existing but also interacting with the human world. The willingness of a scientist to accept the appearance of a god in twenty-first-century America is explained by means of Arthur C. Clarke's famous dictum that 'any sufficiently advanced technology is indistinguishable from magic'. Ancient astronaut theory thus underpins the Hollywood hokum: what our ancestors saw as divine was, the theory goes, the product of highly advanced civilizations that interacted with our world in prehistoric times.

In *Thor,* those advanced beings return to our world, and Thor's hammer (Mjolnir) serves as a quasi-technological instrument. The film hedges it around with moral significance: Odin (Thor's father and chief of the gods) makes the hammer's power dependent upon the worthiness of its possessor. The hero loses Mjolnir when Odin casts him to Earth, and only regains it when he has sacrificed himself to save mortal lives. To invest a weapon with this kind of moral agency is a gesture belonging firmly in ancient myth, encoding as it does an ideology of justified, or even sacred, violence. Whatever one makes of the identification of godlike power with misunderstood technology, Marvel's *Thor* represents divine, or technologically advanced, beings as behaving in a way which replicates some of the most regressive attitudes of modern people: the demonizing of perceived enemies, the relegation of women to little more than passive observers of male action, and the fetishization of murderous technologies.

But cinematic uses of myth can be more subtle. The Coen brothers' *O Brother, Where Art Thou?* (2000) uses humour to distance itself from its ancient precursor. Loosely based on the *Odyssey*, it transplants the action to 1930s America. The story of three convicts on the run from a chain gang is largely played for laughs, episodes from Homer's epic being translated into faintly ridiculous set pieces and plot points. In this version, the Sirens are seductresses who drug the trio, and turn in one of them for the bounty; the Cyclops is a one-eyed Bible salesman turned mugger; the scene in which Odysseus visits the underworld, becomes a gathering of the Ku Klux Klan. The central character (named Ulysses – the Roman version of Odysseus), like his classical forebear, is trying to reach home to save his marriage, although he convinces his companions to come along by spinning them a yarn of buried loot.

There are many other incidental nods to the *Odyssey*, such as a blind man who prophesies the outcome of the story, the pursuit of the hero by a determined lawman (echoing Poseidon's role in Homer), the illegitimate killing of cows, a man apparently turned into an animal (a toad, in this case), Ulysses appearing in his hometown in disguise, and his wife being named Penny. But what this all adds up to is less than clear, as the film's very mixed reviews suggest. I see in it a self-satirizing attempt to mobilize classical models in the service of a modern American mythology. It replaces ancient figures with a series of American archetypes such as the tommy gun wielding bank robber on a wild larcenous spree, the musician selling his soul to the devil at a crossroads, the Klan gathering beneath burning crosses, the dishonest Bible salesman, the complacent, fat-cat politician on the campaign trail and the clever outsider outwitting authority. And, of course, it is a road movie: the modern version of an odyssey, and metaphor for the American Dream. But the humour undercuts any sense of the heroic or sublime, so that the mismatch between classical mythology and modern America is as important as any putative parallels.

The film's self-mocking tone is underlined by the role of religion/divine intervention in the plot. Ulysses' two companions are 'saved' when they encounter a religious group staging a river baptism, prompting a discussion in which the central character rejects any idea of faith. The debate is reprised at the end of the film, when, on the verge of being lynched, Ulysses prays for rescue. A sudden flood carries off the lawmen, and the three comrades, afloat on an empty coffin, re-open the question. Despite the apparent 'miracle' Ulysses remains sceptical. At which point he sees a cow on the roof of a mostly submerged building, recalling the blind man's prophecy delivered early in the film, and proving its accuracy. Divine intervention thus becomes an unanswered question, but the circumstances in which it arises are preposterous. The role of the gods in the *Odyssey* is replaced with all the ambiguity of contemporary America's relationship with Christianity.

The fruitful, if uneasy, coming together of Christian and pagan worlds which shapes *O Brother* characterizes *The Secret of Kells* (2009), too. The latter interweaves Celtic myth with Christian history to reflect the medieval period during which the celebrated *Book of Kells* was produced. The beautiful animation subtly celebrates the achievement of ancient manuscript illuminators, while mythological elements counterbalance the patriarchal monastic setting. A female fairy (Aisling) not only assists the hero (Brendan) in his quest to recover a crystal lens from the demonic Crom Cruach but she also acts as his guide to the world beyond the monastery walls and saves his life on more than one occasion.

Such attempts to offset the gender deficit inherent in mythological tales are rare in films (*O Brother, Where Art Thou?* is relentlessly male-centred) though gestures are sometimes made in that direction. *Hercules* includes an Amazon (Atalanta) in the hero's warband; *Clash of the Titans* has the nymph Io assist Perseus in crucial ways; *Noah* depicts the hero's wife as a counterbalance to his irrational behaviour. Yet these remain undeniably patriarchal stories, firmly focussed on the male heroes to whom the female characters are adjuncts.

In the film named after him, Noah is the only figure given any meaningful agency or psychological depth. Yet, despite that imbalance, and all the weaknesses in its dialogue, characterization and storyline, it does make some attempt to question the morality of the genocidal flood, even if its conclusions are less than clear. The eponymous hero is depicted as a zealot whose moral compass goes haywire in the face of the divinely engineered catastrophe, to such an extent that he comes close to murdering his own grandchildren. His journey towards a more merciful attitude reflects, in some degree, the narrative arc of the biblical story as it moves from judgement to renewal. In a familiar interpretative gesture, the myth is turned into an environmental parable, a silent and absent god coming to stand (perhaps) for the forces of nature meting out retribution for human mistreatment of the planet. But the plot (which supplements the biblical narrative with original elements and material from the *Book of Enoch*) ultimately muddies the ethical waters, engendering doubt as to whether we are meant to understand the killing of most humans as an act of 'justice', or the tragically inevitable outcome of their greed, stupidity and selfishness.

Values

What most of the contemporary novels and films based on mythology have in common is a valuing of the human over the divine. Where the gods are present, they tend to be depicted as vicious in some degree. Frequently selfish, petulant, cruel and reactionary, their behaviour is typically inimical to human interests. Their role often seems to be to contrast (and so to emphasize) traditional human virtues such as love, compassion, courage, humility, loyalty, self-sacrifice and endurance in the face of adversity. *Clash of the Titans* has Perseus elect to live as a human, despite his semi-divine nature, because the gods have shown selfish indifference to the suffering of their subjects. *Gods of Egypt* has a human hero (Bek) who exposes the extent to which Horus and his fellow gods pursue their own interests and disregard the welfare of their mortal charges. Similarly, Madeline Miller's Circe comes to despise the Olympians for their spite and malignity.

Such a disposition towards divinity is broadly in line with the humanism which gradually came to dominate Western cultures from the early modern period on. Reviving myths in the context of scientific, post-Christian modernity necessarily creates a tension between ancient worldviews and current ideas. One response is to reverse the ancient moral hierarchy, making humans more principled than their divine overlords. This not only distances the myths from their origins but also reinforces the most generic and least contentious values deemed fundamental to contemporary Western civilization.

Another revisionary strategy involves playing down (or even dispensing with) divine presences and actions. *Hercules* undercuts the supernaturalism of the stories on which it is based in a series of demythologizing gestures. The hero is leader of a band of mercenaries, one of whom (Iolaus) is a storyteller. His job is to enhance the band's reputation by creating myths such as branding Hercules a son of Zeus and the subject of Hera's ire. Effective propaganda, the richly embroidered tales exaggerate the accomplishments of the group and recast them as the work of a single demigod. In this version of antiquity, much-feared centaurs turn out to be particularly adept mounted warriors, demons nothing more than fierce fighters with elaborately painted bodies, and the three-headed dog, Cerberus, a trio of wolves kept as attack animals by the villainous King Eurystheus. While the light-hearted and spectacle-making treatment of myth in *Hercules* is a long way from Colm Tóibín's reworking of the story of Orestes, they share the modern view of divinity and the supernatural as belonging to a bygone age. Nothing better typifies the uses of myth today.

Notes

1. Christopher Booker has argued at great length that there are just seven basic plots, which he labels: 'Overcoming the Monster', 'Rags to Riches', 'Quest', 'Voyage and Return', 'Comedy', 'Tragedy' and 'Rebirth'. He writes: '[T]here are indeed a small number of plots which are so fundamental to the way we tell stories that it is virtually impossible for any storyteller ever entirely to break away from them' (Booker 2004: 6). As he acknowledges, Booker was not the first to make this kind of claim, but his 700+-page study, based on more than three decades' research, is the most comprehensively argued account of the phenomenon.
2. Commenting on Jacques Derrida's suspicion of the idea of community, John D. Caputo writes: 'After all, a *communitas* is a military formation, referring to the common defence we build against the other, the fortifications built around the city: *munire*, to fortify ourselves, to build a wall, to gather ourselves together (*com*) for protection against the other; to encircle ourselves with a common wall or barrier that protects the same from the incoming (*invenire, invention*) of the other, that keeps the same safe from the other' (1996: 25).
3. Demythologization was an approach to the Bible developed by thinkers such as David Strauss (1808–74) and Charles Hennell (1809–50), who understood its historical and religious significance to be separable from its supernatural aspects. The latter, it was argued, could be rejected without diminishing the moral force of Christian teaching. Strauss' *Das Leben Jesu* (*The Life of Jesus*) was translated into English in 1846 by Marian Evans (better known as the novelist George Eliot). Although the critical practice preceded his work by a hundred years, the term 'demythologization' was coined by the German theologian Rudolf Bultmann (1884–1976).
4. According to Robert Graves, Pylades was the son of Strophius, the husband of Agamemnon's sister. Smuggled out of Mycenae after the murder of his father, the ten-year-old Orestes stayed with his aunt and uncle, forming a close and lasting friendship with his playmate (1992: 419). Tóibín's renaming of the character avoids the implication of a sexual bond between cousins.
5. The revenge film is sometimes considered to be a genre in its own right. Many recent myth-based films fit into that category, including *Immortals, Hercules* and *Oldboy.*

AFTERWORD

In November 2017, UK broadcaster Channel 5 screened a documentary entitled *Eden Revealed* as part of its Ancient Mysteries series. Its subject was the extraordinary archaeological sites at Göbekli Tepe and Karahan Tepe in southeastern Turkey. Believed to be around 11,000 years old they are among the most important sites ever excavated, not least because they date from a time before humans were deemed capable of building anything on such a huge scale. These imposing megalithic structures were erected not by settled farmers but by pre-agricultural hunter-gatherers, challenging established timelines of human development. Archaeologists previously insisted that complex construction and fixed ritual sites could have been built only after animals had been domesticated and crops planted – changes marking the transition from Mesolithic to Neolithic ages. Prior to that, the theory ran, the time and energy needed for such labour-intensive projects would have been devoted to the all-consuming quest for sustenance. Which is, of course, precisely why these discoveries tempt their interpreters towards mythological associations: we reach for myths when science runs out of road. The mythological resonance proved too attractive for many newspapers and websites to resist: the real Garden of Eden, it was surmised, had been found at last.[1] The connection with Eden is both geographical and temporal: the Turkish site might mark the where and when of the putative 'Fall'. Here, some suggest, our ancestors first abandoned the primal modes of existence passively dependent upon, rather than actively manipulative of, their environment. That this is, arguably, a reversal of the biblical story – in which the 'garden' is closed off and nomadic herding is enforced – is less significant than it might seem. If development of the sites helped to initiate the process of settlement, the change was, conceivably, experienced as both loss and gain. Settlement brought the benefits of security, stability and cooperation, but also produced a sense of alienation from the natural world and imposed hard labour on all: from now on, as the book of Genesis puts it: 'By the sweat of thy brow shalt thou eat bread' (Gen. 3.19). Understood thus, these sites might also be thought to mark the emergence of myth itself, since they represent the groundwork of post-dispersion culture: a story in stone of the rupture in time and place which made gathering, dwelling and social order possible. They bespeak fall and exile, but, at the same time, genesis and belonging.

A story in stone but one which, as far as we know, pre-dated writing, poetry and narrative. There are no records of who built Göbekli Tepe, nor of why nor how it was constructed. Yet the myriad strange T-shaped pillars in their cell-like enclosures bear striking representational carvings, mostly of animals. The figures – some in high relief – memorialize unknown concerns, whether with the movement of heavenly bodies, the spiritual power of totemic creatures or even cataclysmic events.[2] This, too, is mythology, perhaps its earliest expression: a way of relating to, understanding or controlling entities, events and processes by rendering them in the symbolic forms and patterns which make ritual possible. We cannot be sure what this most ancient of monuments meant to its creators, any more than we can, with any certainty, define myth, but we can, I think, say that myth is inherent in this earliest vestige of civilization. In such a context myth appears to operate as a kind of mould for culture, expressing, while also producing, human values, meanings and goals. When, eventually, narrative emerged as a conduit for myths, enabling them to be blended with legends, folktales, fairytales and fictions, the pillars of Göbekli Tepe had long been buried, and, along with them, the dark origins and meanings of their depictions. But something of their attempt to fix a set of ideas, beliefs or culturally significant practices survived translation into the storytelling modes by means of which we continue to make sense of our world.

Each enclosure at Göbekli Tepe was, at some point, deliberately buried. When the arena had fulfilled its purpose or ceased to be useful, it was not destroyed but committed to the earth like a human corpse, and, presumably, its successor became the venue for whatever activities shaped the site. We have in such a practice not only the beginnings of myth but also a model for narrative: the unfolding through time of sequenced and preserved episodes in a history of cultural practice. Whatever prompted the serial interments, they turned the landscape itself into a story which archaeologists are slowly learning to read. It is, perhaps, not altogether surprising that one reading takes us back to Eden and to that most enduring of ancient stories – the loss of paradise. It may turn out to be the oldest story of all, as well as the one which speaks most clearly to our now desperate sense of human finitude and ecological fragility.

Notes

1. See, for example, Tom Knox, 'Do these Mysterious Stones Mark the Site of the Garden of Eden?', *Mail Online* (5 March 2009). https://www.dailymail.co.uk/sciencetech/article-1157784/Do-mysterious-stones-mark-site-Garden-Eden.html; Lucy Mangan, 'Ancient Mysteries: Eden Revealed Review – All Round Adam and Eve's for a Gazelle Feast?' *The Guardian* (25 November 2017). https://www.theguardian.com/tv-and-radio/2017/nov/25/ancient-mysteries-eden-revealed-review-adam-and-eve-gazelle-feast
2. See Martin B. Sweatman and Dimitrios Tsikritsis, 'Decoding Göbekli Tepe with Archaeoastronomy: What Does the Fox Say?' *Mediterranean Archaeology and Archaeometry*, 17, no. 1 (2017): 233–50.

GLOSSARY

Definitions adapted from the Oxford English Dictionary.

Allegory Description of a subject under the guise of another which resembles it in some significant ways, e.g., C. S. Lewis' representation of the death and resurrection of Christ by means of the story of Aslan in *The Lion, the Witch and the Wardrobe*.

Epic Narrative poetic composition, represented typically by the *Iliad* and the *Odyssey*, celebrating the achievements of one or more heroic figures.

Euhemerization The treatment of myths as traditional accounts of real figures and events from history.

Folktale Traditional story circulating among ordinary (non-elite) people, typically communicated orally.

Legend An unverifiable traditional story which may be (or have been) taken by some to be historical.

Literary work Imaginative, written composition, sometimes thought of as distinguished by the high quality of its formal and/or aesthetic character.

Mythology A body or collection of myths such as those dealing with the gods and supernatural events of a particular people or culture. Formerly used to denote the branch of knowledge relating to myths.

Mythopoeic Producing or giving rise to myths.

Ritual (1) Pertaining to the performance of rites. (2) A prescribed order for performing religious or devotional acts. (3) Ceremonial and/or symbolic re-enactment of an event considered to be of the highest cultural significance.

REFERENCES

The following list is divided into sections corresponding to the book's chapters. Works referred to in more than one chapter appear in the section devoted to the chapter in which they first appear.

Introduction

Buxton, R. (1994), *Imaginary Greece: The Contexts of Mythology*, Cambridge: Cambridge University Press.

Jacobsen, T. (1976), *The Treasures of Darkness: A History of Mesopotamian Religion*, New Haven, CT: Yale University Press.

Johnston, S. I. (2018), *The Story of Myth*, Cambridge, MA: Harvard University Press.

Leeming, D. (2005), *The Oxford Companion to World Mythology*, New York, NY: Oxford University Press.

Chapter 1: Defining and interpreting myth

Atwood, M. (2005), *The Penelopiad*, Edinburgh: Canongate.

Augustine, Saint (1961), *Confessions*, trans. R. S. Pine-Coffin, London: Penguin.

Campbell, J. (1949), *The Hero with a Thousand Faces*, Princeton, NJ: Princeton University Press.

Caputi, J. (1992), 'On Psychic Activism: Feminist Mythmaking', in C. Larrington (ed.), *The Woman's Companion to Mythology*, 423–38, London: Harper Collins.

Coupe, L. (1997, 2009), *Myth*, 2nd edn, London: Routledge.

Csapo, E. (2005), *Theories of Mythology*, Oxford: Blackwell.

Dalley, S. (1989, 2000), *Myths from Mesopotamia: Creation, The Flood, Gilgamesh, and Others*, rev. edn, Oxford: Oxford University Press.

Deer, S. and L. Murphy (2017), '"Animals May Take Pity on Us": Using Traditional Tribal Beliefs to Address Animal Abuse and Family Violence within Tribal Nations', *Mitchell Hamline Law Review*, 43 (4): 703–42.

Dundes, A. (1997), 'Binary Opposition in Myth: The Propp/Lévi-Strauss Debate in Retrospect', *Western Folklore*, 56 (1): 39–50.

Eisler, R. (1992), 'Introduction', in C. Larrington (ed.), *The Woman's Companion to Mythology*, viii–ix, London: Harper Collins.

Eliade, M. (1963), *The Sacred and the Profane: The Nature of Religion*, trans. W. R. Trask, New York, NY: Harcourt, Brace and World.

Feldman, B. and R. D. Richardson, Jr (1972), *The Rise of Modern Mythology, 1680–1860*, Bloomington, IN: Indiana University Press.

Frymer-Kensky, T. (1992), *In the Wake of the Goddesses: Women, Culture and the Biblical Transformation of Pagan Myth*, New York, NY: Macmillan.

Gentile, J. S. (2011), 'Prologue: Defining Myth: An Introduction to the Special Issue on Storytelling and Myth', *Storytelling, Self, Society*, 7 (2): 85–90.

Goff, B. (2004), *Citizen Bacchae: Women's Ritual Practice in Ancient Greece*, Berkeley, CA: University of California Press.

Hansen, W. (2002), *Ariadne's Thread: A Guide to International Tales Found in Classical Literature*, Ithaca, NY: Cornell University Press.

Harrison, J. E. (1912), *Themis: A Study of the Social Origins of Greek Religion*, Cambridge: Cambridge University Press.

Jung, C. G. (1956–67), *Collected Works of C.G. Jung, Volume 5: Symbols of Transformation*, 2nd edn, ed. and trans. G. Adler and R. F. C. Hull, Princeton, NJ: Princeton University Press.

Katz, M. (1992), 'Ideology and "The Status of Women" in Ancient Greece', *History and Theory*, 31 (4): 70–97.

Klages, M. (n.d.), 'Claude Levi-Strauss "The Structural Study of Myth" and Other Structuralist Ideas'. Available online: https://www.webpages.uidaho.edu/~sflores/KlagesLevi-Strauss.html (accessed 24 Feb 2020).

Lambert, W. G. (2013), *Mesopotamian Creation Myths*, University Park, PA: Pennsylvania State University Press.

Lévi-Strauss, C. (1955), 'The Structural Study of Myth', *The Journal of American Folklore*, 68 (270): 428–44.

Long, C. H. (1963), *Alpha: The Myths of Creation*, Atlanta, GA: Scholars Press.

Magoulick, M. (n.d.), 'What is Myth?' Available online: http://www.faculty.de.gcsu.edu/~mmagouli/defmyth.htm (accessed 03 Jun 2018).

Ricoeur, P. (1974), *The Conflict of Interpretations: Essays in Hermeneutics*, trans. W. Domingo et al., ed. D. Ihde, Evanston, IL: Northwestern University Press.

Segal, R. (1999), *Theorizing About Myth*, Amherst, MA: University of Massachusetts Press.

Sommer, B. D. (2000), 'The Babylonian Akitu Festival: Rectifying the King or Renewing the Cosmos?', *Journal of the Ancient Near Eastern Society*, 27: 81–95.

Tedlock, D., trans. (1985, 1996), *Popol Vuh: The Definitive Edition of the Mayan Book of the Dawn of Life and the Glories of Gods and Kings*, revised and expanded, New York, NY: Simon and Schuster.

Vitaliano, D. B. (1968), 'Geomythology: The Impact of Geologic Events on History and Legend with Special Reference to Atlantis', *Journal of the Folklore Institute*, 5 (1): 5–30.

Vitaliano, D. B. (2007), 'Geomythology: Geological Origins of Myths and Legends', in L. Piccardi and W. B. Masse (eds.), *Myth and Geology*, 273:1–7, London: Geological Society Special Publications.

Chapter 2: Myth and science

Aveni, A. (2019), 'Myth vs. Truth: Science and Stories', *Yale University Press Blog*, 11 Nov. Available online: http://blog.yalebooks.com/2019/11/11/myth-vs-truth-science-and-stories/ (accessed 09 May 2020).

Bacon, F. (1886), *The Wisdom of the Ancients and New Atlantis*. London: Cassell. Originally published 1609 and 1626.

Bacon, F. (1974), *The Advancement of Learning and New Atlantis*, ed. A. Johnson, Oxford: Oxford University Press. Originally published 1605 and 1626.

Briggs, R. (2013), 'As Myth Marries Science, the Origin Story Matters', *Live Science*, 05 Nov. Available online: https://www.livescience.com/40946-the-origin-story-matters.html (accessed 10 May 2020).

Brisson, L. (2004), *How Philosophers Saved Myths: Allegorical Interpretation and Classical Mythology*, trans. C. Tihanyi, Chicago, IL: University of Chicago Press.
Chernyshova, T. (2004), 'Science Fiction and Myth Creation in Our Age', *Science Fiction Studies*, 31 (3): 345–57.
Hawking, S. and L. Mlodinow (2010), *The Grand Design*, London: Bantam Press.
Horton, R. and R. Finnegan (1973), *Modes of Thought: Essays on Thinking in Western and Non-Western Societies*, London: Faber and Faber.
Josephson-Storm, J. A. (2017), *The Myth of Disenchantment: Magic, Modernity and the Birth of the Human Sciences*, Chicago, IL and London: The University of Chicago Press.
Kass, L. R. (2006), *The Beginning of Wisdom: Reading Genesis*, Chicago: University of Chicago Press.
Lewis, C. S. (1961), *An Experiment in Criticism*, Cambridge: Cambridge University Press.
Luminet, J.-P. (2016), 'Creation, Chaos, Time: from Myth to Modern Cosmology', *Cosmology*, 24: 501–15.
Maldamé, J.-M. (2002), 'Myth', in G. Tanzella-Nitti, I. Colagé and A. Strumia (eds.), *INTERS – Interdisciplinary Encyclopedia of Religion and Science*. Available online: https://inters.org/myth (accessed 03 Apr 2017).
Pesic, P. (1999), 'Wrestling with Proteus: Francis Bacon and the "Torture" of Nature', *Isis*, 90 (1): 81–94.
Popper, K. (1963, 1965), *Conjectures and Refutations: The Growth of Scientific Knowledge*, 2nd edn, London: Routledge.
Reiss, J. and J. Sprenger (2020), 'Scientific Objectivity', in E. N. Zalta (ed.), *The Stanford Encyclopedia of Philosophy*. Available online: https://plato.stanford.edu/archives/win2020/entries/scientific-objectivity/ (accessed 09 Apr 2017).
Scarborough, M. (1994), *Myth and Modernity: Postcritical Reflections*, Albany, NY: State University of New York Press.
Schrempp, G. (2012a), *The Ancient Mythology of Modern Science: A Mythologist Looks (seriously) at Popular Science Writing*, Montreal & Kingston: McGill-Queens University Press.
Schrempp, G. (2012b), 'Mythology and Science; Or, What Do We Want From Popular Science?', *Huffington Post*. Available online: http://www.huffingtonpost.com/gregory-schrempp/myths-and-science_b_1949316.html (accessed 20 Apr 2017).
Segal, R. (2004), *Myth: A Very Short Introduction*, Oxford: Oxford University Press.
Thornton, S. (2021), 'Karl Popper', in E. N. Zalta (ed.), *The Stanford Encyclopedia of Philosophy*. Available online: https://plato.stanford.edu/archives/spr2021/entries/popper/ (accessed 23 Mar 2022).
Villarmea, S. (2001), 'The Revolution of Thought: from Mythology to Hellenistic Science', The Mediterranean Program - American University Madrid, October 10. Available online: https://core.ac.uk/download/pdf/58907937.pdf (accessed 26 Mar 2020).
Weber, M. (2004), 'Science as a Vocation', trans. R. Livingstone, in D. Owen and T. B. Strong (eds.), *Max Weber: The Vocation Lectures*, 1–31, Indianapolis: Hackett Publishing Company.

Chapter 3: *The Epic of Gilgamesh*

Abusch, T. (2001), 'The Development and Meaning of the Epic of Gilgamesh: An Interpretive Essay', *Journal of the American Oriental Society*, 121 (4): 614–22.
Ackerman, S. (1989), *When Heroes Love: The Ambiguity of Eros in the Stories of Gilgamesh and David*, New Haven, CT: Yale University Press.
Altes, L. K. (2007), 'Gilgamesh and the Power of Narration', *Journal of the American Oriental Society*, 127 (2): 183–93.

Brisch, N. (2016), 'Anunna (Anunnaku, Anunnaki) (a group of gods)', *Ancient Mesopotamian Gods and Goddesses*, Oracc and the UK Higher Education Academy. Available online: http://oracc.museum.upenn.edu/amgg/listofdeities/anunna/ (accessed 03 Aug 2018).

Cordova, C. E. (2005), 'The Degradation of the Ancient Near Eastern Environment', in D. C. Snell (ed.), *A Companion to the Ancient Near East*, 125–41, Oxford: Blackwell.

Cregan-Reid, V. (2013), *Discovering Gilgamesh: Geology, Narrative and the Historical Sublime in Victorian Culture*, Manchester: Manchester University Press.

Dalley, S. (1989, 2000), *Myths from Mesopotamia: Creation, The Flood, Gilgamesh, and Others*, rev. edn, Oxford: Oxford University Press.

Damrosch, D. (2006), *The Buried Book: The Loss and Rediscovery of the Great Epic of Gilgamesh*, New York, NY: Henry Holt and Company.

Davila, J. R. (1995), 'The Flood Hero as King and Priest', *Journal of Near Eastern Studies*, 54 (3): 199–214.

Finkel, I. (2014), *The Ark Before Noah: Decoding the Story of the Flood*, London: Hodder and Stoughton.

Finkel, I. and J. Taylor (2015), *Cuneiform*, London: The British Museum Press.

Fisher, E. (1970), 'Gilgamesh and Genesis: The Flood Story in Context', *The Catholic Biblical Quarterly*, 32 (3): 392–403.

Foster, B. R. (1993, 1996), *Before the Muses: An Anthology of Akkadian Literature*, 2nd edn, Bethesda, MD: CDL Press.

George, A. (1999), *The Epic of Gilgamesh: A New Translation*, London: Allen Lane.

George, A. (2012), 'The Mayfly on the River: Individual and Collective Destiny in the Epic of Gilgamesh', *Kaskal*, 9: 227–42.

Harrison, R. P. (1992), *Forests: The Shadow of Civilization*, Chicago, IL: University of Chicago Press.

Horry, R. (2013), 'Utu/Šamaš (god)', *Ancient Mesopotamian Gods and Goddesses*, Oracc and the UK Higher Education Academy. Available online: http://oracc.museum.upenn.edu/amgg/listofdeities/utu/ (accessed 05 Aug 2018).

Jacobsen, T. (1949), 'Mesopotamia', in H. Frankfort et al., *Before Philosophy: The Intellectual Adventure of Ancient Man*, 137–234, Harmondsworth: Penguin.

Jacobsen, T. (1981), 'The Eridu Genesis', *Journal of Biblical Literature*, 100 (4): 513–29.

Meador, B. D. (2000), *Inanna, Lady of Largest Heart: Poems of the Sumerian High Priestess Enheduanna*, Austin, TX: University of Texas Press.

Meador, B. D. (2009), *Princess, Priestess, Poet: The Temple Hymns of Enheduanna*, Austin, TX: University of Texas Press.

Moran, W. L. (1995), '*The Epic of Gilgamesh*: A Document of Ancient Humanism', *Canadian Society for Mesopotamian Studies Journal*, 22: 15–22.

Riley, J. M. (2013), '"Love the Child who Holds You by the Hand": Intertextuality in *The Odyssey* and *The Epic of Gilgamesh*', *Studia Antiqua*, 12 (2): 1–12.

Rubio, G. (2005), 'The Languages of the Ancient Near East', in D. C. Snell (ed.), *A Companion to the Ancient Near East*, 79–109, Oxford: Blackwell.

Schmidt, M. (2019), *Gilgamesh: The Life of a Poem*, Princeton, NJ: Princeton University Press.

Tigay, J. H. (1997), 'Summary: The Evolution of *The Gilgamesh Epic*', in J. Maier (ed.), *Gilgamesh: A Reader*, 40–9, Wauconda, IL: Bolchazy-Carducci Publishers Inc.

Van Nortwick, T. (1996), *Somewhere I Have Never Travelled: The Hero's Journey*, Oxford: Oxford University Press.

Chapter 4: The book of Genesis

Alter, R. (1996), *Genesis: Translation and Commentary*, New York, NY and London: W.W. Norton & Company.

Baden, J. S. (2012), *The Composition of the Pentateuch: Renewing the Documentary Hypothesis*, New Haven, CT: Yale University Press.
Ball, B. W. (2015), 'The Origins of Genesis Reconsidered', in B. Ball and R. McIver (eds.), *Grounds for Assurance and Hope: Selected Biblical and Historical Writings of Bryan W. Ball*, 93–113, Cooranbong: Avondale Academic Press.
Berman, J. (2017), *Inconsistency in the Torah: Ancient Literary Convention and the Limits of Source Criticism*, Oxford: Oxford University Press.
Fokkelman, J. P. (1991), *Narrative Art in Genesis: Specimens of Stylistic and Structural Analysis*, 2nd edn, Eugene, OR: Wipf and Stock.
Friedman, R. E. (1987, 1997), *Who Wrote the Bible?* 2nd edn, San Francisco, CA: Harper Collins.
Greenblatt, S. (2017), *The Rise and Fall of Adam and Eve: The Story that Created Us*, New York, NY: W.W. Norton & Company.
Gunn, D. M. and D. N. Fewell (1993), *Narrative in the Hebrew Bible*, Oxford: Oxford University Press.
Hendel, R. (2012), 'Historical Context', in C. A. Evans et al. (eds.), *The Book of Genesis: Composition, Reception, and Interpretation*, 51–82, Leiden: Brill.
Hendel, R. (2013), *The Book of Genesis: A Biography*. Princeton, NJ: Princeton University Press.
Kramer, S. N. (1961, 1972), *Sumerian Mythology: A Study of Spiritual and Literary Achievement in the Third Millennium BC*, rev. edn, Philadelphia, PA: University of Pennsylvania Press.
Rendsburg, G. A. (1986), *The Redaction of Genesis*, Winona Lake, IN: Eisenbraun.
Ricoeur, P. (1990), 'Interpretative Narrative', trans. D. Pellauer, in R. Schwartz (ed.), *The Book and the Text: The Bible and Literary Theory*, 237–57, Oxford: Basil Blackwell.
Rohl, D. (2002), *The Lost Testament: From Eden to Exile – The Five-Thousand-Year History of the People of the Bible*, London: Century.
Ronning, J. (1991), 'The Naming of Isaac: The Role of the Wife/Sister Episodes in the Redaction of Genesis', *Westminster Theological Journal*, 53: 1–27.
Sarna, N. M. (1966), *Understanding Genesis: The World of the Bible in the Light of History*, New York, NY: Schocken Books.
Schmid, K. (2012), 'Genesis in the Pentateuch', in C. A. Evans et al. (eds.), *The Book of Genesis: Composition, Reception, and Interpretation*, 27–50, Leiden: Brill.
Ska, J.-L. (2012), 'The Study of the Book of Genesis: The Beginning of Critical Reading', in C. A. Evans et al. (eds.), *The Book of Genesis: Composition, Reception, and Interpretation*, 3–26, Leiden: Brill.
Stuckenbruck, L. T. (2000), 'The "Angels" and "Giants" of Genesis 6:1–4 in Second and Third Century BCE Jewish Interpretation: Reflections on the Posture of Early Apocalyptic Traditions', *Dead Sea Discoveries*, 7 (3): 354–77.
Woudstra, M. H. (1970), 'The *Toledot* of the Book of Genesis and their Redemptive-Historical Significance', *Calvin Theological Journal*, 5: 184–9.
Yudkowsky, R. (2007), 'Chaos or Chiasm? The Structure of Abraham's Life', *Jewish Bible Quarterly*, 35 (2): 109–14.
Zamazalová, S. (2015), 'The Ziggurat and its Temples', *Nimrud: Materialities of Assyrian Knowledge Production*, The Nimrud Project at Oracc.org. Available online: http://oracc.museum.upenn.edu/nimrud/ancientkalhu/thecity/zigguratandtemples/ (accessed 12 Jan 2019).

Chapter 5: The book of Job

Alter, R. (2010), *The Wisdom Books: Job, Proverbs, and Ecclesiastes: A Translation with Commentary*, New York, NY and London: W.W. Norton & Company.

Britt, B. M. (2022), 'Curses in the Hebrew Bible', *Bible Odyssey*. Available online: https://www.bibleodyssey.org/people/related-articles/curses-in-the-hebrew-bible/ (accessed 13 Sep 2022).

Browning, W. R. F. (1996, 2009), *A Dictionary of the Bible*, 2nd edn, Oxford: Oxford University Press.

Clines, D. (1990), 'Deconstructing the Book of Job', in M. Warner (ed.), *The Bible as Rhetoric: Studies in Biblical Persuasion and Credibility*, 65–81, London: Routledge.

Cooper, A. (1990), 'Reading and Misreading the Prologue to Job', *Journal for the Study of the Old Testament*, 46: 67–79.

Crenshaw, J. L. (2007), 'Beginnings, Endings, and Life's Necessities in Biblical Wisdom', in R. J. Clifford (ed.), *Wisdom Literature in Mesopotamia and Israel*, 93–105, Atlanta, GA: Society of Biblical Literature.

Dick, M. B. (1979), 'The Legal Metaphor in Job 31', *The Catholic Biblical Quarterly*, 41 (1): 37–50.

Dolansky, S. (2022), 'Sheol', *Bible Odyssey*. Available online: https://www.bibleodyssey.org/en/places/related-articles/sheol (accessed 13 Sep 2022).

Fox, M. V. (2005), 'Job the Pious', *Zeitschrift für die Alttestamentliche Wissenschaft*, 117 (3): 351–66.

Fox, M. V. (2013), 'God's Answer and Job's Response', *Biblica*, 94 (1): 1–23.

Good, E. M. (1990), *In Turns of Tempest: A Reading of Job, with a Translation*, Stanford, CA: Stanford University Press.

Gordis, R. (1943–4), 'The Social Background of Wisdom Literature', *Hebrew Union College Annual*, 18: 77–118.

Greenstein, E. L. (2019), *Introduction to Job: A New Translation*, New Haven, CT: Yale University Press.

Habel, N. C. (1975), *The Book of Job: Commentary*, Cambridge: Cambridge University Press.

Lasine, S. (1990), 'The Trials of Job and Kafka's Josef K', *The German Quarterly*, 63 (2): 187–98.

Lawton, D. (1990), *Faith, Text and History: The Bible in English*, London: Harvester Wheatsheaf.

Myerson, G. (1992), *The Argumentative Imagination: Wordsworth, Dryden, Religious Dialogues*, Manchester: Manchester University Press.

Newsom, C. A. (2003), *The Book of Job: A Contest of Moral Imaginations*, Oxford: Oxford University Press.

Rata, C. G. (2008), 'Observations on the Language of the Book of Job', *Scripture and Interpretation*, 2 (1): 5–24.

Robertson, D. (1973), 'The Book of Job: A Literary Study', *Soundings: An Interdisciplinary Journal*, 56 (4): 446–69.

Sanders, J. T. (2005), 'Wisdom, Theodicy, Death, and the Evolution of Intellectual Traditions', *Journal for the Study of Judaism in the Persian, Hellenistic, and Roman Period*, 36 (3): 263–77.

Scheindlin, R. P. (1998), *The Book of Job: Translation, Introduction and Notes*, New York, NY: Norton.

Chapter 6: The *Odyssey*

Adorno, T. W. and M. Horkheimer (1992), 'Odysseus or Myth and Enlightenment', trans. R. Hullot-Kentor, *New German Critique*, 56: 109–41.

Alden, M. (2017), *Para-Narratives in the Odyssey: Stories in the Frame*, Oxford: Oxford University Press.

Bakker, E. J. (2013), *The Meaning of Meat and the Structure of the Odyssey*, Cambridge: Cambridge University Press.

Bremmer, J. N. (2007), 'Greek Normative Animal Sacrifice', in D. Ogden (ed.), *A Companion to Greek Religion*, 132–44, Oxford: Blackwell Publishing.
Clarke, H. (1981), *Homer's Readers: A Historical Introduction to the Iliad and the Odyssey*, Newark, DE: University of Delaware Press.
Combellack, F. M. (1959), 'Milman Parry and Homeric Artistry', *Comparative Literature*, 11 (3): 193–208.
Crane, G. (1987), 'The Odyssey and Conventions of the Heroic Quest', *Classical Antiquity*, 6 (1): 11–37.
Dietrich, B. C. (1979), 'Views of Homeric Gods and Religion', *Numen*, 26 (2): 129–51.
Edmunds, L. (2009), 'Epic and Myth', in J. M. Foley (ed.), *A Companion to Ancient Epic*, 31–44, Chichester: Wiley-Blackwell.
Fagles, R., trans. (1996), *The Odyssey*, London: Penguin.
Finley, M. I. (1963, 1971), *The Ancient Greeks*, rev. edn, London: Penguin.
Frame, D. (2020), 'New Light on the Homeric Question: The Phaeacians Unmasked', Harvard University's Center for Hellenic Studies. Available online: https://chs.harvard.edu/CHS/article/display/4453 (accessed 03 Oct 2021).
Goff, B. E. (1991), 'The Sign of the Fall: The Scars of Orestes and Odysseus', *Classical Antiquity*, 10 (2): 259–67.
Graziosi, B. (2016), *Homer*, Oxford: Oxford University Press.
Griffin, J. (1987, 2004), *Homer: The Odyssey*, 2nd edn, Cambridge: Cambridge University Press.
Hall, J. M. (2007), *A History of the Archaic Geek World, ca. 1200–479 BCE*, Oxford: Blackwell.
Hemingway, C. (2004), 'Women in Classical Greece', *Heilbrunn Timeline of Art History*. Available online: https://www.metmuseum.org/toah/hd/wmna/hd_wmna.htm (accessed 17 Oct 2019).
Hornblower, S. (1983, 1991), *The Greek World, 479–323 BC*, rev. edn, London: Routledge.
Kearns, E. (2004), 'The Gods in the Homeric Epics', in R. Fowler (ed.), *The Cambridge Companion to Homer*, 59–73, Cambridge: Cambridge University Press.
Knox, B. (1996), 'Introduction to Robert Fagles (trans.)', in *The Odyssey*, 3–64, London: Penguin.
Louden, B. (2009), 'The Gods in Epic, or the Divine Economy', in J. M. Foley (ed.), *A Companion to Ancient Epic*, 90–104, Chichester: Wiley-Blackwell.
Myrsiades, K. (2019), *Reading Homer's Odyssey*, Lewisburg, PA: Bucknell University Press.
Nagler, M. N. (1990), 'Odysseus: The Proem and the Problem', *Classical Antiquity*, 9 (2): 335–56.
Nagy, G. (2020), 'Homer and Greek Myth', Harvard University Center for Hellenic Studies. Available online: http://nrs.harvard.edu/urn-3:hlnc.essay:Nagy.Homer_and_Greek_Myth.2007 (accessed 12 Sep 2021).
Powell, B. B. (2004, 2007), *Homer*, 2nd edn, Oxford: Blackwell.
Segal, C. (1962), 'The Phaeacians and the Symbolism of Odysseus' Return', *Arion: A Journal of Humanities and the Classics*, 1 (4): 17–64.
Segal, C. (1983), '*Kleos* and its Ironies in the *Odyssey*', *L'Antiquité Classique*, 52: 22–47.
Segal, C. (1992), 'Divine Justice in the *Odyssey*: Poseidon, Cyclops, and Helios', *The American Journal of Philology*, 113 (4): 489–518.
Shewring, W., trans. (1980), *Homer: The Odyssey*, Oxford: Oxford University Press.
Slatkin, L. M. (2009), 'Homer's Odyssey', in J. M. Foley (ed.), *A Companion to Ancient Epic*, 315–29, Chichester: Wiley-Blackwell.
Vidal-Naquet, P. (1968), 'The Black Hunter and the Origin of the Athenian Ephebeia', *Proceedings of the Cambridge Philological Society*, new series, 14 (194): 49–64.
Wheeler, G. (2002), 'Sing, Muse ...: The Introit from Homer to Apollonius', *The Classical Quarterly*, 52 (1): 33–49.
Zazzera, E. D. (2019), 'The Geography of the Odyssey: Or How to Map a Myth', *Lapham's Quarterly*. Available online: https://www.laphamsquarterly.org/roundtable/geography-odyssey (accessed 13 Sep 2021).

Chapter 7: From myth to romance: *The Life of St Cadoc* and *Sir Orfeo*

Barnes, G. (1993), *Counsel and Strategy in Middle English Romance*, Cambridge: D.S. Brewer.

Barron, W. R. J. (1987), *English Medieval Romance*, London: Longman.

Battles, D. (2010), 'Sir Orfeo and English Identity', *Studies in Philology*, 107 (2): 179–211.

Blumenfeld-Kosinski, R. (1985), 'The Gods as Metaphor in the "Roman de Thèbes"', *Modern Philology*, 83 (1): 1–11.

Bowen, E. G. (1954), *The Settlements of the Celtic Saints in Wales*, Cardiff: University of Wales Press.

Bowen, E. G. (1977), *Saints, Settlements and Seaways in the Celtic Lands*, Cardiff: University of Wales Press.

Burlin, R. B. (1995), 'Middle English Romance: The Structure of Genre', *The Chaucer Review*, 30 (1): 1–14.

Charles-Edwards, T. M. (2013), *Wales and the Britons, 350–1064*, Oxford: Oxford University Press.

Cooper, H. (2004), *The English Romance in Time: Transforming Motifs from Geoffrey of Monmouth to the Death of Shakespeare*, Oxford: Oxford University Press.

Crystal, D. (2018), 'Middle English', Discovering Literature: Medieval. British Library. Available online: https://www.bl.uk/medieval-literature/articles/middle-english (accessed 03 Jun 2021).

Fee, C. R. (2011), *Mythology in the Middle Ages: Heroic Tales of Monsters, Magic, and Might*, Westport, CT: Praeger.

Fee, C. R. with D. A. Leeming (2001), *Gods, Heroes, and Kings: The Battle for Mythic Britain*, Oxford: Oxford University Press.

Finlayson, J. (1999), 'The Marvellous in Middle English Romance', *The Chaucer Review*, 33 (4): 363–408.

Friedman, J. B. (1996), 'Eurydice, Heurodis, and the Noon-Day Demon', *Speculum*, 41 (1): 22–9.

Green, M. (1992), *Animals in Celtic Life and Myth*. London: Routledge.

Hofstee, P. (2014), 'From Myth to Romance: Medievalisation in Sir Orfeo'. Available online: https://www.academia.edu/5764599/From_Myth_to_Romance_Medievalisation_in_Sir_Orfeo (accessed 04 Jun 2021).

Hunt, E. E. (1910), *Sir Orfeo Adapted from the Middle English*, Cambridge, MA: Harvard Cooperative Society.

Jankulak, K. (2003), 'Alba Longa in the Celtic Regions: Swine, Saints and Celtic Hagiography', in J. Cartwright (ed.), *Celtic Hagiography and Saints' Cults*, 271–84, Cardiff: University of Wales Press.

Kay, S. (2000), 'Courts, Clerks, and Courtly Love', in R. L. Krueger (ed.), *The Cambridge Companion to Medieval Romance*, 81–96, Cambridge: Cambridge University Press.

Knight, J. (2013), *South Wales from the Romans to the Normans: Christianity, Literacy and Lordship*, Stroud: Amberley.

Laing, L. (2006), *The Archaeology of Celtic Britain and Ireland, C. AD 400 –1200*, Cambridge: Cambridge University Press.

Laskaya, A. and E. Salisbury (1995), 'Sir Orfeo: Introduction', in A. Laskaya and E. Salisbury (eds.), *The Middle English Breton Lays*, Kalamazoo, MI: Medieval Institute Publications. Available online: https://d.lib.rochester.edu/teams/publication/laskaya-and-salisbury-middle-english-breton-lays (accessed 23 Jun 2021).

Leckie, R. W. (1981), *The Passage of Dominion: Geoffrey of Monmouth and the Periodization of Insular History in the Twelfth Century*, Toronto: University of Toronto Press.

Lerer, S. (1985), 'Artifice and Artistry in Sir Orfeo', *Speculum*, 60 (1): 92–109.

Martí, J. S. (2017), 'Insular Sources and Analogues of the Otherworld in the Middle English Sir Orfeo', *The Grove. Working Papers on English Studies*, 24: 131–52.

McClure, E. (1910), *British Place-names in their Historical Setting*, London: SPCK.

Minogue, J. (n.d.), 'Sir Orfeo and the Power of the Harp', California State University. Available online: http://www.csun.edu/~jm9869/2SirOrfeo.html (accessed 23 Jun 2021).
Partner, N. F. (1977), *Serious Entertainments: The Writing of History in Twelfth-Century England*, Chicago, IL and London: University of Chicago Press.
Pryor, F. (2004), *Britain AD: A Quest for Arthur, England and the Anglo-Saxons*, London: Harper Collins.
Rees, W. J. (1843), *Lives of the Cambro British Saints*, Llandovery: William Rees; London: Longman and Co; Abergavenny: J.H. Morgan.
Rider, J. (2000), 'The Other Worlds of Romance', in R. L. Krueger (ed.), *The Cambridge Companion to Medieval Romance*, 115–31, Cambridge: Cambridge University Press.
Ross, A. (1974), *Pagan Celtic Britain: Studies in Iconography and Tradition*, London: Sphere.
Saunders, C. (2010), *Magic and the Supernatural in Medieval English Romance*, Cambridge: D.S. Brewer.
Selling, K. (1998), 'The Locus of the Sacred in the Celtic Otherworld', *Conference Proceedings of Centre for Studies in Religion, Literature and the Arts*, 293–301. Available online: https://core.ac.uk/download/pdf/229403658.pdf (accessed 30 Jun 2021).
Seznec, J. (1953, 1961), *The Survival of the Pagan Gods: The Mythological Tradition and Its Place in Renaissance Humanism and Art*, trans. B. F. Sessions, New York, NY: Harper and Brothers.
Walker, D. (1990), *Medieval Wales*, Cambridge: Cambridge University Press.
Weston, J. L. (1914), *The Chief Middle English Poets*, Boston, MA and New York, NY: Houghton Mifflin Co.
Wittig, S. (1978), *Stylistic and Narrative Structures in the Middle English Romances*, Austin, TX: University of Texas Press.
Wogan-Browne, J. (2001), *Saints' Lives and Women's Literary Culture c.1150–1300: Virginity and its Authorizations*, Oxford: Oxford University Press.
Zaerr, L. M. (2012), *Performance and the Middle English Romance*, Cambridge: D.S. Brewer.

Chapter 8: The Four Branches of the *Mabinogi*

Ashe, G. (1990), *Mythology of the British Isles*, London: Methuen.
Bollard, J. K. (1996), 'The Structure of the Four Branches of the Mabinogi', in C. W. Sullivan III (ed.), *The Mabinogi: A Book of Essays*, 165–96, New York, NY: Garland.
Bollard, J. K., trans. and Anthony Griffiths, photography (2006), *The Mabinogi: Legend and Landscape of Wales*, Llandysul: Gomer.
Boyd, M. (2010), 'Why the Mabinogi has Branches', *Proceedings of the Harvard Celtic Colloquium*, 30: 22–38.
Breeze, A. (2009), *The Origins of the Four Branches of the Mabinogi*, Leominster: Gracewing.
Breeze, A. (2018), 'The Dates of the Four Branches of the Mabinogi', *Studia Celtica Posnaniensia*, 3 (1): 47–62.
Bromwich, R. (1996), '*The Mabinogion* and Lady Charlotte Guest', in C. W. Sullivan III (ed.), *The Mabinogi: A Book of Essays*, 3–18, New York, NY: Garland.
Brown, A. (2016), 'Guide to the Classics: The Arthurian Legend', *The Conversation*, 07 Dec. Available online: Guide to the classics: the Arthurian legend (theconversation.com) (accessed 10 Jan 2022). https://theconversation.com/guide-to-the-classics-the-arthurian-legend-64289.
Byfield, C. E. (1993), 'Character and Conflict in the Four Branches of the Mabinogi', *Bulletin of the Board of Celtic Studies*, 40: 51–72. Revised. Available online: https://www.academia.edu/5987435/Character_and_Conflict_in_the_Four_Branches_of_the_Mabinogi (accessed 07 Feb 2022).

Carey, J. (1987), 'Time, Space, and the Otherworld', *Proceedings of the Harvard Celtic Colloquium*, 7: 1–27.
Chapman, M. (1992), *The Celts: The Construction of a Myth*, London: Palgrave Macmillan.
Davies, S. (1992), 'Storytelling in Medieval Wales', *Oral Tradition*, 7 (2): 231–57.
Davies, S. (1995), 'Mythology and the Oral Tradition: Wales', in M. J. Green (ed.), *The Celtic World*, 785–91, London: Routledge.
Davies, S. (2007), *The Mabinogion: A New Translation*, Oxford: Oxford University Press.
Dexter, M. R. (1990a), 'The Hippomorphic Goddess and her Offspring', *The Journal of Indo-European Studies*, 18 (3 & 4): 285–307.
Dexter, M. R. (1990b), 'Reflections on the Goddess Donu', *The Mankind Quarterly*, XXXI (1 & 2): 45–58.
Dietler, M. (2006), 'Celticism, Celtitude and Celticity: The Consumption of the Past in the Age of Globalization', in S. Rieckhoff (dir.), *Celtes et Gaulois, l'Archéologie face à l'Histoire, 1: Celtes et Gaulois dans l'histoire, l'historiographie et l'idéologie moderne. Actes de la table ronde de Leipzig, 16–17 Juin 2005*, 237–48, Glux-en-Glenne: Bibracte, Centre Archéologique Européen.
Ford, P. K. (1981–2), 'Prolegomena to a Reading of the Mabinogi: "Pwyll" and "Manawydan"', *Studia Celtica*, 16–17: 110–25.
Ford, P. K. (1996), 'Branwen: A Study of the Celtic Affinities', in C. W. Sullivan III (ed.), *The Mabinogi: A Book of Essays*, 99–119, New York, NY: Garland.
Fulton, H. (2000), 'Cultural Meanings in the Mabinogi', in G. Evans et al. (eds.), *Origins and Revivals: Proceedings of the First Australian Conference of Celtic Studies*, 437–52, Sydney: Centre for Celtic Studies, University of Sydney.
Gantz, J. (1978), 'Thematic Structure in the Four Branches of the Mabinogi', *Medium Aevum* 47: 247–54.
Hamp, E. P. (1999), 'Mabinogi and Archaism', *Celtica*, 23: 96–112.
Huws, B. (2010), 'Manawydan uab Llŷr: A Tale of the Norman Occupation of Deheubarth', *Transactions of the Hon Soc of the Cymmrodorion*, new series, 16: 7–23.
Keefer, S. L. (1996), 'The Lost Tale of Dylan in the Fourth Branch of The Mabinogi', in C. W. Sullivan III (ed.), *The Mabinogi: A Book of Essays*, 79–97, New York, NY: Garland.
McDonald, M. (1986), 'Celtic Ethnic Kinship and the Problem of Being English', *Current Anthropology*, 27 (4): 333–47.
McKenna, C. (1980–2), 'The Theme of Sovereignty in Pwyll', *Bulletin of the Board of Celtic Studies*, 29: 35–52.
Ó Coileáin, S. (1977–8), 'A Thematic Study of the Tale *Pwyll Pendeuic Dyuet*', *Studia Celtica*, 12–13: 78–82.
Parker, W. (2005), *The Four Branches of the Mabinogi*, Oregon House, CA: Bardic Press.
Parker, W. (2010), 'The Mabinogion'. Available online: https://www.mabinogion.info/about.htm (accessed 03 Mar 2022).
Rees, A. and B. Rees (1961), *Celtic Heritage: Ancient Tradition in Ireland and Wales*, London: Thames and Hudson.
Rider-Bezerra, S. (2011), 'The Mabinogion Project: A Brief History of the Mabinogion', The Camelot Project. Available online: https://d.lib.rochester.edu/camelot/text/rider-bezerra-mabinogion-project (accessed 03 Mar 2022).
Roberts, B. (1984), 'From Traditional Tale to Literary Story: Middle Welsh Prose Narratives', in L. A. Arrathoon (ed.), *The Craft of Fiction: Essays in Medieval Poetics*, 225–8, Rochester, MI: Solaris Press.
Roberts, B. (1992), 'Tales and Romances', in A. O. H. Jarman and G. R. Hughes (eds.), *A Guide to Welsh Literature. Volume One*, 203–43, Cardiff: University of Wales Press.

Rodway, S. (2018), 'The Mabinogi and the Shadow of Celtic Mythology', *Studia Celtica*, 52 (1): 67–85.
Sessle, E. J. (1994), 'Exploring the Limitations of the Sovereignty Goddess through the Role of Rhiannon', *Proceedings of the Harvard Celtic Colloquium*, 14: 9–13.
Shack, J. (2015), 'Otherworld and Norman "Other": Annwfn and its Colonial Implications in the First Branch of the Mabinogi', *Proceedings of the Harvard Celtic Colloquium*, 35: 172–86.
Valente, R. (1988), 'Gwydion and Aranrhod: Crossing the Borders of Gender in Math', *Bulletin of the Board of Celtic Studies*, 35: 1–9.
Welsh, A. (1990), 'Doubling and Incest in the Mabinogi', *Speculum*, 65 (2): 344–62.
Welsh, A. (1996), 'Manawydan fab Llŷr: Wales, England, and the "New Man"', in C. W. Sullivan III (ed.), *The Mabinogi: A Book of Essays*, 121–41, New York, NY: Garland.
Wood, J. (1996), 'The Calumniated Wife in Medieval Welsh Literature', in C. W. Sullivan III (ed.), *The Mabinogi: A Book of Essays*, 61–78, New York, NY: Garland.

Chapter 9: Myth today

Abrahams, R. D. (1972), 'Folklore and Literature as Performance', *Journal of the Folklore Institute*, 9 (2/3): 75–94.
Attebery, B. (2014), *Stories about Stories: Fantasy and the Remaking of Myth*, Oxford: Oxford University Press.
Atwood, M. (2011), *In Other Worlds: SF and the Human Imagination*, New York, NY: Doubleday.
Baeten, E. M. (1996), *The Magic Mirror: Myth's Abiding Power*, Albany, NY: State University of New York Press.
Barker, P. (2019), *The Silence of the Girls*, London: Penguin.
Barthes, R. (2000), *Mythologies*, trans. A. Lavers, London: Vintage.
Bolen, J. S. (1985), *Goddesses in Everywoman*, New York, NY: Harper and Row.
Booker, C. (2004), *The Seven Basic Plots: Why We Tell Stories*, London: Continuum.
Caputo, J. D. (1996), 'A Community without Truth: Derrida and the Impossible Community', *Research in Phenomenology*, 26: 25–37.
Filmer-Davies, K. (1996), *Fantasy Fiction and Welsh Myth: Tales of Belonging*, Basingstoke: Macmillan.
Frye, N. (1957), *Anatomy of Criticism: Four Essays*, Princeton, NJ: Princeton University Press.
Graves, R. (1992), *The Greek Myths: Complete Edition*, London: Penguin.
Jones, L. (2006), *Mr Cassini*, Bridgend: Seren.
Larkin, P. (1983), *Required Writing: Miscellaneous Pieces 1955–1982*, London: Faber and Faber.
London, J. (2001), *Gilgamesh: A Novel*, New York, NY: Grove Press.
Magerstädt, S. (2015), *Philosophy, Myth and Epic Cinema: Beyond Mere Illusion*, London: Rowman and Littlefield.
Miller, M. (2018), *Circe*, London: Bloomsbury.
Tobin, B. (2008), *Ice Land*, London: Short Books.
Tóibín, C. (2018), *House of Names*, London: Penguin.
Vogler, C. (1998, 2007), *The Writer's Journey: Mythic Structure for Writers*, 3rd edn, Los Angeles, CA: Michael Wiese Productions.
Workman, M. E. (1981), 'The Role of Mythology in Modern Literature', *Journal of the Folklore Institute*, 18 (1): 35–48.

Films

Brother, Where art Thou? (2000), [Film] Dir. Joel and Ethan Coen, USA: Buena Vista Pictures.
Clash of the Titans (2010), [Film] Dir. Louis Leterrier, USA: Warner Brothers Pictures.
Django Unchained (2012), [Film] Dir. Quentin Tarantino, USA: Columbia Pictures.
Dune (2021), [Film] Dir. Denis Villeneuve, USA: Warner Brothers Pictures.
Eternals (2021), [Film] Dir. Chloé Zhao, USA: Marvel Studios.
Gods of Egypt (2016), [Film] Dir. Alex Proyas, USA: Summit Entertainment.
Hercules (2014), [Film] Dir. Brett Ratner, USA: Paramount Pictures and Metro-Goldwyn-Mayer.
Immortals (2011), [Film] Dir. Tarsem Singh, USA: Universal Pictures.
Noah (2014), [Film] Dir. Darren Aronofsky, USA: Paramount Pictures.
The Secret of Kells (2009), [Film] Dir. Tomm Moore and Nora Twomey, Ireland, France and Belgium: Buena Vista International.
Troy (2004), [Film] Dir. Wolfgang Petersen, USA: Warner Brothers.
Thor (2011), [Film] Dir. Kenneth Branagh, USA: Marvel Studios.

AUTHOR INDEX

SUBJECT INDEX